Buddhayana: Living Buddhism

Also available from Continuum:

Fundamentalisms and the Media, Stewart M. Hoover and Nadia Kaneva
Interpreting the Qur'an, Clinton Bennett
A Mirror For Our Times, Paul Weller
Religious Cohesion in Times of Conflict, Andrew Holden
Religious Diversity in the UK, Paul Weller
Understanding Christian-Muslim Relations, Clinton Bennett
Young, British and Muslim, Philip Lewis

Buddhayana

Living Buddhism

Anil Goonewardene

continuum

Continuum International Publishing Group

The Tower Building	80 Maiden Lane
11 York Road	Suite 704
London SE1 7NX	New York NY 10038

www.continuumbooks.com

© Anil Goonewardene 2010

British Library Cataloguing-in-Publication Data
A catalogue record for this book is available from the British Library.

ISBN: HB: 978-0-8264-2310-8
        PB: 978-1-4411-8795-6

Library of Congress Cataloguing-in-Publication Data
Goonewardene, Anil.
    Buddyahana: Living Buddhism/Anil Goonewardene.
        p. cm.
    Includes bibliographical references and index.
    ISBN 978-0-8264-2310-8 – ISBN 978-1-4411-8795-6
1. Buddhism. I. Title.

    BQ4022.G66 2010
    294.3–dc22
                                                        2009050599

Typeset by BookEns Limited, Royston, Herts
Printed and bound in Great Britain by CPI Antony Rowe Ltd,
Chippenham, Wiltshire

Contents

Detailed Contents

The merit of the work on this book is dedicated with loving-kindness to my parents, family and teachers

Foreword

I have known Anil Goonewardene for some 15 years as a valued friend and co-author of, a number of publications including *Six World Faiths*, an Open University text book that I edited. We have also met at gatherings of the Religious Education Council of England and Wales and I am aware of his many activities at the Buddhist Society in London, where he has run courses in the religion.

Buddhism is a lived faith rather than a philosophy, as it is sometimes incorrectly regarded in the West. When I was beginning my own study of the major religions found in Britain, about 40 years ago, I wrote to Christmas Humphreys, the Founder and the then President of the Buddhist Society, London, who had become a Buddhist in his early days. I asked him for information about Buddhist festivals and stories about the Buddha, only to be put firmly in 'my place' by being told that 'such things are unimportant, even young children should be taught what matters, that is the ideas and concepts'. According to what Anil says in his book, this is a very mistaken perception of Buddhism, which is a living religion.

Anil, a Sri Lankan Buddhist, covers these areas in the second half of his book but he also examines the *Jataka* stories and Gotama's life and the influence these experiences have had on him. We are introduced to Gotama the man as well as the ideal venerated by believers. During its historical development, carefully traced by the author, Buddhism has taken on different forms and expressions, while remaining faithful to the core beliefs. It now faces new and demanding challenges as it moves into a Western society dominated religiously by Christianity and socially and philosophically by secularism, not of the Eastern and particularly Indian kind, where all religions are respected, but one where they are ignored and expected to fade away under the scrutiny of rationalism. It will be interesting to see how Buddhism responds to this situation, one that confronts all non-materialistic life views. Anil considers this in his final chapter.

As the writer reflects upon his childhood influences out of which he has emerged as a man equally at home in London and Sri Lanka, we not only share his authentic rather than idealized Buddhism, but we are, unintentionally, invited to consider our own personal, social and spiritual development if we so wish. I regard this as an added bonus to a sound and helpful introduction to a religion that has attracted Western students of Eastern thought for more years than any other Eastern form of spirituality. We should be grateful to Anil Goonewardene for sharing his insights with us so realistically and clearly.

Dr W Owen Cole
BA, BD, MPhil., PhD, Dip ED, Dip Theology

Dr Cole is Head of Religious Studies Teaching and Senior Research Fellow at the University of Chichester and its constituent colleges. He is author and editor of nine books on religious studies and adviser to several publishers on publishing books on religious studies. His most recent publication is *Cole Sahib: the Story of a Multifaith Journey* (Sussex Academic Press, 2009).

Preface

There are three main reasons for writing this book, in which I have attempted to present the material in a simple, concise and readable form.

First, I was born in Sri Lanka into a family that has been Buddhist for generations and was brought up within the Southern Buddhist tradition. From an early age I was interested in the different traditions of Buddhism and their relationship to one another.

I was lucky enough to have contact with the late Venerable Myokyo-ni, who was a nun ordained in Japan in the Zen tradition and a vice-president of the Buddhist Society in London. We used to meet at the Society on Tuesday evenings when we came there to teach our respective classes. Over several years we discussed the respective merits of the various schools and traditions of Buddhism. 'There is nothing in any one tradition which is not found, in some form or another, in other traditions', she used to say. We agreed that the central teaching of the different schools and traditions of Buddhism is the same or very similar. It comes from the teaching rehearsed and finalized at the Second Council at Vesali, presided over by Venerable Sabbakami, 100 years after the passing away of Gotama (Sakyamuni) Buddha, at which time there was no division in the Buddha Sasana or community. She invited me to present the Buddhist teaching in a book to demonstrate this. This idea of the common foundation of Buddhism has been mentioned by various scholars, including Venerable Dr. Walpola Rahula and Professor Richard Gombrich of Oxford University. I have developed this theme in my publications.

Venerable Bogoda Seelawimala, Head of the London Buddhist Vihara and the Chief Sangha Nayaka of Great Britain, after reading some of my publications and discussing some points on Buddhism with me, suggested about three years ago that I write a book on Buddhism, editing my published papers and writing new material, emphasizing this theme. This is the primary aim of this book, and hence the name *Buddhayana* in the title.

This idea is highlighted in several places in the *Saddharma Pundarika (Lotus) Sutra*, for example, on pages 71 and 168:

> Though by reason of their tactful powers
> They (the Buddhas) display various kinds of ways,
> Really they are (but) the (One) Buddha-vehicle (yana).

> Buddhas by their tactful powers
> Separately preach the three vehicles;
> (But) there is only the One Buddha-vehicle (yana).

I was unable to find a suitable precedent in order to demonstrate the common features of teaching and I had to make my own rules. There is a multitude of books written on Buddhism within the different schools and traditions. For the purposes of my study I had to concentrate on a manageable number of representative books. I have chosen Professor Junjiro Takakusu, sometime Professor Emeritus of Sanskrit at Tokyo Imperial University, *The Essentials of Buddhist Philosophy,* and Beatrice Lane Suzuki, *Mahayana Buddhism,* for Eastern Buddhism; Tenzin Gyatso, His Holiness The XIV Dalai Lama, *The Buddhism of Tibet* and Geshe Tashi Tsering, teacher at the Jamyang Buddhist Centre in London, *The Four Noble Truths,* for Northern Buddhism; and Narada Maha Thera, *The Buddha and His Teachings* and Venerable Nyanatiloka, *Buddhist Dictionary*, for Southern Buddhism. From time to time I have obtained guidance from the Sangha and teachers of Amaravati Buddhist Monastery, Jamyang Buddhist Centre, London Buddhist Vihara, Shobo-an Zen monastery, Sri Saddhatissa International Buddhist Centre and Yakushi-do Tendai temple, regarding the specific teachings in the different traditions.

Second, I taught at the London Buddhist Vihara Dhamma School for over 20 years. The then Head of the Vihara, the late Venerable Dr Hammalawa Saddhatissa, mentioned to me several times that a book should be written presenting Buddhism as a living religion. He explained how this should be done and I have attempted to follow his advice, hence the title *Living Buddhism*. I have set out the material from the point of view of someone born and brought up as a Buddhist who tries to live according to the teaching.

Third, at the London Buddhist Vihara Dhamma School the teaching followed the syllabuses written by the Young Men's Buddhist Association in Colombo, Sri Lanka, for such classes. Students sat examinations at the end of the year. The question papers were set and the answer scripts marked in Colombo. The teaching at the Buddhist Society, where I taught, was according to more flexible class content guidelines. There was no examination at the end of the course. At the London Metropolitan University I taught the Buddhism unit in the South Asian Degree course, in addition to my main teaching in the Law Department. This was according to a published syllabus, which I had written, and there was an examination at the end of the semester. I marked the scripts that were then second marked by an external examiner. I have also been involved in writing syllabuses for teaching Buddhism and guidelines for teaching in schools at national and local level in the UK. Drawing on this experience I have included topics that are often included in these syllabuses.

Finally, I come to the general aim of this book, which is to present Buddhism in all its beauty and nobility; a religion that has guided millions of people over the years.

I am happy to mention the help I have received in preparing the material for this book. Ajahn Anandabodhi and Sister Sumedha of Amaravati Buddhist Monastery read the draft material in sections over two years and made very helpful comments relating to the *Dhamma* and the text. I am most grateful for the advice I received from them and from Rajah Kuruppu. Venerable Sochu of the Shobo-an Zen Buddhist temple, Rev Ganshin Rock of the Yakushi-do Tendai Buddhist temple, Priya Fernando, Rajah Kuruppu and Lakshman Abayawickrema, have read and made comments on some chapters. Rev Prof Kemmyo Tairo Sato of the Three Wheels (Pure Land, Jodo Shin Shu) Buddhist temple, Ven Sochu and Rev Ganshin Rock helped me to clarify some matters relating to Eastern (Mahayana) Buddhism. Mike Murray, a teacher at the Jamyang Buddhist Centre, helped me to understand some matters relating to Northern (Tibetan) Buddhism. Venerable Seelawimala, Head of the London Buddhist Vihara, Venerable Piyadassi of the Sri Saddhatissa International Buddhist Centre, Venerable Dr Pollamure Sorata Mahathero of the Sri Sudharmarama International Buddhist Monastery in Kandy, Sri Lanka, and Rajah Kuruppu gave me advice regarding Southern (Theravada) Buddhism. I learned much in answering questions from my sons Chula, Manoj and Rahal, who attended the London Buddhist Vihara *Dhamma* classes. Dr Desmond Biddulph, the Vice President of the Buddhist Society was unfailing in his help and encouragement. I thank Dr W. Owen Cole for his support and advice and Dr Athula Weerakoon and Nalin Goonewardene for help using computers. I am indebted to relatives and other friends, too numerous to mention, for their interest and support. Finally I thank my wife Sunethra for her encouragement, discussions and answers to my questions on the *Dhamma* and constant reminders to 'get on with the work'.

The background to this book is 30 years' study and teaching of Buddhism, several publications and two-and-a-half years of intensive work on the material. Everything was written out in longhand and typed by me over several years. The scope of the subject matter is wide. I take responsibility for any mistakes and hope the readers will bring them to my attention.

Introduction

Buddhism helps people to understand and come to terms with life and death. Buddhists believe that the purpose of life is achieved through the study and practice of the *Dhamma* (Dharma) and obtaining the fruits of that practice to realize *Nibbana* (*Nirvana*). Buddhism points to a civilization where the emphasis is not on living in luxurious houses, travelling in fast cars, using mobile telephones and microwave ovens and having power over people, but rather on treating all living beings with respect, generosity and loving kindness.

The term Buddha is derived from the Pali word 'budh', which means to know, be aware, understand and be fully awakened. It is the title given to an Enlightened being. When a bodhisatta (bodhisattva) becomes Enlightened and realizes *Nibbana* as a *Samma Sambuddha*, he teaches the *Dhamma* and establishes a Buddha *Sasana* (Buddhist community). This continues for a long time, but over time people understand and practice it less frequently and after many years the teaching is forgotten. This leads to a gap in time when the teaching is not known to living beings. Then another bodhisatta becomes Enlightened and begins to teach the *Dhamma*. In this way there are successive Buddha cycles. The current teaching is that of Gotama (Sakyamuni) Buddha, the last of a long line of Buddhas.

Dhamma is the term for reality and also the teaching of the Buddhas, all of which are intended to awaken one to reality. The teaching consists of intellectual wisdom and practice teachings. The Buddha said that, for a devotee, intellectual study by itself was insufficient. There must also be the practice of the teaching. The devotee needs to understand that, in addition to intellectual understanding, there must be realization of the teachings by mindfulness and meditation, while practising the ethical guidelines. The ethical and moral guidelines lead to the achievement of harmony and peace for the individual and society. The teaching relating to mental culture guides the devotee to experience the truth and to realize *Nibbana*. The living being is considered to be a microcosm of the universe. The Buddha said in the *Rohitassa Sutta* that:

> 'Within this body six feet high endowed with perception and consciousness is contained the world, the origin of the world, the end of the world, and the path leading to the end of the world.'[1]

Gotama did not ask the people to accept his teachings simply because it was the word of a Buddha. He invited them to understand and practise the teachings and realize the truth for themselves.

The Buddha *Dhamma* is the law of nature. Buddhism is not a revealed religion and does not teach of a God or Creator. It has no idea of 'sin', as in some other religions, or punishment, reward or pardon by anyone. Living according to the teaching contributes to one's progress, as a Buddhist pilgrim, to realize *Nibbana*. The *Dhamma* applies to all living beings, as it outlines the laws of nature. It could be said that it applies to all persons, whether they are Buddhists or not, whether they are aware of the *Dhamma* or not. It continues to apply all the time, even when the teaching is not known to living beings.

Is Buddhism a religion? Buddhism comes within the definitions of religion in the *Oxford English Dictionary*. There has been some discussion on whether Buddhism is a philosophy or a religion. The *Dictionary* defines philosophy as an intellectual study of mind and matter. Religion is defined as having an extra element of activity amounting to practice and worship. Buddhism has a vast and complex philosophy. It also has guidance on religious practice for the devotee to progress as a Buddhist. Like all other religions, Buddhism explores the meaning of life and gives guidance on how the devotee should live. Further, the foundation teaching of Buddhism is the Four Noble Truths (see Chapter 5). If the Buddha had stopped at the Third Noble Truth, Buddhism would have been a philosophy but he added the Fourth Noble Truth – the Noble Eightfold Path – which gives the devotee guidance on practice. This makes Buddhism a religion. The courts of law have had to decide whether Buddhism is a religion for the purposes of charity law, where organizations for the advancement of religion are permitted to be registered as charities. They have recognized Buddhism as religion. A Buddhist is understood to be a person who accepts the Triple Gem, the Buddha, *Dhamma* and *Sangha* as guides; has a present and continuing intention to live according to the *Dhamma* as a religion; and makes an immediate and ongoing effort to do so (see Chapter 16).

The Buddha's teaching was oral. He taught for 45 years in different locations, addressing different groups of people and changing the subject matter and presentation to suit the occasion and the listeners. His teachings are not set out as classes or lectures at school or university, to cover a particular subject in an ordered manner and in a given time. Out of necessity, there is therefore much repetition and duplication in the texts. For instance, feelings is the second of the five aggregates and the seventh link in the chain of Dependent Origination. *Dukkha* is the First Noble Truth and the second section of Three Signs of Being. *Metta* is the ninth *Parami*, a section in general moral values, a kind of meditation and the first *brahmavihara*. Some topics appear in different sections of the teachings, for instance the Four Noble Truths appear in the *Dhammacakkappavattana Sutta* and in the *Satipattana Sutta*. Sometimes the meaning of a word depends on the context. For example, the word consciousness in Pali has a different meaning as the fifth aggregate than as the third link in Dependent Origination.

In order to relate the teachings, the evolution of Buddhism and the different traditions, the subject matter in the book is arranged in five parts. The chapter headings describe the contents in a chapter. Part I deals with the lives of the Buddha, history and literature. Part II deals with the intellectual wisdom teachings. Part III gives the practice: ethical life, worship and meditation. Part IV sets out the various sections of the Buddhist community. Part V gives a concluding account. The appendices provide two examples of Buddhist life – one a view of death and the other a true story of rebirth.

The classification of Buddhism adopted in this book is the geographical: Eastern Buddhism (Mahayana), Northern Buddhism (Tibetan Buddhism) and Southern Buddhism (Theravada). Generally the Southern Buddhist teaching is set out first, as this is my background, and then references are made to Eastern and Northern Buddhism, in comparison and to show the similarities.

I have used the word *Dukkha* in the text since the word 'suffering' normally used is misleading and there is no word in the English language that gives the complete, precise and elegant meaning. Generally, skilful, wholesome and profitable are used to describe good qualities; and unskilful, unwholesome and unprofitable are used to describe bad qualities. Sometimes the words good and bad are used for simplicity. The unwholesome roots or defilements are generally referred to craving, hatred and ignorance. Some of my students have said that the words craving and hatred are too strong so I have followed their suggestion to use attachment, ill-will and ignorance. The amount of detail given is what seems to be suitable to a book that deals with this variety of topics.

The publication details of the books referred to in the text are to the editions mentioned in the bibliography. See the end of the Bibliography at p. 276 for recommended Internet website references.

The two languages most important in the Buddhist texts are Pali and Sanskrit. When a technical word is first used, generally both versions of the word are given and thereafter the Pali word is used for convenience, unless the Sanskrit word is more appropriate in the context.

In accordance with the legal rules of interpretation, reference to a male includes the female and *vice versa*, unless the context precludes this.

Ten of the chapters have already been published in the same or modified form in the Buddhism section of *Six World Faiths* (Cassell/ Continuum) or in *The Middle Way*, the journal of the Buddhist Society, London, or in some other journals in Sri Lanka and the UK. These have been edited to fit in as chapters in this book.

Part I

Current Teaching Begins

Chapter 1

Previous Life (Jataka) Stories

Many hundreds of years ago a child was born in a wealthy Brahmin family and named Sumedha. His parents died while he was still young and he inherited all of their wealth. He noticed, however, that they did not take away any of their wealth when they died and he had doubts about the real value of this wealth. He determined to make good use of his inheritance and offered it to the king. When the king refused the offer, Sumedha distributed his entire wealth among the poor people and left for the Himalayan foothills to lead the life of a homeless ascetic.

One day Sumedha heard that Buddha Dipankara was visiting the city of Ramma and so he travelled there to meet the Buddha. On meeting Buddha Dipankara, Sumedha thought, 'May I be able to attain Enlightenment, like this Buddha, and be of service to mankind?' Buddha Dipankara knew of Summedha's wish and, looking to the future, saw that this would come to pass. He addressed the monks and said, 'This ascetic will become a *Samma Sambuddha* by the name of Gotama many years from now,' and later Buddhas made the same prophecy. The ascetic Sumedha was overjoyed to hear this. Over many births, as a bodhisatta, he began to practise and develop the qualities and perfections (*Paramis, Paramitas*) needed to become a *Samma Sambuddha* (see Chapter 17).

After Enlightenment, Gotama Buddha recounted the stories of his many lives as a bodhisatta. These are the *Jataka* stories. There are about 550 stories, with various duplications and some titles having more than one story. In various lives, the bodhisatta was born as an animal and a human being, male and female, breaking the barrier between such different rebirths. The *Jatakas* map the individual's way upwards in mental development over many life times and also traces the lives of his later disciples, who were associated with the bodhisatta in these previous lives. The *Jatakas* are used to teach Buddhist values to children and adults. Many paintings and images, some life sized, in the Buddhist temples in Asia depict scenes from the *Jatakas*. Some *Jatakas* are acted out as plays in schools and Buddhist organizations, bringing living Buddhism to the people. The *Jatakas* were told in circumstances when the Buddha wished to emphasize the theme of the story. Many an Asian Buddhist will remember being taken as a child to the temple by his parents on days of the full moon and, after worship, being seated out of doors in the moonlight under the Bodhi tree listening to a *Jataka* story related by a monk.

Sandy Road (*Vannupatha Jataka*) (No. 2)

This story was told when a monk had given up his effort to progress on the Buddhist path. In the past, when King Brahmadatta was reigning in Benares, the bodhisatta was born into the family of a caravan leader. When he came of age he continued in the same trade, with 500 carts. He transported goods, sold them, bought other goods and returned home.

One day the caravan was passing through a huge sand desert. It was so hot during the daytime that no one could walk on the sand. They took fire wood, oil, rice, food and water in the carts and travelled only at night. At sunrise they drew the carts up in a circle, spread an awning over the top and, after a meal, spent the day sitting in the shade. At sunset they had dinner and, when the ground became cool, yoked the carts and moved on. The caravan had a pilot who mapped the route by studying the stars.

One day the leader was moving his caravan through the desert. The caravan had come a long way and one evening he said, 'In one night we shall pass out of the desert'. The extra fire wood and water were thrown away and the caravan moved forward. The pilot was in the lead caravan and directed it by looking at the stars. He fell asleep and did not notice that the oxen had turned around and were going back the way they had come. At daybreak the pilot woke up and looking at the stars noticed that they were going the wrong way. 'Turn the carts,' he shouted, but it was too late. 'This is where we camped yesterday,' the men said, 'We have no firewood or water'. They arranged the carts in a circle and took shelter under the awning in a state of shock.

The bodhisatta thought, 'If I give up all will be lost'. He noticed a patch of grass and thought, 'There must be water underneath for this grass to grow'. He asked the men to start digging to find water. They dug a deep hole, came upon a rock and disheartened gave up. The bodhisatta was not one to give up so easily, however. He put his ear to the rock and heard the sound of water flowing underneath the rock. He spoke to one of the men and said, 'If we give up all will be lost. We must keep up the effort. Take this hammer, climb down to the rock and strike the rock with all your might'. The man did this, the rock split in the middle and a spout of water rose up to the sky. They all drank the water, bathed and, breaking up a part of a cart for firewood, cooked and ate a meal. The caravan fed the oxen, set up a flag near the water hole and at sunset continued their journey. They reached their destination, sold the goods, bought more to take back and returned home. They each then proceeded according to their respective *kammas*. The bodhisatta then spoke the following words:

> In the sandy desert digging though tired
> On the road was the water found.
> So the wise man with effort and with strength
> Works untiring till he finds peace of heart.

The Buddha then said, 'The man who had not given up the effort was the monk who now had given up. The others in the caravan were my present disciples and I was the caravan leader in a previous birth.' He explained that Buddhists must maintain the effort to progress on the Buddhist path.

Wise Partridge (*Tittira Jataka*) (No. 37)

This story was related by the Buddha when he heard that Venerable Sariputta, his senior disciple, had to sleep out of doors under a tree because the junior monks had occupied all of the accommodation in a new monastery.

A long time ago, on the slopes of the Himalayas in a wooded forest through which ran a stream with crystal clear water there lived three good friends – an elephant, a monkey and a partridge. They would forage for food during the day and in the evening, after their dinner, they would sit by the river under a banyan tree and chat to one another. They would speak freely, were kind, friendly and never argued among themselves. By and by they began to feel that this way of life was not quite proper because there was no one among them who could be obeyed and respected by the others. They thought that they ought to find out which of them was the senior, so that he could be respected and honoured.

One day while they were chatting under the banyan tree, the three friends began to wonder who the eldest among them was. Suddenly they were struck with an idea how this problem could be solved. The partridge and the monkey asked the elephant, 'How big was this banyan tree when you first saw it?' The elephant replied, 'When I was a baby this banyan tree was only a little plant. When I used to walk over it the topmost branches used to touch the underside of my tummy. So I have known this tree since it was a little plant.'

Next, the monkey was asked the same question by the other two. He replied, 'When I was young, as I sat on the ground, I had only to stretch my neck and I could eat the topmost leaves of this tree. So I have known this tree since it was a small tree.'

Now it was the partridge's turn to be asked this question. He said, 'Dear friends, long ago there was a huge banyan tree not far from here. I ate its fruit and by accident dropped a seed in this spot. That seed has grown into this tree. My knowledge of this tree goes back before it sprouted its first leaves. That proves I am older than either of you.'

Upon this, the monkey and the elephant said to the partridge, 'Friend, you are without doubt the oldest among us. Being the most senior you will receive from us honour, respect, obedience, service and attention due to a senior and an elder. Further we shall consult you and expect you to give good advice when we need it.'

The three friends, the elephant, the monkey and the partridge, continued to live happily together and often listened to the wise counsel of the partridge.

The Buddha then explained that he wished the monks to pay respect to the senior of them in the same way. He went on to say that Venerable Moggallana was the elephant, Venerable Sariputta was the monkey and that he himself was the partridge.

Gutthila (*Gutthila Jataka*) (No. 243)

This story was told to illustrate that respect should be shown to teachers.

Once upon a time the bodhisatta was reborn in Benares in a family of musicians, where he was named Gutthila. He learnt to play the veena (a stringed instrument like the lute) and on growing up became a fine musician. When he played the veena everyone listened spellbound. He did not get married but looked after his blind parents. The king appointed him the chief court musician.

Some merchants from Benares went to a nearby town called Ujjeni for trade. They attended a celebration there and heard the chief musician Musila play the lute. When he had finished playing, the merchants asked him to play the instrument now that he had finished tuning it. 'Do you know of a better musician?' Musila asked. The merchants explained that in Benares there was a musician called Gutthila who was much, much better. Impressed, Musila persuaded the merchants to take him to Benares to meet and study under Gutthila.

When Musila arrived at Gutthila's home he had gone out. Musila explained the nature of his visit and Gutthila's parents invited him in, made him comfortable and gave him food and drink. He saw Gutthila's veena placed against the wall and began to strum a few notes and play a tune. Gutthila's parents, thinking that mice were attacking the instrument, came rushing into the room to drive them away. When Gutthila returned Musila said that he had come from Ujjeni to take lessons on the veena from Gutthila. Gutthila did not like the look of the man, however, and refused to give him lessons. Musila then appealed to Gutthila's parents, requesting they ask their son to take him on as a pupil. Gutthila did not wish to refuse his parents' request so he reluctantly agreed to teach Musila.

Musila was an apt pupil and after some time was able to play the veena almost as well as his teacher. One day he expressed a wish to enter the king's service and to remain in Benares permanently. Gutthila introduced him to the king as his pupil and an accomplished veena player who wished to enter the king's service. The king agreed to give employment to Musila at half the salary paid to Gutthila. But Musila said, 'My talent and skill is equal to my teacher and that merits equal pay'. The king was surprised and said, 'Why do you challenge your teacher, who has been so kind and taught you all these skills?' Musila insisted that he was a better musician than Gutthila and challenged his teacher to a public performance. The king asked Gutthila whether he was willing to take part in such a contest, and he agreed.

Gutthila was worried because he was old now and felt that his younger pupil would outshine him in a public contest. He retired into the forest and began to think of his pupil's ingratitude. A person in the form of an ascetic then appeared and questioned him as to the reasons for his troubled state of mind. When Gutthila explained, the ascetic said that he was a senior deity, Sakra by name, and advised Gutthila to take part in the contest. He said, 'As you play, snap the strings of your instrument one by one and the sweetest music will be heard.' Then, handing him three magic dice, he said, 'Throw these up in the air as you play and 900 deities will appear in the sky and dance to your music.' Sakra then returned to his heavenly home and Gutthila returned to his earthly abode.

The day of the contest was a big celebration. A platform had been built for the musicians; the king and all the royal family were there, all the people of Benares and even some individuals from neighbouring districts.

The musicians began to play one at a time. At the start there was not much to choose between them. The people had never heard such superb music. Then Gutthila snapped the strings of his veena one by one, as directed by Sakra, and his music continued to be beautiful and excellent as before. Musila followed and snapped the strings on his instrument and his music became like the noise of cats howling at night. Gutthila then threw the magic dice given by Sakra up in the air and 900 beautiful deities came and danced in the sky to his music. The king and the people were delighted. The people chased Musila out of Benares saying that there was no place in their city for such an ungrateful person.

After relating the story, the Buddha identified the persons associated with him in his current life with the characters in the story, and said, 'Musila was Venerable Devadatta, the king was Venerable Ananda and I was the kind musician Gutthila in a previous birth.'

Hare (Sasa Jataka) (No. 316)

This story was told to illustrate the importance of generosity.

Once upon a time the bodhisatta was reborn as a hare and lived in a forest. On one side of the forest was a mountain and on the other a village with the Ganges running beside. He had three friends – a monkey, a jackal and an otter. These four gathered their respective food during the day and met in the evenings. One day the hare explained a lesson to them, 'There should be giving of gifts, we should live an ethical life and observe the holy days.' That night the hare observed the moon and said, 'Tomorrow is a holy day. We must observe the moral rules and also be generous to strangers.' The other three agreed.

The next day the otter went out early to the banks of the Ganges. He found some fish there and brought them home, hoping to eat them in due course. The jackal going in search of food came across some roasted meat and some milk, with no obvious owner in sight. He brought these items home for a meal later. The monkey brought a bunch of mangoes that he hoped to eat in due course. The hare went out and came back with some of his favourite dabba grass, which he stored for a later meal.

Sakra, the chief of the deities, saw all that was happening and decided to test the ethical values of the hare. In the form of an ascetic, he went to the otter's home first. On enquiry, he said he would like to have some food and the otter offered him the fish. The ascetic thanked him and, saying he would come back later, went away. Next he went to the jackal and likewise asked for some food. The jackal happily offered him the roasted meat and milk. Again the ascetic thanked him and went away, saying that he would come back later. He then went to the monkey and similarly asked for some food. The monkey was happy to offer him the mangoes and some water. The ascetic thanked him and again went away, saying he would come back later.

Now the ascetic went to the hare. This was to be the test. He asked the hare for some food. The hare said, 'I have only some dabba grass and I cannot offer that to you as food. Please collect some wood and make a fire. I shall leap into the fire and when my body is roasted you may eat my flesh.' The ascetic made a fire with some wood and when it was burning fiercely informed the hare that the fire was ready. The hare came to the fire, shook his body so that any insects in his fur would fall away and not be burned, and leapt into the fire. But the fire was not hot; it was as cold as ice.

The hare spoke to the ascetic and said, 'This fire is not hot. It is cold and will not roast my body. How is this?'

'I am not just any ascetic,' Sakra said, 'I am Sakra and have come to test how far you have progressed on the Buddhist path. You have offered me your body and this shows that you have gone far on this path. Come out of this fire and continue with your life. I wish you well.'

Then Sakra, squeezing the hillside, took some essence and etched the shape of the hare on the moon. The four friends continued to live in the forest fulfilling the moral code and progressed according to their respective *kamma*.

This is why on days of the full moon you can see the shape of a hare etched on it.

The Buddha then identified the persons associated with him in his current life who were the characters in the story. The otter was Venerable Ananda, the jackal was Venerable Moggalana, the monkey was Venerable Sariputta and the hare was himself.

Nandiya (*Cula Nandiya Jataka*) (No. 222)

This story was told by the Buddha to illustrate the law of *kamma* and to explain that children should look after elderly parents.

Once there lived in the Himalayan forests two monkeys who were brothers. They headed a large band of monkeys and lived with their mother, who was elderly, frail and blind. They looked after their mother and brought food for her.

One day, the brothers went to a distant forest with their group in search of food. They sent fruits and nuts to their mother by giving them to other monkeys to deliver. When they returned home they found that their mother was much weaker and thinner. She said that she had not received any of the food that they had sent her. The other monkeys had been eating the food.

The elder brother Nandiya decided that it was far more important to him to look after his mother than to rule the colony. He said to his brother, 'You rule the colony. I shall take our mother to the distant forest and look after her.' His brother replied,' I care not for ruling the colony, so I shall join you in looking after our mother.' So the brothers led their mother to the distant forest and tended her.

In a nearby city there lived a man who had received a very good education from a famous teacher. When he had completed his education, the teacher, seeing that his pupil was a violent and cruel person, had said, 'Do not do anything cruel that you will regret. People who do that do not do well in life.'

Although he was educated, because of his nature the man was not able to carry on a good trade or profession. He had to earn his living as a hunter. He used to kill animals in the forest with his bow and arrow, sell the flesh and provide for his family.

One day he came to the forest on a hunting trip and saw the three monkeys high up on the branch of a tree. At the same time the monkeys saw him. As he was preparing to use his bow and arrow Nandiya jumped in front of him and said, 'Please do not kill my mother or brother. Instead, please kill me and sell my flesh.' The hunter shot Nandiya and then prepared to shoot his mother. Then the brother jumped down and said, 'Please do not kill my mother, kill me instead.' The cruel hunter, without thinking about what he was doing, shot the brother and the mother as well. He tied the monkeys together and started on his way home.

Before he reached home a thunderbolt struck his house, destroying it completely and killing everyone in his family. When he reached home and saw what had happened he was overcome by grief. He remembered his teacher's words not to do anything cruel that he might regret. 'So this is what my teacher meant,' the man thought, 'Bad actions have unhappy consequences and good actions have happy consequences.'

The Buddha, having related the story, identified the persons associated with him in his current life with the characters in the story. The famous teacher was Venerable Sariputta, the cruel hunter was Venerable Devadatta, the mother monkey was Queen Prajapati Gotami, the brother monkey was Venerable Ananda and Nandiya was he himself.

Vessantara (*Vessantara Jataka*) (No. 547)

This is the story of the bodhisatta's life immediately before his birth as Prince Siddattha, when he attained Enlightenment and realized *Nibbana* as Gotama Buddha. It was related by the Buddha to illustrate the Buddhist virtues of generosity, charity and non-attachment. Attachment is one of the two causes of *kamma*, the Second Noble Truth and an element of Dependent Origination. This is probably the best known story in Buddhist Asia and is often acted out in schools and Buddhist organizations.

Once upon a time in India there lived a king called Sandumaha who ruled the kingdom of Jayatura. The bodhisatta was born as his son, Prince Vessantara. He grew up to be a very learned, kind and generous person. The king entrusted the prince with many duties of government, which the prince fulfilled to perfection. In time he married Princess Mantridevi and the couple were blessed with two children: a daughter, Princess Krishnajina, and a son, Prince Jalia.

Prince Vessantara practised the virtues of generosity and charity to the extreme. He helped his people and waged war against hunger, thirst, poverty, sickness and want. The people loved him. On holy days, after performing the religious rituals he used to ride around the city on his favourite elephant and ensure that the religious practices were being correctly performed and almshouses were providing food and drink for the people.

His fame spread beyond the kingdom. In a neighbouring country, a king who was jealous of Prince Vessantara's popularity with the people heard that the young prince would never refuse a request for help. He sent some of his men, dressed as ascetics, to ask the prince for his elephant. On a holy day while the prince was riding his elephant and inspecting the places of religious celebration, these men came to the prince mumbling blessings. The prince asked whether they were in need of anything, whereupon the men asked for the elephant. The prince could not understand why these men wanted the elephant, but did not wish to refuse the request. He gave them the elephant and walked back to the palace.

When the people and the king's ministers heard of this they were furious. They asked that the prince be punished for doing something that was politically unwise and because he could not distinguish between reasonable and unreasonable charity. The king loved his son very much and said that he would instruct his son to be more discriminating in his charity. But this was not enough – the people asked the king to banish his son to the forest. The king was greatly distressed but agreed to do this. With a heavy heart he sent his chief minister to the prince to inform him of the decision. The minister, who had great affection for the prince gave the message to the prince with tears in his eyes.

The prince was surprised but accepted the decision. When he explained the position to his faithful wife Princess Mantridevi, she insisted on accompanying him together with their children, Princess Krishnajina and Prince Jalia. They gave away their considerable wealth to the needy, took leave of their parents and started the journey to the forest in his horse-drawn chariot.

The deities decided to test the prince. On the way some people begged him for the horses. Again, he could not refuse the request and gave the horses to these people and began to pull the chariot himself. The deities, who were watching all this, came to his rescue and sent four deer to pull the chariot. When they neared the forest another group of people asked for his chariot. The prince could not refuse this request either and gave the chariot to these men. The parents carried their children and made their way to the forest.

Sakra, the chief of the deities, had arranged for a little wooden hut with a thatched roof to be constructed in the middle of the forest. This became the royal family's home amid the fruit trees, flowering bushes and friendly animals. One day when Princess Mantridevi had gone into the forest to collect fruits and nuts, a travel-stained person arrived at their door. The prince invited him in and gave him food and drink. He asked the person what help he could give him. After a short silence the person said, 'I have heard that you never refuse a request for help. I wish to have your two children to attend on my elderly wife.' The prince was stunned and heartbroken but because of his generous nature he said that he would grant the request. The prince and the children wanted to await the return of Princess Mantridevi, but the person fearing that she might prevent the children from being given away, said that he was in a hurry and wanted to take the children away forthwith.

In his previous lives the bodhisatta had sacrificed his body as food for hungry animals and people. Now he was giving away his children to work for this ascetic's wife. According to normal social practice and family love this seems heartless. But the prince was a bodhisatta at the highest level of perfection and his perception of life was different from that of ordinary people. He was able to look into the future and saw that his father, the king, would rescue the children. As the ascetic led the children away the prince asked him to take the children to his father, who would pay enough money for the ascetic to employ people to help his wife and recover the children.

When Princess Mantridevi returned the prince, with a heavy heart and in tears, related what had happened. She fell in a faint and the prince had to revive her by splashing water on her face. They were both heartbroken and sat in silence in the hut that had echoed with the happy voices of the children. Princess Mantridevi had begun to understand the level of her husband's spiritual development and accepted the situation. Their prayers for the welfare of their children were heard by Sakra and the other deities, who gazed down on them with awe and amazement, rejoicing that the prince had reached this level of development.

The final test, however, was yet to come. Sakra understood that Prince Vessantara was only one life away from becoming a Buddha and decided to test him. He appeared before the prince in the guise of an ascetic coming to ask for a gift and said, 'Yesterday you gave away your two children. Today I wish you to give me your wife as a gift.' The prince and princess were dumbfounded. How could any person make such a request? However, because of the qualities of generosity and non-attachment in his heart, the prince said that he would grant the request.

He had now passed this final test. In admiration, Sakra said, 'Only those whose hearts have been purified can understand your actions. Because of your generosity and non-attachment you have given away your nearest and dearest.' Revealing his identity the deity said, 'I am Sakra the chief of the deities. I give back your good wife. Do not grieve over your children, your father has recovered them and will be here soon with them.' As he said this, Sakra thought 'Surely, the bodhisatta is now on the threshold of Buddhahood. We all, the deities, human beings and all other creatures, bow before you in admiration.'

Having spoken these words Sakra returned to his heavenly home. Soon after King Sandumaha and his queen arrived, bringing the children with them. Prince Vessantara, Princess Mantridevi and the children accompanied the king and queen back to the palace.

The people and the ministers now understood the meaning of the prince's actions and asked for forgiveness. The prince gladly forgave everyone.

Prince Vessantara followed his father on the throne and, with Princess Mantridevi as his queen, governed the kingdom of Jayatura for many years. He had now perfected all of the qualities necessary to become a Buddha. On passing away, the bodhisatta was born in the *Tusita* heaven. There he lived until it was the correct and auspicious time to be born as a human being, a life in which he would attain Enlightenment as a *Samma Sambuddha*.

Having related this story the Buddha identified those associated with him in his current life with people in the story. Princess Mantridevi was Princess Yasodhara, Princess Krishnajina was Venerable Uppalavanna, Prince Jalia was Venerable Rahula and he himself was Prince Vessantara.

Chapter 2

Life of Gotama (Sakyamuni) Buddha

Birth, Naming and Growing Up

Appreciation of the life of Gotama Buddha is important for the understanding of Buddhism. The historical details provide a picture of the transformation of a bodhisatta, born as a human being, into a *Samma Sambuddha*. The various ideas and concepts woven into the story lay the foundation for the study of Buddhism. In Buddhist communities the life story and the *Jataka* stories are the materials used for teaching Buddhism to young children.

After his life as Prince Vessantara, the bodhisatta was born in the *Tusita* heaven. He had perfected all of the qualities needed to become a Buddha. The teaching of Kassapa Buddha was no more and the time was right for the appearance of the next Buddha. All of the deities and heavenly beings assembled together, approached the bodhisatta and invited him to be born in the human world, to become Enlightened as a *Samma Sambuddha*, and then to establish a Buddha *Sasana* for the benefit of living beings. The bodhisatta accepted the invitation and decided on the circumstances relating to his new birth.

He was born on the day of the full moon in the month of May (*Vesak*) in 623 BCE.[1,2] in Lumbini Park, Kapilavastu, in the Indian borders of present-day Nepal. A pillar erected by King Dharmasoka stands to this day to commemorate the sacred spot.

The king and queen were overjoyed at the birth of the baby and there was much rejoicing among the people to celebrate the event. This was his last life. He was a bodhisatta, ready to become a Buddha. An ascetic called Asita, also known as Kaladivela, who had been a tutor to the king was pleased to hear the happy news and visited the palace. The king brought the baby to pay reverence to the ascetic and to everyone's surprise the baby's legs turned and became planted on the hair of the ascetic.

Asita understood why this had happened. He arose from his chair and saluted the child bodhisatta with joined palms. The king worshipped his son the same way. Asita at first smiled and then tears came to his eyes. He explained that the fortunate child will become a Buddha but that he himself would not live to see that. On Asita's advice, his nephew Nalaka retired from worldly life to become an ascetic and, later, an ordained disciple of the Buddha.

The naming ceremony, an auspicious celebration, was arranged for the fifth day after birth. In keeping with custom, many learned Brahmins and ascetics were invited to the ceremony. Among them were eight distinguished holy men. Seven of them prophesied that the prince would become a universal monarch or a Buddha. The youngest of them, Kondanna, prophesied that the prince on growing up would see certain signs and then leave the palace, retiring from worldly life, and later become Enlightened as a Buddha. The prince was named Siddhattha (Siddhartha). His family name was Gotama (Gautama).

Queen Maha Maya, his mother, passed away seven days after his birth and was reborn in the *Tusita* heavenly world. Later on she was reborn in the *Tavatimsa* heavenly world and, on attaining Buddhahood, Gotama Buddha travelled there to teach her the *Dhamma*. The prince was looked after by the Queen's younger sister Queen Maha Prajapati Gotami, who was also a queen of King Suddhodana. Her own son Nanda later became an ordained disciple of the Buddha.

A ploughing ceremony marked the commencement of the festival, in which everyone participated, which was held to celebrate the start of the agricultural season. The king and royal family were there, including young Siddhattha, who was attended by nurses. The nurses placed the prince, who was still a baby, on a couch under the shade of a rose apple tree. When he was asleep the nurses stole away to watch the celebrations. On returning they saw the prince seated cross-legged on the couch deep in meditation. He was concentrating on his breath, on inhalations and exhalations, through which he obtained the pointedness of mind known as Samadhi, and thus developed the first *jhana* or higher consciousness. The nurses reported the matter to the king, who hurried to where his son was and saw him lost in meditation. The king worshipped his son saying, 'My dear son, this is the second time I pay my respects to you.' No one had taught the young prince meditation. It was a skill he had brought with him from a previous life. This illustrates the belief among many Buddhists that skills acquired in one life can be carried over to later lives.

When the prince was about eight years old the king arranged for the learned Brahmin, Sarvamitra by name, to attend to his education. Young Siddhattha had a talent for education. He quickly mastered reading, writing, mathematics, the arts, science and developed his physical skills, as was fitting for a royal prince at that time. His special boyhood friends were his cousins Ananda and Nanda, and the Prime Minister's son Kaludayi.

When the ascetics prophesied at the naming ceremony that the prince might leave household life, the king asked them what would make him do that. They explained that the prince would see four signs – an old man, a sick man, a corpse being taken for cremation and then a peaceful ascetic who had by that time given up worldly life – and that this would make the prince unhappy and dissatisfied with lay life.

The king wanted his son to become a universal monarch so he ordered that no old people, sick people, corpses or ascetics be allowed inside the city gates where they might be seen by the prince, so that the prince would not see any signs of ageing, illness, death or escape from such *Dukkha*. The king did everything to make the life of the prince comfortable and enjoyable. The prince had the best food and drink, the richest clothes, attendants and entertainers. He had three palaces to live in during the different seasons. Amid all this, however, the prince felt that there was more to life than all this material luxury.

Even at an early age he had a great compassion for living things, another quality developed during his past lives. Once Siddhattha was playing with his cousin Devadatta when the latter wounded a bird with his bow and arrow. They both rushed to the bird, Devadatta to capture him and Siddhattha to save his life. Their quarrel over the bird was taken to the king and his Council, who decided that the bird should belong to the person who wanted to save its life. This illustrates the Buddhist principle of compassion for living beings.

To increase Siddhattha's attachment to family life, the advisers and elders in the royal court suggested that he should get married. At the age of 16 he was married to his beautiful cousin Princess Yasodhara, the daughter of King Suppabuddha of the Koliyas. They were born on the same day in the present life and had been husband and wife in previous births too. They continued to live a life of luxury, but Siddhattha was not completely happy with his style of life and often reflected on the real value of this luxury. 'Why do I, being subject to birth, decay, illness, death, sorrow and impurities, search for things of a like nature?' he wondered. 'If I am subject to things of such nature, I should realize their disadvantages and seek the unattained, unsurpassed perfect security of *Nibbana*.' (Majjhima Nikaya, Part 1, *Ariya Pariyesana Sutta*, No. 26, p. 163.)

Four Signs

One day, bored with his life in the palace, Siddhattha suggested to his friend and charioteer Channa that they go for a ride outside the city gates in the country. The deities knew that the time for the Renunciation was drawing nigh and understood that the Four Signs should be shown to the bodhisatta for him to understand the realities of life. Some deities who were keeping an eye on him informed the others that Siddhattha was about to leave the palace for a ride in the country.

When he was out in the country one of them took the form of an old man, grey haired and bent, and appeared on the route. Siddhattha had not seen such a man before and asked Channa who that was. 'He is an old man. We all grow old,' Channa replied.

Siddhattha asked 'Will I, Yasodhara and all of us grow old like this?'

'Yes we all grow old. This is the way of life. Right from the time we are born we are growing old,' said Channa.

. Siddhattha was greatly distressed, and they returned to the luxury of the palace.

On later journeys they saw a sick man and then a funeral procession bearing a corpse for cremation. Channa explained similarly that sickness and death were common to all beings. Siddhattha was greatly disturbed by Channa's explanations. He understood that actual life was not full of the luxuries to which he was accustomed, that the pleasures he enjoyed were superficial and that old age, illness and death were the common lot of all living beings.

On the fourth journey they encountered a holy man dressed very simply in a robe and carrying an alms bowl together with his few other possessions. Again Siddhattha inquired of Channa who that might be. 'He is a man who has given up worldly life because he was not satisfied with such a life. He has no home and has few possessions. He travels from place to place leading a life of great simplicity and discipline. By means of leading a good life and mental development he strives to understand and realize the meaning of life and how to transcend its imperfections of rebirth and *Dukkha*. As he goes from village to village he teaches the people what he has realized.'

A thought hit the bodhisatta's mind like a thunderbolt. It suddenly dawned on Siddhattha that this was what he was looking for. This was the way to find an answer to the imperfections of life.[3]

On returning to the palace he was informed that Princess Yasodhara had given birth to a son. In addition to his great happiness, he felt that this was a bond to tie him further into family life.

The Great Renunciation

Despite his great love for his wife, son, parents, family and friends, Siddhattha felt that because of his compassion for them and for humankind, he had a duty to find the truth about life. This could only be done by becoming an ascetic so he decided to renounce his luxurious life in the palace and go forth to find the truth, knowing that his father would look after his wife and son.

He wished to take leave of his wife and son, so he walked softly to the bedchamber where the princess was sleeping with her baby son. He opened the door and saw her deep in sleep with her hand covering the face of the baby. He did not wish to disturb them, so he turned away after a silent farewell and left with a heavy heart without even seeing his son's face.

It was the day of the full moon in the month of July in the year 594 BCE. Prince Siddhattha, now 29-years-old, asked Channa to saddle his favourite horse Kanthaka. In the middle of the night, riding Kanthaka and with Channa in attendance, he left the palace. The deities opened the palace gates for him and ensured that the horses' hoofs did not make a clatter on the road. At the gates he stopped his horse, pausing for a moment. He turned around to look at the palace where his loved ones were asleep and thought aloud to himself, 'I go now because of my compassion for you and for all human kind. I shall be back only after I have realized the truth and shall teach you how you can do the same. Look after yourselves, I shall return soon.'

Siddhattha and Channa journeyed through the night until they reached the river Anoma. Having crossed the river they came to a forest. Here they stopped and Prince Sidhattha addressed Channa, 'I am going to retire from worldly life and live the life of an ascetic in order to realize the truth. Hand over my clothes and Kanthaka to my father.' He refused Channa's request to accompany him into his new life. He cut off his hair with his sword, changed into the simple robes of an ascetic and, carrying an alms bowl, walked into the forest to a life of voluntary renunciation.

Channa returned to the palace with Kanthaka, who understood what had happened, their eyes streaming with tears. Channa reported what had happened to the king and other members of the royal family. They all were greatly saddened by what had happened. When Princess Yasodhara heard the news, though deeply grieved, she understood his reasons for leaving. She too gave up a luxurious way of life, wore simple robes and led a simple life in the palace.

In the mean time, Siddhattha had reached the gates of Rajagaha, which was ruled by King Bimbisara. The king came out to meet the ascetic and during their conversation the ascetic gave his name as Siddhattha, son of King Suddhodana, a friend of King Bimbisara's. The ascetic explained that he had renounced lay life and luxuries in order to work towards realizing the truth of life. King Bimbisara offered half his kingdom to the ascetic. The offer was refused, but the ascetic promised to return after completing his quest.

Enlightenment

There were at that time, and there are today, ascetics and holy men teaching spiritual progress and meditation and living with their disciples. The bodhisatta Gotama, as we shall now call Siddhattha because at this point he was close to becoming a *Samma Sambuddha*, trained with Alara Kalama and Udakka Ramaputta, two well-known meditation teachers. He very quickly learnt what they had to teach and then moved on because he felt there was more to learn. In his previous lives he had perfected many qualities of spiritual development and was now progressing from that position.

Bodhisatta Gotama wandered into the kingdom of Maghada and arrived at Uruvela, the market town of Senani. There he met five ascetics, one of whom was Kondanna who had prophesied at the naming ceremony that he would become a Buddha. The others were Bhaddiya, Vappa, Mahanama and Assaji. There was an understanding in India at the time that a life of severe austerity and self-mortification was conducive to spiritual progress. These five ascetics were leading a very hard life, eating little, wearing rags, not taking shelter from the sun and rain, meditating for long periods and punishing their bodies as much as they could. The bodhisatta joined them and over the next six years led a similar, strict ascetic life. He grew very thin and weak and eventually found that this was not helping his spiritual progress.

He had not been happy with his luxurious life in the palace. He now felt that this austere lifestyle was not conducive to spiritual development either. He decided on a Middle Way – between a luxurious life and an austere one – and began to eat sufficient food and look after himself physically, at the same time continuing with his meditation. The five ascetics left him, thinking that he did not have the stamina for spiritual development. Later, on attaining Enlightenment, he was to say in the *Dhammacakkappavattana Sutta*, (see Chapter 5) that:

There are two extremes which should be avoided
1. Indulgence in sensual pleasures – this is base, vulgar, worldly, ignoble and pointless, and
2. Addiction to self-mortification – this is painful, ignoble and profitless.

This is the reason why Buddhism is called the Middle Way.

When bodhisatta Gotama arrived at Buddha Gaya on the banks of the river Neranjara, he recalled the occasion when he was lost in meditation at the ploughing festival and felt that this was the way forward in realizing the truth. He accepted a bowl of milk rice from Sujatha, a lady from Senani. A grass cutter called Sotthiya gave him a bundle of kusa grass. This he spread the kusa on the ground at the foot of a pipal tree to form a seat and sat cross legged in the lotus position, determined not to rise until he realized the absolute truth. This was to be his final effort. The progress was difficult as his mind was drawn to many worldly distractions. Mara was trying to entice him to return to worldly life but he soldiered on, intent on his goal.

It was now the day of the full moon in the month of *Vesak* (May) in the year 588 BCE and the bodhisatta had spent 35 years as a human being. That night the moon shone with greater brilliance than normal and lit up all around. The deities had gathered there as they felt that something extraordinary was about to happen. Animals from near and far had come to witness the bodhisatta's final effort. The leaves in the trees rustled in the gentle breeze. Now the bodhisatta commenced his meditation. In the first watch of the night the bodhisatta remembered his previous existences. In the middle watch he realized the appearance and disappearance of living beings. In the last watch he realized the Four Noble Truths. At a time when the *Dhamma* was not known to living beings. By his own unaided efforts bodhisatta Gotama attained Enlightenment, realized *Nibbana* (a fully awakened awareness and the absolute truth of reality) and became a *Samma Sambuddha*. From now on he was known as Gotama (Sakyamuni) Buddha.

Immediately after Enlightenment – explaining attachment, life and the end of rebirth – Gotama Buddha exclaimed these words of victory:

> Through many a birth I wandered in *Samsara* (existence),
> Seeking, but not finding, the builder (attachment) of this house (body).
> Sorrowful is birth again and again.
> O' attachment, you are seen. You shall build no house (body) again,
> All your defilements (passions) are ended. Your ignorance is gone.
> My mind has attained *Nibbana*
> Achieved is the end of attachment.
>
> *The Dhammapada*, v. 153.154

Teaching Life

Gotama Buddha spent seven weeks under the tree, now called the Bodhi tree, under which he attained Enlightenment. Most of this time was spent in meditation. He often looked at the tree with gratitude for having given him shelter during his meditations.

He was at first reluctant to teach the *Dhamma* he had realized, because it was subtle and not easily understood. A heavenly being, Brahma Sahampati,[4] read the thoughts of the Buddha and, fearing that mankind might not have a chance to hear the *Dhamma*, came to him and invited the Buddha to teach the *Dhamma*, explaining that there were some people who had the ability to understand it. The Buddha explained that the *Dhamma* could not be easily understood by those whose minds were dominated by attachment and ill will. Brahma Sahampati appealed to the Buddha a second time, and the Buddha made the same reply. Then Brahma Sahampati appealed a third time. The Buddha now surveyed the world of human beings with his Buddha vision and saw that though many would not understand the *Dhamma*, there were indeed some who would understand the teaching and benefit from it. Brahma Sahampati was delighted to hear that the Buddha had changed his mind.

The Buddha was seated under the rajayatana tree when two merchants, Tapassu and Bhallika, happened to pass that way. A certain female deity who was a blood relative of theirs in a previous birth invited them to offer alms to the Buddha who had very recently become Enlightened. The two delighted merchants offered food to the Buddha, who related his experience to them. Afterwards they sought refuge in the Buddha and the *Dhamma* and requested that the Buddha to accept them as lay disciples. The Buddha agreed, and they became his first lay disciples reciting the twofold formula (Buddha and *Dhamma*).

The *Jataka* commentary relates that when these two first lay disciples asked the Buddha for an object of worship, the Buddha presented them with some hair from his head. These relics are now enshrined in the Shwe Dagon Pagoda in Yangon, Myanmar, the most sacred Buddhist site in Myanmar. This site the pride and joy of Burmese Buddhists. Its enormous bell-shaped *cetiya* appears like a golden mountain from a distance, rises 98 metres above its base and is covered with over 60 tons of pure gold paint.

The Buddha now searched for someone to whom he could teach the *Dhamma*. The two ascetics Alara Kalama and Udakka Ramaputta with whom he had first learnt meditation in this life were no longer living. He journeyed from place to place and finally arrived at the deer park at Isipatana in Benares. The five ascetics with whom he had led a life of severe austerity were there. At first they ignored him, but seeing his noble bearing they agreed that it was worth listening to him. The first formal teaching was to these ascetics. It was the day of the full moon in the month of July in the year 588 BCE (exactly six years after the renunciation) and seven weeks after the Buddha's Enlightenment.

His first teaching was the *Dhammacakkappavattana Sutta*, (the Teaching Setting in Motion the Wheel of Truth), where he explained the Four Noble Truths including the Noble Eightfold Path (see Chapter 5). A few days later he gave these ascetics another teaching, the *Anattalakkhana Sutta*, about the Three Signs of Being, namely impermanence, *Dukkha*, and no self (see Chapter 5). All five ascetics understood the teachings well and each attained the state of *arahatship* (see Chapter.17). So Kondanna, Bhaddiya, Vappa, Mahanama and Assaji became Gotama Buddha's first disciples and were ordained as the first members of the *Sangha* under the twofold formula (Buddha and *Sangha*).

In Benares Yasa, the son of a millionaire, led a luxurious life. One morning he arose early and saw his attendants and musicians asleep in repulsive attitudes, snoring loudly, mouths open and tongues hanging out. He was disgusted with the spectacle. He left home and proceeded towards Isipatana, where the Buddha was residing, having ordained the first five monks. The Buddha, seeing Yasa approaching, took his usual seat. Yasa explained his distress to the Buddha, who invited him to have a seat and said, 'I shall explain the *Dhamma* to you.' The Buddha began with the simpler elements of the *Dhamma*, such as the Five Precepts and general morality, and progressed to the Four Noble Truths and Three Signs of Being.

Yasa's mother noticed his absence from the house and reported the matter to her millionaire husband. He dispatched attendants in all directions and went himself in search of his beloved son. He travelled towards Isipatana. The Buddha saw him approaching and by his mental powers willed that the father could not see his son Yasa. The millionaire approached the Buddha and inquired whether he had seen Yasa. He invited Yasa's father to sit down and said that soon he will be able to see his son. The Buddha then delivered a teaching on the *Dhamma*, at the end of which the millionaire, understanding the excellence of the teaching, requested the Buddha to accept him as a lay disciple. The Buddha acceded to his request and he was the first lay disciple to seek refuge under threefold formula of the Buddha, *Dhamma* and *Sangha*.

On hearing the teaching given to his father, Yasa attained *arahatship*. The Buddha then withdrew his willpower and the father was able to see his son seated near him. The millionaire thereupon invited the Buddha and his disciples to his home for alms food the next day and repaired home.

After the departure of his father Yasa, now an *Arahat*, requested and received higher ordination. He was the sixth Bhikkhu *Arahat* to be ordained (the first outside the original group of five) and the first to be ordained under the threefold formula of the Buddha, *Dhamma* and *Sangha*.

As invited, the Buddha with his six disciples attended at the millionaire's house the next day for alms food. After the meal the Buddha gave a *Dhamma* teaching. Venerable Yasa's mother and

Yasa's former wife attained the first stage of sainthood on hearing this teaching and became the first two female lay disciples. Venerable Yasa's sisters at first did not understand what was happening. Their beloved brother had gone from home and had now come back dressed in the simple robes of a Buddhist monk, with five other monks dressed likewise. He sat with the other monks and took his food; he did not sit with his sisters as before. On hearing Buddha's teaching they too began to understand and appreciate the *Dhamma* and they became lay disciples of the Buddha. In time all of these lay disciples became *Arahats*. Friends of Venerable Yasa came to hear the *Dhamma* from the Buddha, then requested and were granted ordination. The Buddha's teaching was so powerful that just one talk convinced the person of the benefit of becoming a disciple and following the *Dhamma*.

The Buddha wandered from place to place in that part of India teaching those he met. Kings, nobles, men and women came to listen to him, accepted the teaching and became his disciples. Some men requested ordination into the *Sangha*. He accepted people from all backgrounds, rich and poor, with no caste or other distinctions, as lay disciples or members of the *Sangha*.

Soon the order numbered 60 monks. With further teaching they all became *Arahats*. The Buddha founded the Order of the *Sangha* with these disciples. Due to his compassion for humankind he encouraged them to go forth in all directions to teach the Dhamma. The creation of the Order of the *Sangha*, with a democratic constitution enshrined in the Vinaya, the monastic rules, was the first recorded example of democracy in the world.

At Uruvela the three Kassapa brothers were ordained. Keeping the promise he made to King Bimbisara, he proceeded to Rajagaha. On hearing the Dhamma, the king became his first royal disciple. The king donated the bamboo grove to the Buddha and the first monastery, Veluvanarama, was built there. Venerable Sariputta and Venerable Moggallana were ordained and later appointed the two chief disciples of the Buddha.

The Buddha's Homecoming – Return to Kapilavastu

King Suddhodana heard that the Buddha was residing and teaching at Rajagaha. He sent messengers inviting the Buddha to Kapilavastu. The Buddha had not forgotten the promise he had made to his loved ones in the palace – that he would return after attaining Enlightenment and teach them the way to *Nibbana*. About seven years after leaving home Gotama Buddha returned to Kapilavastu, the capital city of his father's kingdom. On hearing the *Dhamma* his father King Suddhodana and stepmother Queen Prajapati Gotami became his disciples.[5] He went to meet his former wife Princess Yasodhara. The king commented on her loyalty and how she had lived the life of an ascetic in the palace, wearing simple clothes, having one meal a day, using low couches, not using adornments and perfumes and refusing gifts from other princes as she considered herself a widow. The Buddha explained that they had been married in previous lives and that she had been devoted and faithful to him in these as well. She expressed a desire to join the Order and become a nun, but the Buddha remained silent. He knew that the time was not yet right.

She dressed her son young Prince Rahula, now seven years old, in suitably smart clothes and sent him to the Buddha, saying, 'That holy man you see is your father. He has given up all his wealth to lead a holy life. This wealth should now be yours. Go and ask him for your inheritance.' The prince went up to the Buddha and after a friendly conversation said, 'Give me my inheritance.' The Buddha got up and started to leave the palace and the prince followed him. The Buddha thought, 'I shall give him a much better inheritance than wealth and a kingdom,' and asked Venerable Sariputta to ordain the prince into the *Sangha*.

When King Suddhodana and Princess Yasodhara heard of this they were greatly saddened. The king had lost his son and now his grandson, and the princess her husband and her son. The king spoke to the Buddha and obtained a promise that children would not be ordained without the consent of their parents. The Buddha took a special interest in Venerable Rahula's progress, guiding him and giving him special teachings on honesty and truthfulness.

Teaching Continues

The Buddha had a special concern for the care of the sick. A monk called Putigatta Tissa Thera had a skin ailment that was so unpleasant that some monks carried him out of the monastery and laid him on the ground. When the Buddha heard of this he, with the assistance of some monks, bathed the patient and made him comfortable, saying 'Whoever attends on the sick attends on me.'

Some of the teaching was very down to earth. King Pasenadi of Kosala liked his food and used to eat enormous quantities of rice and curries. One morning after such a meal he came to see the Buddha and could hardly keep his eyes open. The king complained that he always felt like this after meals. 'Your trouble is you are eating too much,' the Buddha said. 'It is wise to observe moderation in food, because therein lies contentment. A person who is moderate in eating will grow old slowly and will not have a lot of physical trouble and discomfort.'

Very early on the Buddha ordained several relatives, including his stepbrother Nanda and his cousins Ananda and Devadatta. Devadatta, whom we met in the story of the wounded bird, created various difficulties for the Buddha. For some time he led a break-away group of monks, but later realized the error of his ways.

When the Buddha was 55 years old he felt the need for a personal attendant. Venerable Ananda, his cousin and the son of Maha Prajapati Gotami, was chosen for the task and attended on the Buddha with great devotion for the rest of Buddha's life. Venerable Ananda was privileged to hear much of the Buddha's teaching because of his position and it was he who recited the *Dhamma* at the First Council.

When the people asked him whether he was a deity or a god, the Buddha explained that he was neither but that he was a *Samma Sambuddha*. A monk, Venerable Vakkali by name, was in the habit of coming to the Buddha and gazing at him day after day. When the Buddha asked him why he did this Venerable Vakkali replied, 'I gaze at you because you are so smart in appearance.' Then the Buddha said, 'Venerable Vakkali, what is the use of gazing at my body, which is something transient and impermanent? If you really want to see me, look at my teaching' (*Samyutta Nikaya*).

One individual, Angulimala, due to unfortunate circumstances, started killing people and collecting their fingers to make a necklace. He stalked the Buddha, who was to be his last victim. The Buddha, preventing Angulimala from doing any harm, taught him the *Dhamma*, whereupon Angulimala became a lay disciple, was later ordained as a monk and attained *arahatship*.

A certain monk came to the Buddha and said that he wished to go on a tour of the country and then further afield because he wished to see the world. The Buddha responded that he did not have to do all that to see the world, and said:

Within this body, six feet high, endowed with perception and consciousness, is contained the world, the origin of the world and the end of the world, and the path leading to the end of the world.

(Rohitassa Sutta)[6]

The Buddha taught village folk, learned people, monks and nuns. He visited heavenly worlds to teach the *Dhamma* to deities. He adapted the style and content of the teaching to suit his audience. For instance, he might teach the lay people about ethical matters connected with their daily lives, while to the monks and nuns he might talk about complex philosophical matters and meditation. The *Saddharma Pundarika Sutra* (p. 290) states that to those who sought to be *Sravakas* he taught the Four Noble Truths for escape from birth, old age, disease and death leading finally to *Nirvana*; to those who sought to be *Pratyeka Buddhas* he taught the law of twelve causes; and to bodhisattvas he taught the *Paramitas* for perfecting Buddha wisdom. Each talk consisted of an introduction, the main teaching and a conclusion, being a fine example of a logical exposition of a subject, with illustrations and examples so that the talk could be easily understood. The teaching was oral and anyone reading the *Sutta* texts will agree that intellectually and presentation wise they are comparable to any good lecture in a university anywhere in the world. He asked the people not to accept the teaching because it came from him but to consider the teaching and practise it in order to see its value.

He had many lay supporters. Anathapindika arranged for the construction of the famous Jetavana monastery where the Buddha spent 19 rainy seasons. During the rainy season, or *Vassa*, the *Sangha* did not go out to teach but remained in a monastery. This practice continues today. Visakha, who had the Pubbarama monastery constructed, was the most prominent female supporter and played an active part in the affairs of the community.

Women – The Order of Nuns

The position of women socially and in religion was low in that society. The Buddha considered men and women to be of equal status, intellectually, spiritually and socially, and accepted women as lay disciples right from the start. He later accepted them as nuns. Once when King Kosala was talking to the Buddha, a messenger informed the king that his wife Queen Mallika had given birth to a baby girl. Seeing that the king was not too happy about having a daughter, the Buddha explained to him that women were the equal of men in intelligence and goodness, and sometimes even superior.

A number of ladies led by Queen Maha Prajapati Gotami, who had looked after the bodhisatta when he was a baby and was the mother of Venerable Ananda, and Princess Yasodhara requested ordination as nuns. The Buddha refused at first because he did not wish to go against the social trend at that time and because it might destabilize the newly created Order of *Sangha*. The ladies, having cut off their hair and wearing simple yellow clothes, were leading the life of ascetics and persisted in their request for ordination, but the Buddha refused again. Venerable Ananda found Queen Maha Prajapati Gotami weeping outside the Pinnacled Hall in Vesali. He now spoke on their behalf and asked the Buddha to ordain these ladies. At first the Buddha refused but Venerable Ananda tried a different approach. He asked, 'Are women, Sir, capable of realizing the highest fruits of the teaching (*Nibbana*)?'

'Yes, they are so capable Ananda,' replied the Buddha.

'Then Sir why not ordain Queen Maha Pajapati Gotami and the other ladies? She looked after you so well on the passing away of your mother when you were a baby, and she and the other ladies have been living such exemplary lives.'

The Buddha agreed and, having formulated a few extra rules to protect the order, first ordained Queen Maha Pajapati Gotami and Princess Yasodhara into an order of nuns and later ordained the other ladies. Venerable Khema and Uppalavanna were appointed the two senior nuns soon after this. The *Saddharma Pundarika Sutra* (p. 216–17) states that the Buddha predicted that both Bhikshuni Mahaprajapati and Bhikshuni Yasodhara would, in time, become well known teachers of the *Dhamma*, bodhisattvas and finally Buddhas.

Practical Teaching

Sometimes the Buddha set a person a task to perform so that the person would realize some aspect of the *Dhamma*. The story of Kisa Gotami is an excellent example. Kisa Gotami was a young woman from a wealthy family married to a successful merchant. When a son was born to her she was overjoyed and cared for him with great love. When he was about one year old he fell ill and suddenly passed away. Kisa Gotami was overcome with grief. She refused to accept that her son was dead and went from person to person asking whether they knew of a medicine that would cure her son who was ill.

Finally a wise person told her to go to the Buddha for help. She then went to the Jetavana monastery, where the Buddha was residing at that time, and related her story. The Buddha understood that no explanation of death being universal and irrevocable would be understood and accepted by Kisa Gotami in her frame of mind and decided to teach this to her in an indirect way.

'I know of a medicine for your son,' the Buddha said. 'Go and get some mustard seeds from a household in which no one has died.'

So Kisa Gotami went from house to house carrying the body of her little son. When she explained her quest for the mustard seeds and asked whether anyone had died in that household the answer was always the same: 'We are sorry but one of our family died sometime ago.' Kisa Gotami realized that in each family and in each house someone had died. She returned to the Buddha and said, 'Sir it is impossible to obtain mustard seeds from a house in which no one has died, for in each family someone has died. Death seems to be common to all beings.'

'That is the lesson I wished to teach you,' the Buddha said. 'Death is common to all living beings. All things are impermanent.' He gave her a teaching on the *Dhamma* and granted her request to be admitted to the order of nuns. One day, much later, it was her turn to light the lamp in the meeting hall and observing the movement of the flame, taking that as a subject of meditation, she thought, 'Even so it is with living beings, they arise and pass away, and on realizing *Nibbana* they are no more.' The Buddha, understanding her thoughts, made an image of himself appear before her and giving another teaching on the *Dhamma*, said:

> Rather than live a hundred years,
> And not realize Nibbana,
> Better is the life of a single day,
> For one who has seen Nibbana.

> *The Dhammapada*, v. 114

Parinibbana, Passing Away

In the year 543 BCE, Gotama Buddha reached the age of 80 years. He had taught for 45 years. Gotama Buddha was mortal, subject to illness and death as all beings. He was conscious that he would pass away in his eightieth year. Venerable Sariputta and Venerable Moggallana, his two chief disciples, had passed away, as had Venerable Rahula and Bhikkhuni Yasodhara.

Rajagaha, the capital of Maghada, was the starting point of his last journey. Accompanied by Venerable Ananda and the other monks he travelled on foot to Nalanda, crossed the Ganges and arrived at the village of Nadika. There, questioned by Venerable Ananda, he explained the mirror of the *Dhamma*:

1. Perfect confidence in the Buddha and reflecting on his virtues
2. Perfect confidence in the *Dhamma* and reflecting on its characteristics
3. Perfect confidence in the *Sangha* and reflecting on the virtues of the *Sangha*.

The details that he gave for each section were the same as we use for worship of the Three Refuges (see Chapter 12).

From Nadika the Buddha travelled to the flourishing town of Vesali and stayed at a grove owned by Ambapali, a well-known lady. After a meal at her residence the next day she offered her spacious mango grove to the Buddha and his followers. The Buddha advised the monks to spend the retreat around Vesali there and he himself travelled to a little hamlet called Beluva to spend his last retreat there. At Beluva he fell ill and realized that his life on earth will soon come to an end. He summoned Venerable Ananda and said, 'What does the *Sangha* need from me? The *Dhamma* I have taught is clear. There is no secret part of it that I have not explained to you. I have not kept a closed fist on anything. Now I am old Ananda, I am past 80 years... so Ananda, let each of you be an island, be a refuge to yourself. Let the Dhamma be your refuge. Seek no other refuge.' The Buddha laid special emphasis on the importance of individual striving. There was no use praying to others or depending on others.

The Buddha then spoke to the assembled monks, 'Whatever truths have been taught by me, study them well, practise, cultivate and develop them so that this Buddha *Sasana* will last long, out of compassion for the world, for the good and happiness of many, and for the good and happiness of deities and humankind. These truths are:

Four foundations of mindfulness,
Four kinds of fight effort,
Four means of accomplishment,
Five faculties,
Five powers,
Seven factors of Enlightenment, and
The Noble Eightfold Path.

He then publicly announced the time of his death to the *Sangha*, explaining to Venerable Ananda that he would pass away in three months' time. He recovered from his illness and continued the walk, arriving at Pava where he and his disciples were entertained by Cunda, the smith. Cunda had prepared an especially delicious dish called *sukaramaddava*. He served the Buddha this dish and was advised by the Buddha to bury the balance. None of the other monks ate this dish. After the meal the Buddha developed a stomach complaint.

Though ill, he walked to Kusinara. He lay down on a couch placed between two sala trees in the sala grove. He explained how people should respect and worship him (see Chapter 12). The deities had assembled in large numbers to pay their respects to the Buddha. He then spoke of four places made sacred by his association that his followers should visit on pilgrimage:

1. Lumbini, his birth place on the Indian borders of Nepal
2. Buddha Gaya, where he attained Enlightenment, about eight miles from Gaya station
3. Saranath, where he established the *Dhamma* by teaching the *Dhammacakkappavattana Sutta*
4. Kusinara, where the Buddha attained *Parinibbana*.

He spoke to Venerable Ananda, saying 'People might say when I am gone that you now have no teacher. This is not so. The *Dhamma* will be your teacher when I am gone.' His last words were, 'Subject to change are all component things. Strive on with diligence.' It was now the day of the full moon in the month of May (*Vesak*) in the year 543 BCE. Attended by the faithful Venerable Ananda, amidst his ordained disciples (monks, nuns and lay people) and in front of the tearful deities who had come to pay their last respects, Gotama Buddha passed away peacefully attaining *Parinibbana (Parinirvana)*.

At this moment Venerable Anuruddha, recited these words:

When he who from all attachment was free,
Who to Nibbana's tranquil state had reached,
When the great sage had finished his span of life,
No grasping struggle troubled that steadfast heart.

All resolute and with unshaken mind,
He calmly triumphed over pain of death,
Even as a bright flame dies away, so was
The last freeing of his heart.

Mahaparinibbana Sutta (Mahaparinirvana Sutra)

Chapter 3

History and Development

Geographical Development

Buddhism spread from India to other Asian countries and is now found in many countries outside Asia.

India

In the present Buddha cycle, Buddhism arose in North India where Gotama Buddha lived and began to teach the Dhamma in about the sixth century BCE. At the time of his *Parinibbana*, or passing away, Buddhism was well established in the north eastern part of India.

Emperor Asoka, the grandson of the Mauryan King Candragupta and son of King Bimbisara was born about 304 BCE. In order to fulfil his ambition for supreme sovereignty he killed most of his brothers. He came to the throne about 273 BCE and reigned until his death about 232 BCE. Waging fierce wars against neighbouring kingdoms, he established a kingdom the size of present-day India. He was called *Candasoka*, meaning Asoka the wicked, because of the brutality of his campaigns.

After the victorious battles of Kalinga he ventured into the city and, on seeing the burnt out houses and scattered corpses, he cried out: 'What have I done?' He was haunted by the grief he had caused by his deeds. On receiving teachings from Buddhist sages and a young Buddhist ordained novice, called Nigrodha, who happened to be his nephew brought up in a Buddhist temple, he embraced Buddhism. This changed his philosophy and outlook on life altogether. We gather much about his later rule from the numerous rock edicts and pillars he established throughout his kingdom, on which were inscribed words of the Dharma (see Chapter 13). The main principles of his new philosophy, Dharma, were non-violence, tolerance of all sects and opinions, respect for parents, friends and all others, and generosity to all. He became an ideal Buddhist monarch, giving state support to Buddhism, building numerous Buddhist temples, shrines, monuments and pilgrim residences. He established an immense public works programme, building schools, universities, hospitals, roads and various other facilities for the development of the people. The essence of his new philosophy of government was non-violence and generosity, and he now came to be known as *Dharmasoka*. He initiated the holding of the Third Buddhist Council (see later in this chapter).

Buddhism flourished in India until about the seventh century when there was a decline. This was due to a reduction in the vigour of the *Sangha*, dwindling lay support, the spread of Jainism, and the emergence of devotional and philosophically coherent forms of Hinduism, which gradually absorbed the followers of Buddhism. The Buddhist university monasteries, such as Nalanda, Valabhi and Taxila, continued their religious and scholastic activities. The foreign invasions and the spread of Islam from about the eleventh century ended the leading position of Buddhism in the main cultural life-stream of India, although it did continue its influence in parts of the country and in neighbouring northern kingdoms, such as Bhutan and Ladakh.

Since about 1850 there has been a revival of Buddhism in India in line with renewed Buddhist activity in Asia. Some important features of this revival have been:

- the conference in Adyar, Madras, in 1891 to agree on fundamental Buddhist beliefs common to different schools and traditions
- archaeological discoveries
- restoration of Buddhist shrines, and
- the adoption of Buddhist symbols as national symbols, for example, the four-lion emblem on the pillar of *Sarnath* and the 'Asoka chakra' wheel (see Chapter 13).

Many Indians led by Dr Ambedkar and others have embraced Buddhism in recent years.

South and South East Asia

Sri Lanka

The ancient chronicle of Sri Lanka, *the Mahavansa*, relates that Gotama Buddha predicted the Dhamma becoming established in Sri

Lanka. The same chronicle relates how the son and daughter of Emperor Asoka, Venerable Mahinda and Venerable Sanghamitta, respectively, both of whom had entered the Order of the *Sangha*, brought Buddhism to Sri Lanka in about 240 BCE during the reign of King Devanampiyatissa of Sri Lanka. The country has been a stronghold of Buddhism since then and it was in Sri Lanka that the Dhamma was written down for the first time in the first century BCE.

The monks and nuns of Sri Lanka played an important role in the spread of Buddhism in Asia and the rest of the world. Since 1850 there has been a Buddhist resurgence in Sri Lanka. This has seen:

- the Buddhist-Christian debates culminating in the Panadura debate of 1873
- The work of Anagarika Dharmapala and the Maha Bodhi Society, which he established
- The establishing of Buddhist schools and universities
- The inauguration of the World Fellowship of Buddhists in 1950
- An increase in Buddhist publications, including the setting up of the Buddhist Publication Society in Kandy
- The start of Buddhist organizations, such as the Young Men's Buddhist Association
- The increased activity in Buddhist archaeological work, and
- The recognition by international organizations such as UNESCO of the importance of Buddhist archaeological sites and shrines as evidence of the development of civilization.

Similarly in other South Asian countries, such as Cambodia, Indonesia, Laos, Myanmar, Thailand and Vietnam, Buddhism has played an important role in the religious and cultural development of those societies.

Cambodia

The same Asokan mission reached Cambodia. From about the sixth century Buddhism filtered into Cambodia and Laos from the east coast of India and became established there by the tenth century. From about the thirteenth century there was further Buddhist influence, this time from Burma, Sri Lanka and Thailand. The year 1969 saw the completion of the translation of the Buddhist Pali Canon into the Khmer language in Cambodia.

Indonesia

Buddhism reached Indonesia about the fifth century and was well established during the great Buddhist kingdoms of Sri Vijaya, Syailendra and Majapahit, from the eighth century until about the fifteenth century. There was then a decline in Buddhism. The archaeological site of Borobodur temple, built in the eighth century, a huge Buddhist monastery in Indonesia is considered one of the wonders of the world. Since 1959 there has been a small-scale revival, with regular celebration of festivals at the Borobudur temple.

Myanmar

The town of Bagan (also known as Pagan), the former capital of Myanmar, which is on the eastern bank of the Ayeyarwaddy river in the central Mandalay division is one of the richest archaeological sites in Asia. The first Bagan city was established about the second century BCE during the reign of King Thamudarit. The whole space within the city limits is thickly studded with pagodas of all shapes and sizes. At one time there were 13,000 temples, pagodas and Buddhist structures. Today over 2,000 well-preserved pagodas and temples from the eleventh–twelfth centuries remain, including the famous Shwe Zigon Pagoda dated 1087 and the equally famous Ananda Temple dated 1090. In Yangon is the famous Shwe Dagon Pagoda (see Chapter 2) is found in Yangon.

Several Buddhist Councils have been held in Myanmar and after the Council in 1871 the Pali Canon was inscribed on marble slabs. The Burmese Buddhist *Sangha* is known for developing and teaching special meditation techniques.

Thailand

One of Emperor Asoka's missions was to Thailand, where there are archaeological Buddhist sites dating from the first century BCE. Thailand, where Buddhism has received strong and continuing State support, has been a centre for the development of teaching and practice of the Dhamma. The numerous Buddhist temples and shrines in Bangkok and across Thailand is evidence of the importance of Buddhism in the cultural life of the people.

Buddhism is a State institution in Thailand, with a *Sangharajah* (head of the *Sangha*) – who is often a member of the royal family – managing Buddhist affairs. The senior member of the *Sangha* holds the office of Supreme Patriarch and even the Prime Minister greets the Supreme Patriarch with a prostration. In keeping with the custom where a young man spends some time as a Buddhist monk, the king His Majesty Bhumibol Adulyadej, the only Buddhist king in the world today, was himself ordained as a monk for some time.

Vietnam

An inscription in Vietnam refers to the introduction of Buddhism there in the fourth century. Monks from China visited Vietnam during this period and the main influence seems to have come from this country. In the fifth century a Kashmiri monk Venerable Gunavarman studied Buddhism in Sri Lanka and the spent a long time in Vietnam, arriving in China later. There was also a Sri Lankan monk, Venerable Gunabhadra, who arrived in Vietnam from China.

Buddhism was made the State religion in the eleventh century and has remained firmly established here.

Nepal, Bhutan, Ladakh, Afghanistan and Kashmir

Gotama Buddha's birthplace was in Lumbini Park, Kapilavasthu, in present-day Nepal. Buddhism became established in Nepal and continues to be influenced to some extent by Hinduism in this country. Gotama Buddha was from the Sakya clan, which is still exists in Nepal.

Bhutan and Ladakh, situated in the foothills of the Himalayas, have been Buddhist countries from the earliest times.

Buddhism came to Afghanistan and Kashmir about the third century BCE and was well established there by the first century, when these areas were part of Emperor Kanishka's kingdom. The Fourth Council in the Mahayana tradition (see later in this chapter) was held in Kashmir. The influence of Buddhism declined after the tenth century.

China

Buddhism came to China first overland from North India along the silk route and later from South Asian countries across the seas. Official histories of China record the presence of Buddhism there in the first century. China saw a remarkable expansion and development of Buddhism. In some Chinese kingdoms Buddhism was accepted as the State religion. In the second century the Sanskrit texts started to be translated into Chinese, which took almost 1,000 years to complete. New traditions developed and new texts were written.

Nuns from Sri Lanka journeyed by sea to China in the fifth century to establish an Order of Nuns in the country. In the same century an invading Chinese army defeated Kucha in Central Asia and, on the express instructions of the Chinese Emperor, captured the famous scholar monk Venerable Kumarajiva and carried him back to China to organize Buddhist work, including translations, there. This is the only recorded instance of a Buddhist monk being taken as a hostage.

Monks from Southern Asian countries went to China to teach. Chinese pilgrims, including Fa-hsien in the fifth century and Hsiian-tsang and I-tsing in the seventh century, spent many years on study pilgrimages in South Asian countries. There was a close and dynamic exchange of Buddhist teaching, learning, scholarship and practice between China and countries such as India and Sri Lanka until about the twelfth century. From this time Buddhism in China became influenced by Confucianism and Taoism. The Ming dynasty, from 1368, saw the gradual decline in the position of Buddhism although it continued to influence Chinese culture.

Since around 1980 there has been a resurgence of Buddhism in China. There is a Buddhist Association of China officially recognized by the State. Many Chinese Buddhists participate in a 'Going for Refuge and Five Precept' ceremony. An increasing number of temples are active today, including Fayuan Si which houses the Beijing Buddhist Academy. There are about 40 monks, most in their late 20s or early 30s in residence at the Longhua monastery in Shanghai. This monastery, dating back to the eighth century, is typical of the Tang dynasty. The monks' training continues despite a shortage of books and teachers. Longhua is a focal point of religious activity and each day many people visit to make offerings, worship and meditate.

Other important sites include:

- Jiuhua Shan, the sacred mountain of Bodhisattva Kshitigarbha, which is an eight-hour journey from Shanghai
- A newly renovated Buddhist academy below the town of Jiuhua Shan
- A monastery in Hangzhou dating back to the fourth century, which is active in Buddhist teaching and is a major tourist attraction for visitors from China and elsewhere.

Korea and Japan

Buddhism was introduced to Korea in the fourth century from China. It became established quickly, blending with the indigenous Shamanism, and was accepted as the State religion by the seventh century. Buddhism has maintained its dominant influence in Korean culture and today Korea has a flourishing *Sangha* of monks and nuns.

It was from Korea that Buddhism was introduced to Japan in the sixth century. It was immediately accepted in royal circles and was given enthusiastic support by Prince Shotoku who, as regent, ruled Japan from 592–622. It was Chinese Buddhism that had the most influence on the development of Buddhism in Japan. Many Japanese monks went to study in China and returned with Chinese texts. There was also some influence from the indigenous Shintoism, which continues as a separate religion today. Buddhism, made up of different traditions, however, remains the main religion in Japan today. Some families have a Buddhist celebration at the birth of a baby and on marriage, then a Shinto ceremony when a person dies. Several universities, such as Otani and Koyasan, specialize in Buddhist studies and scholarship.

Tibet, Mongolia and Central Asia

Buddhism was first introduced to Tibet in the seventh century through the matrimonial alliances of King Sron-btsan-gam-po with Nepal and China. It did not become widely recognized at this time, however. Later, in the eleventh century, it was introduced again and then became firmly established, becoming a major part of Tibetan culture. The teachings came mainly from Northern India and all of the Buddhist traditions in Tibet were introduced during the eleventh century, evolving over time into Tibetan Buddhism, with its special teaching and practices of *Vajrayana* and *Tantrayana* (see later in this chapter).

The Tibetan alphabet was formulated primarily to copy the Buddhist texts into the local language. Tibetan Buddhists were very active in translation and literary work, scholarship, building and maintaining temples and monasteries, and in the study and practice of Buddhism. The practice of combining spiritual eminence with political leadership evolved in Tibet, signified in the office of the Dalai Lama.

One of the missions sent by King Kanishka in the first century was to Mongolia. Buddhism became established there and has remained the main religion.

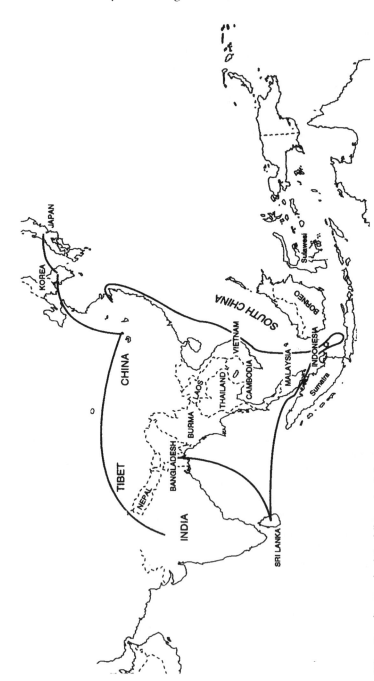

Directional spread of Buddhism in Asia

There has been a resurgence of Buddhism in recent years. There were several Buddhist kingdoms in Central Asia and recent archaeological findings indicate the importance of Buddhism in this area in the past going as far back as the first century. Archaeologists from Moscow University have unearthed several palm leaf Buddhist manuscripts in Prakrit and Sanskrit, dating from the fifth century, along with various other Buddhist relics and artefacts.

United Kingdom

Since about 1826 there have been an increasing number of English translations of Buddhist texts by various scholars and a growing scholarly interest in Buddhism in the UK. The formation of the Pali Text Society in 1881 and the teaching of Pali, Sanskrit and Buddhism in some universities fostered this interest.

The first English person to become a Buddhist monk was Gordon Douglas, who was ordained in Sri Lanka in 1899 as Bhikkhu Asoka.

In 1898 Allan Bennett left London to study Buddhism in Sri Lanka. He then travelled to Burma in 1901 and soon after was ordained Venerable Ananda Metteyya. He led a Buddhist mission to the country of his birth in 1908 and in that year was the first Buddhist monk to teach the *Dhamma* in the UK.

The Buddhist Society was established in its present form in 1926 by Christmas Humphreys. Also in 1926, as a consequence of a mission from Sri Lanka, led by Anagarika Dharmapala, the London Buddhist Vihara was established. From about this time Buddhism has been accepted as a religion by an increasing number of people in the UK. Since 1960 Buddhism has come to the UK from various Asian countries, mainly with Asian Buddhists who have come to live here, and there has been ever-increasing interest, study and practice of this religion by British people. The *Buddhist Society Directory* in its 2007 edition listed over 649 Buddhist temples, monasteries, centres and groups.

Continental Europe

Buddhism is found throughout Europe, with Buddhist societies functioning in the Czech Republic, Greece, Hungary, Poland, Romania, Spain and Switzerland, among others. The European Buddhist Union was formed to provide a forum for the discussion of Buddhist activities in Europe. It has an annual meeting, mainly for teachers of Buddhism.

Germany

In Germany Buddhist studies began around 1850 and many texts were translated into German. A Buddha House was founded in Berlin in about 1925.

In the 1ninth century Venerable Nyanatiloka and Venerable Nyanaponika, both German nationals, were ordained as monks in Sri Lanka. They established various monasteries. These include the Island Hermitage in Dodanduwa in the South of Sri Lanka, situated on a wooded island in a lagoon and so accessible only by boat, and the Forest Hermitage at Udawattekelle behind the Sri Dalada Maligawa (see Chapter 14) in Kandy. They published their own writings and translations.

When the Buddhist Publication Society (BPS) was founded in Kandy in 1958 to publish Buddhist literature in English, the founders invited Venerable Nyanaponika, who was residing at the Forest Hermitage, to be the Society's spiritual director and editor. He steered the BPS, whose current worldwide membership is over 5,000, until his retirement in 1984 due to ill health. Venerable Nyanatiloka's *Buddhist Dictionary*, written in 1946 and Venerable Nyanaponika's *The Heart of Buddhist Meditation* are two Buddhist classics that are greatly valued by English-speaking Buddhists the world over.

These two monks also influenced the development of Buddhism in Germany, where new temples have been established recently. Buddhism is studied in a number of universities, for example the University of Hamburg.

France and Belgium

Buddhist studies started in France in about 1875. The main interest was in the Buddhism of China, Japan and Vietnam, and the study of Sanskrit and Tibetan texts. There was notable Buddhist scholarship in universities, such as Sorbonne. The first Buddhist temples were established by Vietnamese who settled in France and more recently temples of other traditions have been established. Professor de la Vallee Poussin, who held a Chair in Oriental Studies at the University of Ghent, Belgium, in 1893, pioneered many scholarly studies in Buddhism.

Italy

In Italy Buddhism has been taught in the universities including the Roman Catholic Gregorian University, and now there are some temples and monasteries in Italy.

Scandinavia

In countries such as Denmark, Netherlands and Sweden interest in Buddhism was first apparent in academic circles. The University of Arhuus in Denmark has an oriental studies faculty teaching Pali and Buddhism.

In recent times people have become interested in Buddhism as a religion. The Buddhist Society of Sweden was founded in 1957 as the result of an interest in Buddhism kindled by a lecture by Venerable Narada of Sri Lanka.

Russia and Adjoining Countries

In some parts of Russia and the adjoining countries, Buddhism has been established as a religion since the earliest times. Archaeological work directed by universities has unearthed some exciting finds, including some Buddhist pottery and artefacts dating back to the first century in Central Asia. There has also been a large volume of academic work in the oriental studies faculties of the Universities of Leningrad and Moscow.

In the 1990s Buddhist temples were re-established in Leningrad and Moscow, and the Buddhist Religious Board was set up to co-ordinate Buddhist activities in the area.

The United States and Canada

Interest in Buddhism was kindled in the United States when Professor Rhys Davids lectured there in 1881 and when Anagarika Dharmapala spoke at the Parliament of World Religions in 1893 in Chicago. At about the same time Japanese people, who were finding new homes on the western coast, brought Buddhism to their new country. From about 1890 the oriental studies faculties in universities such as Harvard and Yale have contributed to the development of Buddhism through scholarship, translations and publications.

In this century different traditions of Buddhism have come to the USA, where now one sees representatives of all of the schools and traditions as well as some new movements. Centres for the study of world religions have been established in universities, such as Harvard and Yale, and there are Chairs in Buddhism in California and Wisconsin. The last 50 years has seen has seen an increasing number of Buddhist temples, monasteries and meditation centres.

The position in Canada is similar. Asian Buddhists who now live in Canada have established temples and have organized Dhamma classes. Some have contributed new books and other publications on Buddhism.

South America

The Japanese finding new homes in South America brought Buddhism with them from about 1900. New traditions have become established in recent times. In Brazil the first Buddhist Society was formed in 1956. In Sao Paulo there are several Buddhist temples catering mainly to Japanese Buddhists. In 1967, a Sri Lankan Buddhist temple was established in Rio de Janeiro. There are Buddhist Societies in Argentina, Chile and Columbia.

Africa

In Africa there are Buddhist societies, groups and centres in Ghana, South Africa and Zimbabwe.

Australia and New Zealand

People from China and Sri Lanka who came to live in Australia brought Buddhism with them early in the ninth century. A temple was established in Melbourne in 1856. In 1910, Venerable U Sasana Dhaja, an English Buddhist monk, arrived in Australia and started teaching Buddhism.

Recent years have seen many Buddhist temples, monasteries, meditation centres and groups with different traditions set up throughout Australia, enthusiastically supported by Asian people who have come to live in Australia amid the increasing interest in Buddhism as a subject of study and practice among all Australian Buddhists.

Buddhism arrived in New Zealand a little later and has developed in the same way.

Buddhist Councils

Introduction

Councils have been held from time to time to discuss Buddhism teaching and practice and are a feature of the development of

Buddhism in southern Asia. Their composition and nature has varied. Sometimes only ordained members of the *Sangha* have taken part while at other times lay Buddhists have also been involved.

Councils have been held for various purposes, for instance to recite, rehearse and authenticate the teaching, settle disputes, write the teaching, reorganize the *Sangha*, to unify the *Sasana* (the Buddhist community and teaching) and to preserve the teaching. Until the Fourth Council in Sri Lanka, the teaching was handed down from generation to generation as an oral tradition.

First Council

Even during the Buddha's lifetime there were differences of opinion among some members of the *Sangha* on matters of discipline. A few days after the Buddha passed away, a monk called Venerable Subhadda was heard to say that now the teacher was no more they could do as they wished. On hearing this, the senior monks decided to call a Council to protect the *Sasana* by determining and authenticating the teaching.

The First Council was held at Rajagaha, the capital of Magadha, under the patronage of King Ajatasattu about three months after the Buddha passed away. Venerable Maha Kassapa presided and the *Vinaya* (rules of monastic discipline) and Dhamma were rehearsed. Venerable Upali dealt with the *Vinaya* and Venerable Ananda dealt with the Dhamma. In the presence of the senior monks, who were members of the Council, these two monks recited and explained their respective parts of the teaching. They were questioned systematically by Venerable Maha Kassapa and the other members of the Council. After much discussion the Council, consisting of 500 *Arahats*, arrived at a final definitive version of the *Vinaya* and Dhamma. The Dhamma included *Abhidhamma* (higher philosophy). At the end of the Council all of the monks recited or chanted the complete teaching.

Second Council

About 100 years later there were some differences of opinion among the *Sangha* about certain aspects of the teaching, specifically relating to the interpretation of certain monastic rules and the proper spiritual status of the Buddha. A Second Council was called to meet at Vesali during the reign of King Kalasoka. Venerable Sabbakami, the most senior monk, presided. The *Vinaya* and the Dhamma, including the *Abhidhamma*, were recited, rehearsed and authenticated. At the end of the Council the monks chanted the whole of the teaching. The *Sangha* were united at this time and the *Vinaya*, Dhamma and *Abhidhamma* agreed at this Second Council forms the foundation of the teaching in all of the schools and traditions of Buddhism. There were divisions in the *Sangha* later.

Third Council

By the third century BCE some undesirable elements had entered the *Sangha* and were disturbing the unity, peace and status of the Buddhist community with their improper views and unorthodox lifestyles. A Third Council was called by Emperor Asoka of India to purify the *Sangha* and reaffirm the texts. It was held at Pataliputra, now called Patna, and the senior monk Venerable Moggallputta Tissa presided. The undesirable elements of the *Sangha* were excluded and various matters of conflict sorted out. The *Vinaya*, Dhamma and *Abhidhamma* were rehearsed and the *Abhidhamma* was dealt with separately as the third part of the teaching.

After the Council missions were sent to Kashmir and other areas in the north nest, to Syria, Greece and Egypt in the West, to Sri Lanka in the south and to countries such as Myammar and Thailand in South East Asia.

The mission to Sri Lanka was led by Emperor Asoka's son, Venerable Mahinda, and was followed by a further mission led by Emperor Asoka's daughter Sanghamitta Theri. She brought with her a branch of the Maha Bodhi tree at Buddha Gaya. This was planted at Anuradhapura and flourishes today as the Sri Maha Bodhi tree, the oldest historically authenticated tree. It is venerated by many pilgrims.

Fourth Council

A Fourth Council was held at Aluvihara, near Matale, in Sri Lanka in the first century BCE. Venerable Rakkhita Mahathera presided. Now for the first time the teaching was written down in Pali as the *Vinaya Pitaka* (rules of monastic discipline), *Sutta Pitaka* (the Dhamma) and the *Abhidhamma Pitaka* (higher philosophy) in three sections known as the *Tipitaka* (three baskets) and collectively as the Pali Canon.

In the first century, during the reign of Emperor Kanishka in

North-West India, another Council (Fourth Council in the Mahayana tradition) was called to resolve some differences of opinion and to commit the teaching to writing. This Council was presided over by Venerable Vasumitra. The teaching was written down in Sanskrit in three sections, namely the *Vinaya Vaibhasha* (rules of monastic discipline), *Upadesa Vaibhasha* (Dhamma) and *Abhidhamma Vaibhasha* (higher philosophy), showing the same divisions as the Pali Canon. This version came to be known as the Sanskrit Canon. After the Council Emperor Kanishka sent Buddhist missions to Central Asia, China and Mongolia.

Other Councils

In the twelfth century a Fifth Council was held in Sri Lanka at Anuradhapura, under the patronage of famous King Parakramabahu I. It was presided over by Venerable Dimbulagala Kasyapa. The purpose of this Council was to reform the *Sangha* and settle certain disputes between different schools of Buddhism in Sri Lanka. At this time there were, in Sri Lanka, the teachings of all the schools of Buddhism. This Council came down in favour of the Southern Theravada school, as a result of which other traditions declined and ceased to exist in Sri Lanka.

A Sixth Council was held in Burma in 1871 to rehearse the Pali Canon and to inscribe it on marble slabs.

Finally in 1954 there was a Seventh Council in Burma to study the *Tipitaka*.

Schools and Traditions

Introduction

Sometime after the Second Council, held about 100 years after the Buddha passed away, there was a division in the *Sangha* between the *Sthaviras* or elders, who in time formed the *Sthaviravadin* school, and the other monks known as the *Mahasanghas* (greater community), who in time formed the *Mahasanghika* school. The main points of difference were the *Sthaviravadins'* refusal to agree to any change in the rules of monastic discipline and the *Mahasanghikas'* views that gave a reduced status to the *Arahat* (one who had attained *Nibbana*) and promoted the Buddha to a super-human transcendental status.

In the development of Buddhism over the centuries several schools and traditions have arisen. Most of them have now ceased to exist, being absorbed by others. What we have today are the three main schools of Buddhism. The traditional classification is into Theravada Buddhism (the teaching of the elders) in South Asia, Mahayana Buddhism (the Greater Vehicle) in the East (sometimes understood to include Tibetan Buddhism), and Tibetan Buddhism in the North. Other classifications may be used. First, they can be classed geographically, as the Eastern (Mahayana), Northern (Tibetan) and Southern (Theravada) Buddhism. This is the classification adopted in this book. Second, according to the three turnings of the wheel – first turning (Theravada), second turning (Mahayana) and third turning (Tibetan) Buddhism. The reference to first, second and third relate to the language of the texts, Pali Canon (Theravada), Sanskrit/Chinese/Japanese Canon (Mahayana) and Tibetan Canon (Tibetan).

The schools, and the traditions within the schools, have a different emphasis and style of practice, with a great deal of overlap. There is nothing in any tradition of Buddhism that is not found in the others. The Northern (Tibetan) school is sometimes considered to be a part of the Eastern (Mahayana) school. Within each school we find sub-divisions and different traditions.

Southern (Theravada, Sravakayana) School

After the Third Council, at the time of Emperor Asoka in the third century BCE, missions were sent to various parts of South Asia taking the teaching as finalized at that Council to different countries. This teaching, sometimes referred to as early Buddhism or *Sravakayana*, was that of the *Sthaviravadin* school (the teaching of the elders). It was this teaching, brought to Sri Lanka by Venerable Mahinda and Venerable Sanghamitta, that was written down in Pali in Sri Lanka in the first century BCE as the Pali Canon. Teachings of other traditions reached the South Asian countries but did not become established there.

The school of Buddhism in South Asian countries, such as Cambodia, Laos, Myanmar, Sri Lanka and Thailand, based on the Pali Canon is known as the Southern (Theravada) school. Vietnam has a mixture of Southern and Eastern Buddhism.

Eastern (Mahayana) School

In the first century BCE the important schools of Buddhism in India were the *Mahasanghika* and *Sarvastivada* Schools. The language of these schools was Sanskrit. At about this time there were new developments within the existing schools. New interpretations of Buddhist ideas were developed in India in a religious environment that included Brahminism and, later, Hinduism. These new developments went to form the Mahayana (great vehicle or career) teachings.

The special characteristics of the new Mahayana School were the emphasis on the bodhisattva ideal, the aim of each person to become a Buddha, the promotion of the Buddha to a super-human transcendental status, and an elaborate and complex philosophy. The importance given to the bodhisattva ideal has led to the Mahayana school also being referred to as *Bodhisattvayana* (bodhisattva path or career). New Sutras (texts) were composed similar in form to the existing ones but expounding the new ideas. The older non-Mahayana traditions of Buddhism in India at that time were collectively referred to as the *Sravakayana* (path or career of the disciples).

The Mahayanists, because of their aim to become a Buddha and to work for the happiness and welfare of all beings, considered their teachings to be superior to that of the Sravakas, whose aim was to attain *Nibbana*. The Mahayanists referred derogatorily to the Sravakayana teaching as *Hinayana* (lesser vehicle or career). Venerable Dr Walpola Rahula of Sri Lanka has explained that it is incorrect to refer to the Theravada as *Hinayana*, since the Theravada teaching was formulated and finalized before, and quite independently of, these developments in India.

The growth of the Mahayana was gradual and was not accompanied by violent disagreements. The Mahayana was an extension of the Sravakayana teaching. They were, more than anything else, differences of outlook and attitude, rather than substantive or institutional differences. Chinese Buddhist monks, such as Hsuan-Tsang and I-tsing who travelled in India in the seventh century, write that both Mahayana and Sravakayana monks lived in the same monasteries. Those who accepted the Mahayana teachings were Mahayanists and the others were Sravakayanists.

The special characteristics of the developed Eastern (Mahayana) Buddhism are:

- The bodhisattva ideal and path
- Aim to become a Buddha

- Trikaya concept (see Chapter 18)
- Compassion and wisdom
- Devotion, worship of multiple Buddhas and bodhisattvas
- The importance of lay persons
- New ideas in philosophy
- Relationship of Nirvana to Samsara, and
- Special Sutras.

The doctrines of the different schools of Buddhism at the time of development in North India fell into four schools of philosophy:

- *Vaibasika* (Sarvastivada School), which upheld realism and accepted the existence of phenomenal objects on direct perception.
- *Sautrantika*, which explained that examples are adequate proof for a thesis and that external objects are mere appearances and their existence has to be proved by inference. It also explained that subtle forms of matter were transferred from existence to existence until they ceased to exist on attainment of *Nibbana*.
- *Madhyamika*, which held that reality was a void or emptiness. This explained that the life of the world was the same as *Nibbana* and that the bliss of *Nibbana* was available to everyone.
- *Yogacara*, which held that reality was a void or emptiness that was without origin, decay or destruction and hence beyond description. This reality was pure consciousness.

In China it was the Mahayana version of Buddhism that became established. Different traditions developed, each having its own monasteries and teaching facilities. Each tradition was based on one or more of the Mahayana Sutras. Similarly, the Mahayana became established in Korea and Japan. The main Chinese traditions influenced the development of corresponding traditions in Japan. In addition there were new traditions in Japan. The main traditions in Japan today are:

- *Jodo Shinshu*, which was founded by Shinran (1173–1263) based on pure land, practising devotion to Amida Buddha. This is the largest tradition in Japan.
- *Nichiren*, which involves practising devotion to the founder Nichiren (1222–1282) and to the truth as revealed in the *Saddharma Pundarika Sutra*.
- *Zen*, which emphasizes meditation and developed from the Chinese Chan tradition.

- *Tendai*, which practices devotion and meditation and dates from the sixth century.
- *Shingon*, which is a tantric tradition dating from the seventh century.

The teachings of all these traditions collectively comprise the Eastern (Mahayana) School or Eastern Buddhism.

Northern (Tibetan) School

In about the seventh century there were new developments from within the Mahayana. This was the growth of Buddhist tantra activated by the mutual influence of Mahayana and Hinduism. It drew on the Mahayana *Madhyamika* philosophy and incorporated Hindu yoga practices involving working with subtle mental processes. Buddhist Tantra or *Tantrayana* (tantra path) is also referred to as *Mantrayana* (mantra path) or *Vajrayana* (thunderbolt or diamond path). The aim of *Vajrayana* is the same as that in Mahayana – to attain Buddhahood – but the Tantric practices provided a quick way to achieve this end. New Tantric Sutras were written expounding these new ideas.

The teachings of the different traditions of Buddhism that went to form Tibetan Buddhism were:

- *Sravakayana* – a path that serves for achieving liberation from cyclic existence for its own sake
- *Mahayana* – a path seeking the rank of Buddhahood for the sake of others
- *Tantrayana* – a quickened path to Buddhahood involving complex tantric practices and meditations.

The different traditions of Buddhism in Tibet are as follows:

- Kadam
- Kagyu
- Nyingma
- Gelug.

The teaching of all of these traditions collectively comprise the Northern (Tibetan) School or Northern Buddhism.

New Developments in the West

There are new developments in the West that emphasize different aspects of the Dhamma. The Western Buddhist Order is well established in the UK and there have been other developments in the Americas.

Common Features

Although there are different schools and traditions, the central and fundamental parts of the *Vinaya*, Dhamma and *Abhidhamma* go back to the Second Council before there was any division in the *Sangha*. This central part of the teaching is therefore common to all schools and traditions. Different traditions give varying emphasis to different aspects of the teaching and practices. There are also additional teachings and explanations specific to particular traditions.

A conference was arranged by Col. H. S. Olcott in Adyar, India in 1891 and a document entitled *The Buddhist Catechism* was published setting out the fundamental Buddhist teachings. This document was agreed, accepted and signed by representative members of the *Sangha* in Burma, Sri Lanka, Japan, and Chittagong (in Bangladesh). Its contents, apart from the date of the Buddha, were accepted by Mongolian Buddhists.

In 1945 Christmas Humphreys at the Buddhist Society in London drafted the *Twelve Principles of Buddhism*. These were accepted as correct by representative Buddhists in China, Japan, Myanmar, Sri Lanka and Thailand. Professor Hajime Nakamura, who was the Professor of Indian philosophy in the 1950s in the University of Tokyo, Japan, discusses these matters in great detail in the chapter entitled 'Unity and Diversity in Buddhism' in the *Path of The Buddha* (Morgan, 1956). Finally, we go back to the words in the *Saddharma Pundarika (Lotus) Sutra*: 'There is only one yana, Buddhayana', the path of the Buddha.

Chapter 4

Literature

Oral Tradition

The Buddha's teaching was oral (spoken). The area where he lived was called Magadha and the language he spoke was called Magadhi. This was a spoken form of Sanskrit, one of the classical languages of India. The Buddha advised the *Sangha* to teach in the language of the people they taught. As Buddhism spread to various parts of India, Asia and the world, the *Dhamma* was translated into various other languages.

Memory training was, and still is, an important part of the education in Asia. The *Sangha* memorized the teaching, some of them specializing in certain parts of it. The First and Second Councils revised and authenticated the whole teaching (see Chapter 3). Each Council ended with the chanting of the whole teaching. Over the years there was group chanting of the *Dhamma* at festivals and other special occasions. These groups or communal chanting helped the *Sangha* to remember the teaching. If one of them had forgotten a section he could learn it during chanting. This oral tradition depended on a continuous stream of the *Sangha*, with the senior members passing down the teaching to junior members. Teaching was handed down from generation to generation accurately by means of this group chanting.

The oral tradition of Buddhism continues today. The *Sangha* memorize sections of the *Dhamma* and chant texts at festivals and ceremonies, in the temples, at public Buddhist ceremonies and at private ceremonies in the homes of Buddhists. They take turns in leading the chanting. Some Buddhists recite or chant sections of the texts daily. The *Karaniya Metta Sutta*, the *Mangala Sutta* and Chapter 25 of the *Saddharma Pundarika Sutra* are favourite texts for chanting.

The chanting, known as *pirith*, is a sacred act. It also helps to teach children and adults the texts, because after hearing it several times they begin to remember the words. They also associate different circumstances, celebrations and occasions in their lives with the chanting. Sometimes lay people join in the chanting. The sound of the chanting has a calming effect on the mind and many Buddhists find it to be a very beneficial devotional and meditative experience. Some listen to chanting on cassettes and CDs at home and when going about daily tasks. Some listen to recorded chanting as a part of their daily worship, generally the first thing in the morning.

Chanting of selected texts is often arranged when a person is ill. The author knows of an instance when this was done for a patient after brain surgery to drain the blood following internal haemorrhage in the brain. The patient had been in a coma for over ten days and the family were gathered around her bed. Her eldest daughter began to chant the *Maha Mangala Sutta* and the patient opened her eyes. After the chanting of several other texts, the patient smiled, closed her eyes and passed away peacefully.

This shows the power of the chanting to penetrate the conscious and the unconscious mind. The Buddha himself gave a *Dhamma* teaching to his dying father. It is common to chant Buddhist texts, especially the *Satipatthana Sutta* (see Chapter 15), in the last moments of a person's life.

Many Buddhists feel that reciting and listening to the chanting of specially selected texts from the scriptures, or *pirith*, is a blessing, gives them protection and produces a sense of mental well being. In Sri Lanka, on special occasions such as an important family matter, birth, marriage, death anniversary of a relative or moving into a new house, a *pirith* ceremony is arranged as a blessing. This sometimes involves chanting overnight.

In Japan some Buddhists chant the title of the *Saddharma Pundarika Sutra* (Lotus Sutra) in Japanese – '*Namu Myoho Renge Kyo*' (I seek refuge in the Lotus Sutra) – at their worship. They also chant long passages of the *Sutra*, especially Chapter 25. The spelling *Sutra* is used in the title of a Sanskrit text, and *Sutta* in the title of a Pali text. They both mean a *Dhamma* text.

In Tibet the chanting of, '*Om mane padme hum*' (Hail the jewel in the lotus) is often accompanied by ritual gestures to increase the effect of the spoken words.

In Japan the Pure Land Buddhists (*Jodo-shinshu* tradition) have a ritual chant called the Nembutsu: '*Namu Amida Butsu*' (Praise the Amida Buddha).

In Buddhist communities chanting is a part of the funeral service to bless the dead person. This is especially important as Buddhists believe in rebirth and the continuity of life (see Chapter 8).

Southern School Literature (Pali Canon)

The teaching was written down for the first time at the Fourth Council in Sri Lanka in the first century BCE in Pali The writing was in three sections – *Vinaya Pitaka, Sutta Pitaka* and *Abhidhamma Pitaka (Pitaka* meaning basket or collection) – following the division at the Councils, and is called the *Tipitaka* (three baskets).

The *Vinaya Pitaka* consists of about 227 rules of conduct and discipline applicable to the monastic life of monks (*bhikkhus*) and nuns (*bhikkhunis*). It is divided into three parts and, in addition to the rules, gives accounts of the circumstances under which a rule was promulgated and exceptions to the rule.

The *Sutta Pitaka* consists of the main teaching or Dhamma. It is divided into five *Nikayas* or sections. These are:

- The long teachings *(Digha Nikaya)*
- Medium length teachings *(Majjhima Nikaya)*
- Groups of shorter teachings according to common topics *(Samyutta Nikaya)*
- A collection arranged according to subjects discussed *(Anguttara Nikaya)*
- A collection of a variety of shorter texts in verse and prose *(Khuddaka Nikaya)*.

The *Abhidhamma Pitaka* consists of seven books called the higher or further teaching. This is a philosophical analysis and systematization of the teaching.

In the first century BCE, the writing was on strips of dried palm leaves cut into rectangles, etched with a metal stylus and rubbed over with carbon ink. A thread was passed through the pages to keep them in order and elaborately painted wooden covers were fixed at the ends. This tradition has carried on and is even done today. It is considered to be a meritorious activity. If one visits the Aluvihara temple near Matale in Sri Lanka one can see monks copying the texts onto such palm leaves and preparing the original-style books.

The Pali Canon was recited, checked and agreed at the Fourth and later Southern Buddhism Councils. It was engraved on marble slabs in Myanmar. The entire Canon has been translated into

English. The Pali Canon has been put onto a single CD-ROM disk, published by the American Academy of Religion and Scholar's Press in Atlanta.

Some important *Suttas* in Southern Buddhism (sometimes the word *maha*, meaning great, is added in front of the name of the *Sutta* and sometimes the name of the *Sutta* may be one word or separated into several words) are:

SN 22.59

MN 135

SN 56.11

KN 1.8
KHP 5
Sn 1.6

SN 6.15

SN 12.2

MN 10

DN 31

- *Anattalakkhana Sutta* – the second teaching, which explains impermanence, Dukkha and selflessness (see Chapter 6)
- *Cullakamma Vibhanga Sutta*, which is about actions and results (see Chapter 7)
- *Dhammacakkappvattana Sutta*, the first teaching, which is about the Four Noble Truths (see Chapter 5)
- *Karaniya Metta Sutta*, on loving- kindness (see Chapter 11)
- *Mangala Sutta*, on the blessings of life (see Chapter 11)
- *Parabhava Sutta*, which sets out the causes of one's downfall (see Chapter 11)
- *Parinibbana Sutta* – the last teaching. This emphasizes some important aspects of the Dhamma, gives final advice to followers, bids a fond farewell and describes the *Parinibbana* of Gotama Buddha (see Chapter 2)
- *Paticca Samuppada Vibhanga Sutta*, which sets out the teaching on dependant origination (see Chapter 6)
- *Satipatthana Sutta*, the fundamental text on meditation and mindfulness (see Chapter 15)
- *Sigalovada Sutta* – a lay person's ethical code that explains the guidelines for social relationships (see Chapter 16).

Sanskrit Canon

The Buddha advised the monks to teach in the different languages of the people. Oral teaching continued in India in the form of oral Sanskrit. At the Fourth Council in India (see Chapter 4) the teaching was written down in Sanskrit and was known as the Sanskrit Canon. There were different versions of the Sanskrit Canon, all similar in form and content. Both the Pali and the Sanskrit Canons can be traced to the common original teaching of the Buddha.

The Sanskrit *Tripitaka*, or Canon, displayed the same three divisions as the Pali Canon, namely:

- *Vinaya Vaibasha* – monastic rules

- *Sutra Vaibasha* – the Dhamma, the five *Agamas* corresponding to the five *Nikayas* of the Pali Canon, and
- *Abhidhamma Vaibasha* – the scholarly philosophical analysis.

The Sanskrit Canon does not exist in a complete form in India, but does exist in translation in Chinese, Japanese and Tibetan. Sections of it have been unearthed by archaeologists in Central Asia.

Eastern School Literature (Mahayana Texts)

With the growth of the Mahayana, new Sutras were written. Teaching in the Sanskrit Canon was incorporated into the Mahayana teaching. The new *Sutras* were based on the existing texts but new material was added to incorporate the Mahayana ideas. In Japan the *Sangha* copy out the texts by hand and this is considered to be a very meritorious activity.

The most popular and important of the *Sutras* in Eastern Buddhism are:

- *Brahmajala Sutra*, which sets out the Eastern (Mahayana) Buddhist disciplinary Precepts (see Chapter 11).
- *Dasabhumika Sutra*, where Vodhisattva Vajragarbha explains the ten stages in the path of the Bodhisattva (see Chapter 17).
- *Lankavatara Sutra*, the revelation of the teaching in Sri Lanka.
- *Lalitavistara Sutra*, the life of the Buddha.
- *Mahaparinirvana Sutra*, understood to be Buddha's last teaching, which sets out a summary of the whole teaching. The scene of the *Sutra* is Kushinara as the Buddha is about to enter *Parinirvana*. The Buddha asserts the indestructibility of the Buddha's body and tells of the bodhisattva's virtues. He explains that the ten stages of the bodhisattva's path lead to the highest wisdom. He asserts that all beings have the Buddha nature (*Bodhicitta*) and the capacity to realize *Nirvana*.
- *Prajna Paramita Sutra* (Perfection of Wisdom or Heart *Sutra*), which sets out the teachings of emptiness (see Chapter 6, the section on Selflessness, where the importance of the *Sutra* is explained and the *Sutra* is quoted in phonetic Japanese and English).
- *Saddharma Pundarika Sutra* (Lotus *Sutra*). This Sutra consists of a set of teachings given by the Buddha towards the end of his teaching life to a multitude of disciples, deities and other beings. The setting and scope are cosmic and the teachings

presented in both prose and verse are full of parables and graphic anecdotes. It sets out the teaching, explains the oneness of the teachings referred to as the *Buddhayana* or 'one buddha vehicle' or 'Buddha-way', and praises the bodhisattva. Eastern Buddhism considers this to be the supreme teaching and it is understood as the most important *Sutra* in China and Japan. In all Zen temples selected portions are chanted daily, and Chapter 25 Fumonbon (Avalokitesvera homage) is often selected by other traditions for chanting. The three major concepts of the Eastern (Mahayana) Buddhism are set out in this Sutra. They are: (a) all Sentient beings can attain perfect Enlightment – i.e. Buddhahood – and nothing less than this is the appropriate final goal of believers; (b) the Buddha is eternal, having existed from the infinite past and appearing in many forms throughout the ages to guide and help beings to understand the *Dhamma*; and (c) the noblest form of Buddhist practice is the way of the bodhisattva, one who devotes oneself to attaining Enlightenment not only for oneself but also for all Sentient beings.

- *Sukhavati Sutra*, which teaches that Buddha Amida's Pure Land was open to all believers, however the duration of the sojourn in Pure Land is not eternal – it is a field of purification and illumination and return to the human world is possible in order to help others.
- *Vimalakirtinirdesa Sutra*, which explains that the practice of the Buddha path is not only for ordained *Sangha* but for lay people also, and that a lay person can live a bodhisattva life.

The three most important Eastern Buddhist *Sutras* are said to be the *Parinirvana Sutra*, which sets out the true way, *Prajna Paramita Sutra*, which explains the true view and *Saddharma Pundarika Sutra*, which reveals the ultimate truth.

Buddhism came to China in the first century. The Sanskrit texts of different traditions were taken to China and the translation of the texts into Chinese went on from about the 2nd to the 13th century. At first non-Chinese and later Chinese, monks working individually and in teams carried on the translation work. State translation projects were established. Original Chinese *Sutras* were added. The development of Buddhism in China and recording of the teaching in Chinese literature is one of the great achievements of human civilization.

The Chinese *Tripitaka*, or Canon, that was compiled followed the same pattern. There were the *Vinaya, Sutra* and *Abhidhamma Pitakas* and it included the original Chinese *Sutras*. In the eighth century the Chinese invented wood-block printing in order to make multiple copies of the *Sutras*. The oldest printed book in existence is the *Diamond Sutra* dated 868. The vast Chinese Canon is in the process of being translated into English.

The Chinese *Tripitaka* was translated into Korean in the tenth century and later the Korean *Tripitaka* was printed. The Chinese *Tripitaka* was brought to Japan, and translated into Japanese. Sutra copying became, and still is, an important religious and meritorious activity in Japan. The Chinese *Tripitaka* was first published in the seventeenth century. The Pali *Tripitaka* was translated into Japanese in the last century.

Many of the Japanese texts have been translated into English.

Northern School Literature (Tibetan and Mongolian Texts)

With the growth of Tantric Buddhism in the eighth century in North India, new tantric texts came into being dealing with the new ideas. They covered:

- *Kriya tantra* – ceremonies and rites
- *Carya tantra* – practical rites
- *Yoga tantra* – practice of yoga
- *Anuttarayoga tantra* – higher mysticism.

Tantric Buddhism, called *Tantrayana* or *Vajrayana*, emphasizes individual personal teaching and the relationship with a teacher or guru. These texts are difficult to read and understand because they need to be complemented by oral teaching.

Examples of tantric texts are: *Hevajra Tantra* (emptiness), *Guhya Samaja Tantra* (union of the triple body of the Buddha) and *Kalacakra Tantra* (wheel of time). The Sanskrit texts were translated into Tibetan and edited in the fourteenth century into about 333 volumes. The Tibetan literature is in two parts:

- *Kanjur* (translation of the word of the Buddha) includes the *Vinaya, Sutra* and *Abhidhamma* and also the tantric texts.
- *Tanjur* (translation of commentaries), which consists of commentaries on the main texts, hymns and writings on medicine, grammar and related topics.

The first printed edition was published in Beijing in the fifteenth century. Only a small portion of the Tibetan Canon has been translated into English. The Tibetan *Tripitaka* was translated into Mongolian in the eighteenth century.

Books and Commentaries

As a result of study and scholarship, there are a vast number of books and commentarial matter published over 2,500 years by Asian scholars in different countries and in different languages. A notable work is the *Visuddhi Magga* by Venerable Buddhaghosa on mental training. Over the last 150 years in the West a great deal of commentarial literature and books on Buddhism has been published. There have also been original works, such as Sir Edwin Arnold's *The Light of Asia*.

Abhidhamma

Abhidhamma, as the name indicates, is the higher teaching of the Buddha. It is understood that seven years after Enlightenment the Buddha ascended to the *Tavatimsa* world and gave the teaching on *Abhidhamma* to the deities assembled there, one of whom had been his mother. He returned to this world daily and gave Venerable Sariputta the gist of the teaching. The latter taught the principles to some of the monks, who in turn passed on the teaching to other monks. Venerable Sariputta set out the *Abhidhamma* teaching in six books and these, together with the *Kathavatthu* compiled by Venerable Moggaliputta Tissa after the Third Council, comprise the *Abhidhamma Pitaka*.

The *Sutta* texts are a collection of teachings given by the Buddha to various individuals and groups on various subjects at different times and places during his teaching life. The texts are not connected and there is a great deal of repetition and duplication. On the other hand, the *Abhidhamma* teaching takes a different approach. It is a systematic, precise scientific analysis of mind and matter that constitute a living being. The *Suttas* explain the *Dhamma* in the language of ordinary usage; whereas the *Abhidhamma* uses precise, scientific and specific language. The *Suttas* deal with all aspects of the wisdom, ethical and practice teaching; whereas the *Abhidhamma* deals with consciousness, thoughts, mental states, thought processes, with matter, namely units of matter, material forces, properties and sources of matter, and the relationship between mind and matter.

Abhidhamma teaches that there are two kinds of reality: the conventional reality of ordinary everyday speech and understanding; and absolute reality, being the actual intrinsic nature of things and understandings. It explains that there four types of absolute reality:

- Consciousness – *citta*
- Mental factors – *cetasika*
- Elements of matter – *rupa*
- Supreme happiness - *Nibbana*

All seven books of the *Abhidhamma Pitaka* were summarized by Venerable Anuruddha in the *Abhidhamma Sangaha*, which is accepted as the best introduction to the study of *Abhidhamma*. Some teachings of the *Abhidhamma* are incorporated into the material in this book in certain chapters.

Part II

Teaching (Dhamma, Dharma)

Chapter 5

Four Noble Truths

The Four Noble Truths, the first teaching of Gotama Buddha, is the foundation of Buddhist teaching and practice in all schools and traditions.

The Dhammapada, v. 190–192 and 273 say, respectively,

> He who has gone for refuge to the Buddha, the Dhamma and the Sangha, sees with right knowledge the Four Noble Truths, Dukkha, the Cause of Dukkha, the Transcending of Dukkha and the Noble Eightfold Path which leads to the ending of Dukkha.

> Of paths the Eightfold is the best, of truths the Four Sayings (Four Noble Truths) are the best; non-attachment (Nibbana) is the best of states and of beings the Seeing One (the Buddha).

The Dhammacakkappavattana Sutta

The first teaching given by the Buddha was to the five ascetics on the day of the full moon in the month of July, about eight weeks after he realized *Nibbana*. This was the *Dhammacakkappavattana Sutta*, called the '*Sutta* Setting in Motion the Wheel of Truth' or the 'Four Noble Truths *Sutta*'. The teaching of the Four Noble Truths also appears in other *Suttas*, such as the *Satipatthana Sutta* as a subject of mindfulness and meditation. The *Dhammacakkappavattana Sutta* may be summarized as follows:

> On one occasion the Buddha was residing at Benares in the deer park at Isipatana. There he addressed the group of five ascetics and said:
> > Ascetics, these two extremes should be avoided by one who has renounced and gone into homelessness,
> > (i) Indulgence in sensual pleasures, which is inferior, low, vulgar, ignoble, unprofitable, and

(ii) Addiction to self-mortification, which is painful, ignoble and unprofitable.

The Middle Way discovered by the Buddha avoids both of these extremes; it promotes vision, knowledge, leads to peace, direct knowledge, Enlightment and *Nibbana*. What is this Middle Way? It is the Noble Eightfold Path, which is namely:

- Right view
- Right intention
- Right speech
- Right action
- Right livelihood
- Right effort
- Right mindfulness and
- Right concentration.

This is the Middle Way discovered by the Buddha that gives rise to vision and knowledge, leads to peace, direct knowledge, Enlightment and *Nibbana*.

This, ascetics is the Noble Truth of *Dukkha*: birth is *Dukkha*, ageing is *Dukkha*, illness is *Dukkha*, death is *Dukkha*, sorrow, lamentation, pain, grief and despair are *Dukkha*, association with the unpleasant is *Dukkha*, separation from the pleasant is *Dukkha*, not to get what one wants is *Dukkha*. In brief, the five aggregates of attachment are *Dukkha*.

This, ascetics, is the Noble Truth of the origin of *Dukkha*. It is this attachment, wanting, craving which produces rebirth accompanied by enjoyment and passionate greed and wanting, finding fresh delight and enjoyment; attachment to pleasures of the senses, attachment to existence and attachment to non-existence.

This, ascetics, is the Noble Truth of the ending of *Dukkha*. It is the remainderless ending, giving up, relinquishing, letting go and liberating oneself from this attachment.

This, ascetics, is the Noble Truth of the way leading to the end of *Dukkha*. It is this Noble Eightfold Path, namely, right view, right intention, right speech, right action, right livelihood, right effort, right mindfulness and right concentration.

This *Dukkha* has to be perceived and understood. The origin of *Dukkha* has to be abandoned. The ending of *Dukkha* has to be realized and the path leading to the ending of *Dukkha* has to be developed.

So long, ascetics, as my knowledge and vision of these Four

Noble Truths was not fully perceived I did not claim perfect Enlightment. But when my knowledge and vision of these Four Noble Truths was fully perceived, I claimed to have perfect Enlightment. There arose in me the knowledge and insight Unshakeable is the liberation of my mind. This is my last birth, and now there is no further existence.

The ascetics understood his words and were delighted. Venerable Kondanna understood that, 'Whatever is subject to origination is subject to ending.' The earthly and heavenly deities raised a cry, 'At Benares, in the deer park at Isipatana, the Wheel of Truth has been set in motion by the Buddha.'

The Four Noble Truths are the briefest summary of the entire Buddhist teaching. The rest of the teaching is, directly or indirectly, developed from and connected to this teaching. These four truths are:

- *Dukkha*
- The origin of *Dukkha*
- The ending of *Dukkha*
- The Noble Eightfold Path leading to the ending of *Dukkha*.

The First Truth deals with the nature of life and teaches that all forms of existence are unsatisfactory and subject to *Dukkha*. The Second Truth teaches that rebirth and all *Dukkha* are the result of attachment. It deals with the mental attitude of the person to external objects that come to the notice of the senses – a powerful force latent in living beings over past, present and future births, and connected to the teaching of *kamma* and rebirth. The Third Truth teaches that the ending of attachment necessarily results in the transcending and ending of rebirth and *Dukkha*. This is the state of *Nibbana*. This truth has to be self-realized by ending attachment to the external and internal world. The Fourth Truth sets out the method and practice to be followed to realize *Nibbana* and explains the eight mental elements and way of life that have to be developed and practised for this purpose. It is this Fourth Truth that makes Buddhism a religion and not simply a philosophy.

These four truths relate to the individual and can be verified by experience. They were taught by previous Buddhas, but that teaching had been lost. They were not known in the world at the time of Gotama Buddha's Enlightenment and he discovered them for himself, and for us, by his own untiring and persistent effort.

The Four Truths have to be treated differently. *Dukkha* has to be examined and understood. The origin of *Dukkha* has to be abandoned. The ending of *Dukkha* has to be realized and the Noble Eightfold Path has to be practised, cultivated and perfected.

The Visuddhimagga, XV1, 87 and 90, explains it further. *Dukkha* is compared to a disease – its origin is compared to the cause of the disease, the ending is the cure and the path the medicine. In the ultimate sense these truths are to be considered as empty of self. There is no one who is experiencing *Dukkha*, no one having attachment, no one realizing *Nibbana* and no one who follows the path. Hence it is said:

> Mere Dukkha exists, but no one experiencing it;
> Deeds are done, but no doer is there;
> Nirvana is, but no one experiencing it;
> The Path is there, but no traveller on it.

After this first teaching, the senior ascetic Kondanna (we remember him as the ascetic who at the naming ceremony of the bodhisattva prophesied that he would become a Buddha, see Chapter 2) understood that teaching and achieving *sotapanna* status was the first stage of *arahatship*. It was only after the second teaching given a few days later, the *Anattalakkhana Sutta*, on impermanence, *Dukkha* and selflessness that the five ascetics realized *Nibbana*.

The Buddha explained later that his teaching was like a raft for worldly beings to cross the river of Samsara and reach the bank of *Nibbana*. Perhaps we could consider that the raft is made as follows. There are three logs crossways being the first three of the Four Noble Truths. There are three logs in line being the Three Signs of Being. The logs are tied together with the rope of the Noble Eightfold Path. The individual gets on the raft at this bank and using the teaching in the *Satipattana Sutta* as a paddle crosses the river of Samsara and reaches the bank of *Nibbana*. After reaching the other bank the raft is abandoned because it is of no further use.

The Four Noble Truths is the foundation of the teaching in Eastern Buddhism. Professor Junjiro Takakusu states in *The Essentials of Buddhist Philosophy*, p. 26:

> What is the Truth? What is the Way?
> The Buddha organized these ideas into the Fourfold Truth as follows:
>
> 1. Life consists entirely of suffering (Dukkha);
> 2. That suffering (Dukkha) has causes;

(The above two are the description of reality.)

3. That the causes of suffering (Dukkha) can be extinguished;

4. That there exists a way to extinguish the causes.

(The last two express the ideal)

These constitute the Fourfold Truth to be believed by the *ariya* or those who pursue the way toward Nirvana. (*Takakusu*)

He then goes on to set out the Noble Eightfold Path in the same way that it is set out in Southern Buddhism.

Similarly, the Four Noble Truths form the foundation of the Northern Buddhist tradition. Tenzin Gyatso, HH XIV Dalai Lama, *The Buddhism of Tibet*, p. 23.explains:

> The Blessed One said, 'These are true sufferings (Dukkha), these are true sources, these are true cessations, these are true paths. Sufferings (Dukkha) are to be known, their sources are to be abandoned, their cessations are to be actualised, the paths are to be cultivated.'

Geshe Tashi Tsering states in *The Four Noble Truths*, pp. 7 and 8 that:

> The *Four Noble Truths Sutra* is the Buddha's first and most essential teaching. It contains the framework of all the many discourses he gave during his forty-five-year teaching career ...
>
> The Four Noble Truths are:
>
> 1. The Noble Truth of suffering (Dukkha)
> 2. The Noble Truth of the origin of suffering (Dukkha)
> 3. The Noble Truth of the cessation of suffering (Dukkha) and the origin of suffering (Dukkha)
> 4. The Noble Truth of the path that leads to the cessation of suffering (Dukkha) and the origin of suffering (Dukkha).

The First Two Noble Truths [...] really reflect the nature of our present life – they function continually within us. The truth of cessation and the truth of the path that leads to cessation are the methods to eliminating suffering (Dukkha) and its origin.'

He sets out the three trainings (pages 125–126), divided into ethics, concentration and wisdom, which is the same as the Noble Eightfold Path in Southern Buddhism.

Dukkha

> This, ascetics, is the Noble Truth of Dukkha. Birth is Dukkha, ageing is Dukkha, illness is Dukkha, death is Dukkha, sorrow, lamentation, pain, grief and despair are Dukkha, association with the unpleasant is Dukkha, separation from the pleasant is Dukkha, not to get what one wants is Dukkha. In brief, the five aggregates of attachment are Dukkha.
>
> *Dhammacakkappavattana Sutta*

Dukkha is the First Noble Truth and the second element of the Three Signs of Being. The *Dhammacakkappavattana Sutta* enumerates nine aspects of *Dukkha*, and if the last is taken as five they add up to thirteen. They are:

- Birth
- Ageing
- Illness
- Death
- Sorrow, lamentation, pain, grief and despair
- Association with the unpleasant
- Separation from the pleasant
- Not to get what one wants and
- The five aggregates of attachment.

The first four – birth, ageing, illness and death – constitute the cycle of life in Buddhism. The second, third and fourth – ageing, illness and death – are the first three signs seen by the bodhisatta, which together with the fourth, the ascetic, made him renounce his luxurious life in the palace. The ninth refers to the five aggregates that make up a living being. Birth by itself is associated with pain and is the beginning of ageing, illness and death.

The *Satipattana Sutta* in the section on the mindfulness of the Four Noble Truths gives details of these elements:

- Birth is birth in different orders of beings – their being born, origination, conception, springing into existence, manifestation of the aggregates and acquisition of the sense bases.
- Old age is the ageing of beings in different orders of beings – their getting frail, weak, grey and wrinkled, the failing of their vital force and wearing out of their sense faculties.
- Death is the departing and vanishing of beings in different orders of beings – their destruction, disappearance, death,

completion of their life period, dissolution of the aggregates and discarding of the body.

- Sorrow arises from this or that loss or misfortune beings encounter – the sorrowing, the sorrowful state of mind and the inward sorrow.
- Lamentation arises from loss or misfortune that beings encounter.
- Pain is bodily pain, bodily unpleasantness and the painful and unpleasant feeling produced by bodily contact.
- Grief is mental pain and mental unpleasantness, and painful and unpleasant feeling produced by mental contact.
- Despair arises through the loss or misfortune that beings encounter.
- The *Dukkha* of not getting what they wish is in those born the wish not to be born and in beings subject to ageing, illness, death, sorrow, lamentation, pain, grief and despair, the wish not to be subject to these things. This cannot be got by mere wishing; and when a being cannot get what he wishes it is *Dukkha*.
- The five aggregates of attachment are:
  - the body
  - feelings
  - perceptions
  - volition
  - consciousness.

Dukkha is often translated by the word suffering. This is only one of its meanings and is misleading in that it has led people to believe that Buddhism is melancholy and pessimistic in outlook. On the contrary, the Buddha asked his followers to be joyful and happy because he, the teacher, had found the remedy for the illness. There are other words that can be used to translate *Dukkha*, such as impermanence, imperfection, stress, dissatisfaction, emptiness, insecurity, insubstantiality, non-ease and unsatisfactoriness.

Dukkha includes bodily or mental pain and also imperfection and suffering. It is not limited to painful experiences but also includes happy experiences because these must come to an end. It refers to the unsatisfactory nature and general insecurity of all conditioned things that, on account of impermanence, are liable to cause *Dukkha*. The stress of anticipation of *Dukkha* is itself *Dukkha*.

There are three aspects of *Dukkha*:

- Ordinary *Dukkha*. This includes all forms of physical and mental *Dukkha*. Birth, ageing, illness, death, sorrow, lamentation, pain, grief, association with the unpleasant, separation from the loved ones and pleasant conditions, not getting what one wants – all this is *Dukkha*. We notice this constantly in our daily life.
- Change produces *Dukkha*. This is the impermanence in life. The sensual pleasures and happy physical and mental states come to an end. People have to continually adjust to this change and this gives the mind no rest. In practical life a Buddhist has to understand this in a balanced way. We know that ordinary happiness will come to an end, as will unhappiness and sorrow. This helps us to see life in a detached manner and not react too fiercely or violently to the ups and downs of life: it helps us to maintain a certain equanimity of mind.
- Conditioned states are *Dukkha*. The combination of the ever-changing physical and mental energies of the five aggregates that make up the living being are impermanent, imperfect and *Dukkha* due to continual arising and passing away.

The Buddha mentions various kinds of happiness – family life, attachment to worldly things, mental and intellectual happiness, pleasures of the senses, physical happiness, renunciation and the life of an ascetic. The Buddha said that if there was not some happiness in this world people would not be attached to worldly life, but these are all temporary and impermanent, and therefore *Dukkha*. Because most people are intoxicated by worldly pleasures they cannot see life in a balanced way.

High levels of consciousness achieved by meditation where there is no sorrow and there is unmitigated happiness, with neither sensation nor lack of sensation, is also unsatisfactory and imperfect since one cannot remain in that state permanently. We have to return to ordinary levels of consciousness since a human being needs food, drink and sleep. Even life in heavenly planes full of pleasant companions and surroundings is *Dukkha* because these states come to an end. Further, although a person may be happy himself, the *Dukkha* of family members, relatives, friends and others, including animals, may cause *Dukkha*. The Buddha reduced all of the problems of the world into one single problem, *Dukkha*, which is the result of attachment

The Buddha asked his followers to be joyful and happy because he, the teacher, had found the remedy for the illness. Buddhists should not be sorrowful and melancholy, but happy people who understand the reality of life as impermanent, *Dukkha* and selfless. They should view life with calmness and equanimity and face life with understanding and fortitude. Contemporaries describe the Buddha as ever-smiling. The Buddha advised his followers not to be angry or impatient with *Dukkha* because this would not overcome it but aggravate an already disagreeable situation.

What is required is a clear understanding of *Dukkha*, its causes, how to transcend it, as explained by the Buddha, and to work towards this end with perseverance and diligence. This effort should be pleasurable because we know that we are proceeding on the correct path. If living as a Buddhist is stressful and painful, something is wrong with the person's understanding and practice. It can be stressful and painful at times when we are working through a strong attachment or heavy *kamma*, but there is an inner knowing that it is right to go through this and the result is letting go. This is sometimes called the *Dukkha* that leads to the end of *Dukkha*. The Buddha gave his teaching not to punish people but to help them and enable them to be happy in this life as well as in the lives beyond.

Origin of Dukkha – Samudaya

This, ascetics, is the Noble Truth of the Origin of Dukkha. It is this attachment, wanting, craving which produces rebirth accompanied by enjoyment and passionate greed and wanting, finding fresh delight and enjoyment; attachment to sense pleasures, attachment to existence and attachment to non-existence.

Dhammacakkappavattana Sutta

The conscious mind shows us a stable world of identifiable things due to ignorance. Perception of identifiable things through the senses creates an emotional reaction that sets up attachment. This attachment or mental thirst in its various forms is a powerful mental force that is the immediate and principle, although not the only, cause of *Dukkha*. Attachment is an incessant process. As soon as one desire is satisfied the wanting for something else begins.

The *Satipattana Sutta,* in dealing with contemplation of the Four Noble Truths, explains how this attachment arises and becomes established:

Wherever in this world there are delightful and pleasurable things, there this attachment arises and takes root. Eye, ear, nose, tongue, body and mind are delightful and pleasurable: there this attachment arises and takes root.

Satipattana Sutta

It goes on to refer to the six different matters noticed by the senses, the six different types of consciousness and the sixfold contact, feeling, will, attachment and thoughts. It says that attachment becomes established through the senses because these are delightful and pleasurable.

Attachment is the chief cause of *Dukkha* and the continuing cycle of rebirths. It is the eighth element in the formula of Dependent Origination. It is dependent on feeling and gives rise to grasping and becoming (see Chapter. 6). No first beginning of attachment for existence can be identified. It is first conditioned by ignorance. The elements of ignorance and attachment are the main ones that provide power to the cycle of life.

Attachment can never be satisfied. The satisfaction of an attachment feeds the attachment, like adding fuel to a fire. If one attachment is satisfied another arises. Attachment has an infinite variety, and can be aptly described in the words used by Shakespeare to describe Cleopatra, when Enobarbus says in *Antony and Cleopatra*, Act II, Scene 2, 'Age cannot wither her, nor custom stale Her infinite variety . . .' Attachment can be to sense pleasure, wealth, power, physical and mental objects, ideas, opinions, theories, concepts, beliefs, individual personal matters and national or international matters. Attachment is directed towards:

- Pleasures of the senses
- Existence and continued existence
- Non-existence (ending of existence).

Four ingredients fuel the attachment to existence, continuity and rebirth:

- Ordinary material food
- Contact of our sense organs with the external world
- Consciousness
- Mental volition or will.

Mental volition is the wanting to continue, become and accumulate more and more. It thus equates to attachment.

Attachment forces us to continue existence in a good or bad direction. This continuity is *Dukkha*.

This volition, will, attachment to exist and to continue is a powerful force. It is the greatest energy in the world. In the case of living beings it does not end with the death of the physical body but continues producing not one but many rebirths.

The teaching on attachment is related to teaching on:

- Action and results (*kamma* and *vipaka*) (see Chapter 7)
- Rebirth, rebecoming (see Chapter 8), and
- Dependent Origination (see Chapter 6).

The teaching of Dependent Origination in its serial order, starting with ignorance and ending with rebirth and *Dukkha*, is a detailed analysis of the second of the Four Noble Truths: the arising of *Dukkha*.

Ending of Dukkha – Nirodha

This ascetics is the Noble Truth of the ending of Dukkha. It is the remainderless ending, giving up, relinquishing, letting go and liberating oneself from this attachment.

Dhammacakkappavattana Sutta

The Third Noble Truth follows logically from the first two. If attachment causes *Dukkha* then *Dukkha* must be eliminated; if attachment is transcended and eliminated there will be no *Dukkha*. The state of ending of *Dukkha* is *Nibbana*. *Nibbana* is the complete ending of attachment, ill will and ignorance. It is also referred to as Enlightment, realization of the *Dukkha*, realization of absolute reality, liberation and fully awakened awareness.

The *Satipattana Sutta*, in dealing with the contemplation of the Four Noble Truths, explains where this attachment may be abandoned and extinguished:

Wherever in this world there are delightful and pleasurable things, there this attachment may be abandoned and extinguished. Eye, ear, nose, tongue, body and mind, are delightful and pleasurable; there this craving may be abandoned and extinguished.

Satipattana Sutta

It goes on to refer to the six different matters noticed by the senses, the six different types of consciousness and the sixfold contact, feeling, will, attachment and thoughts. It says that these things are delightful and pleasurable, so attachment may be abandoned and extinguished there.

Language has been devised by human beings to express human mental and intellectual ideas. Language cannot adequately explain the real nature of *Nibbana*. For instance, it is not possible to explain to someone who has not seen ice that ice is cold. The person has to touch the ice to realize what cold means. Similarly *Nibbana* has to be realized by a Buddhist, and cannot be understood intellectually. *Nibbana* is expressed in negative terms so many make the mistake of thinking that it is a negative concept. This is not correct because the expressions negative and positive cannot be used to describe *Nibbana*. According to the Buddha, the purpose of life is to study and practise the *Dhamma*, to help others to do the same and finally to realize *Nibbana*.

Living beings are caught in cycle of rebirth, ageing, disease, death and rebirth, known as *Samsara*. Attachment, ill will and ignorance are referred to as the Three Fires, unwholesome roots or delusions that bind a living being to this continued existence in *Samsara*, and consequent *Dukkha* (see Chapter 9). Transcending and eliminating them is *Nibbana*. It is a realization of a state of consciousness that is aware of the happiness associated with complete freedom from any sort of attachment whatsoever. At the point of *Nibbana* the whole of the *Dhamma* is realized, including the Four Noble Truths, impermanence, selflessness, *kamma*, rebirth and Dependent Origination.

Venerable Nyanatiloka (*Buddhist Dictionary*, p.105), gives the classic explanation of *Nibbana* as understood in Southern Buddhism. *Nibbana* constitutes the highest and ultimate goal of all Buddhist aspirations: the absolute ending of life-affirming will, which manifests as attachment, ill will and ignorance, and clinging to existence, the ultimate and absolute deliverance from all future rebirth, ageing, disease, death and *Dukkha*. *Nibbana* is explained as transcending *Samsara*. *Nibbana* is attainable during life and the person, now known as an *Arahat*, continues to live to the end of that life and is not reborn.

The teaching in Eastern and Northern Buddhist traditions gives the same meaning to *Samsara* as the cycle of rebirth, ageing, disease, death and rebirth. It explains that to be caught in this cycle is *Dukkha*. When these teachings in Eastern and Northern Buddhism use phrases like 'attaining *Nirvana*' or 'cessation' they are referring to various degrees of freedom from delusions and *karma*, eradication of defilements and compulsive rebirth in unEnlightened states. It is similar to the understanding in Southern

Buddhism. This freedom is gained through increasing under-standing and experience of the ultimate reality that all phenom-ena, events and processes are empty of being self-constituted. The most powerful experience of this ultimate reality or truth, which is that state of emptiness, is a direct, non-conceptual realization of the absence of a fixed nature or self in all phenomena. The teachings explain that the absolute truth realized on Enlight-enment was the wisdom of suchness (*sunyata*, emptiness), which is to see things as they really are. When the idea of suchness developed the teachings said that both *Samsara* and *Nirvana* were included in suchness and developed a positive meaning to Nirvana – that it was of the same nature as *Samsara*.

Both the Southern Buddhist teaching of *Nibbana*, that it is the release from *Samsara*, and the Eastern and Northern Buddhist teaching of *Nirvana*, that it is of the same nature as *Samsara*, is that both are empty of self-nature. In essence they both point to the same thing, that *Nibbana* (*Nirvana*) is the transcending and eradication of delusions, unwholesome roots and defilements in the heart that prevent a person from seeing clearly in the six sense bases.

There is, however, one difference. In the teaching of the Southern traditions the *Arahat* having attained *Nibbana* is not born again. In the teaching of the Eastern and Northern traditions the bodhisattva who has attained *Nirvana*, although free from compulsive rebirth, is able to be reborn (manifest) voluntarily in any state and in any form to help Sentient beings.

There are two stages of *Nibbana*. The first *sa-upadi-sesa-Nibbana* is when the negative qualities are extinguished with the groups of aggregates intact (as body and mind) and life continues. This happens when *arahatship* or Buddhahood is attained. The second, *an-upadi-sesa-Nibbana*, is when the groups of aggregates come to an end. It is the end of the physical and mental processes, *Parinibbana*, when the *Arahat* or Buddha passes away. Sometimes both stages may take place at one and the same moment. The Buddha realized *Nibbana* on attaining Enlightenment and his teaching was given after realizing *Nibbana* and until his *Parinibbana* (passing away). Many of his disciples carried on teaching after realizing the first stage of *Nibbana*. Therefore *Nibbana* is not something to be achieved at or after death. It can be realized in this very life.

The teaching of Dependent Origination in its order of ending, starting with the ending of ignorance and terminating with the ending of rebirth and *Dukkha* is an analysis of the third of the Four Noble Truths – the ending of *Dukkha* and realizing *Nibbana* (see Chapter 6).

The Noble Eightfold Path – Magga

This, ascetics, is the Noble Truth of the way leading to the end of Dukkha. It is this Noble Eightfold Path, namely, Right View, Right Intention, Right Speech, Right Action, Right Livelihood, Right Effort, Right Mindfulness and Right Concentration.

Dhammacakkappavattana Sutta

The Fourth Noble Truth, known as the Middle Way between indulgence in sensual pleasures and addiction to self-mortification, sets out how Buddhism has to be practised. It is this Fourth Truth that makes Buddhism a religion; a way of life to be practised diligently.

The Buddhist teaching consists of the wisdom teachings, the intellectual explanations, and the way of practice. The Buddha criticized those who merely studied the teaching and emphasized that the practice, to live as an ordained or lay Buddhist according to the teaching, was even more important. Practice makes for a deeper understanding of the wisdom teachings. Mere knowledge without practice does not take the Buddhist very far on his journey. Practice must be in the context of the *Dhamma* teaching, so that the person understands the reason, purpose and aims of practice. No one has realized *Nibbana* by just reading, listening to talks, discussing and thinking about Buddhism. All the *Arahats* and Buddhas have realized *Nibbana* by practice over several lives. The Buddhist practice consists of the development of morality and mental development of mindfulness and meditation. This is the key that opens the door to *Nibbana*. The Buddha gave an example of a person standing at the beginning of a road, who thinks, 'What a nice broad, straight road this is. It has broad pavements and is lined with tall trees with flowers and fruit. It is well sign-posted and has no ruts. The houses on either side are spacious and attractive with well kept gardens and are the homes of good and clever people. How inviting such a road is for walking along.' Just looking and not walking down the road is not enough. The person must get on the road and travel it, otherwise he will not get to the end.

The Wheel — symbol of *Dhamma*

The wheel is the symbol of the *Dhamma*. It is shown with eight spokes representing the different elements of the Noble Eightfold Path, which can be depicted diagrammatically as:

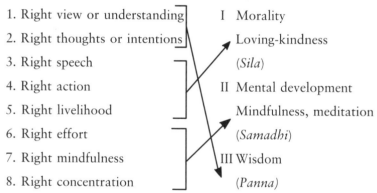

1. Right view or understanding   I Morality
2. Right thoughts or intentions   Loving-kindness
3. Right speech   (*Sila*)
4. Right action   II Mental development
5. Right livelihood   Mindfulness, meditation
6. Right effort   (*Samadhi*)
7. Right mindfulness   III Wisdom
8. Right concentration   (*Panna*)

Right View or Understanding (Samma Ditthi)

This is the understanding of all aspects of the teaching, including the Four Noble Truths, Three Signs of Being, Dependent Origination, *kamma*, rebirth and all that is understood by a person realizing *Nibbana*. Right view means at first to develop wisdom, which is the ability to distinguish between skilful and unskilful actions, and then to develop insight, leading to the realization of *Nibbana*.

Right Thoughts or Intentions (Samma Sankappa)

This is the thoughts that pollute or purify a person (*The Dhammapada*, v. 1&2). Right thoughts refer to a state of consciousness that is clear, cool and free from the limiting considerations of self-interest. It means eliminating unwholesome thoughts and developing wholesome thoughts, renouncing worldly pleasures, overcoming attachment ill will and ignorance (the Three Fires), and developing generosity, loving-kindness, unselfishness, goodwill, compassion and wisdom. These then become the framework of intention and the basis of speech and action.

Right Speech (Samma Vaca)

This means a person should always speak the truth. They should use language that is kind, polite and promotes harmony, peace and happiness. They should avoid telling lies, defamatory talk, talk that may result in disharmony or ill will, harsh, rude or impolite talk and idle gossip. Speech includes all forms of communication, oral or written, publications, cartoons, radio, television, the internet and also silence, when it is not appropriate to say anything. This element relates to the fourth of the Five Precepts (see Chapter 11).

Right Action (Samma Kammanta)

This means to live according to the *Dhamma*, especially the Five Precepts. Buddhists should avoid harming living beings, taking what is not your own, misusing senses, improper speech and consuming drinks or drugs (except medicines) that interfere with the proper working of the mind (see Chapter 11). It means Buddhists should help living beings, be content with what they have, make proper use of the senses, use the correct speech, take wholesome food and drink in the correct quantity to sustain the body, and avoid all actions that go against the *Dhamma*.

Right Livelihood (Samma Ajiva)

This means making a living in a way that does not, directly or indirectly, cause any harm to other living beings. Five occupations are expressly prohibited, namely dealing in arms and weapons, human beings, fish or meat (animal flesh), intoxicating substances or poison.

Right Effort (Samma Vayama)

This involves developing insight, energy, intuition and will, and making an effort to develop mental states that promote progress as a Buddhist. Buddhists should:

- Make the effort to prevent unwholesome states of mind based on attachment, ill will and ignorance from arising
- Get rid of such unwholesome states of mind that have arisen
- Develop wholesome states of mind based on generosity, loving-kindness and wisdom, and
- Maintain such wholesome states of mind that have risen.

Right Mindfulness (Samma Sati)

This means developing your awareness until every thought, word and action is performed with this conscious awareness. Mindfulness acts as a control over the other elements of the path. The *Satipattana Sutta* sets out the four foundations of mindfulness, namely the mindfulness of the body, feelings, mind and mind objects (*Dhammas*, intellectual topics) that result in increased awareness and mindfulness (see Chapter 15).

Right Concentration (Samma Samadhi)

This involves developing the mind and heart by mindfulness and meditation so that you can achieve higher states of awareness and insight. Meditation is a more concentrated form of mindfulness that clears, refines and tunes the mind so that it sees things as they are, perceives absolute reality and realizes *Nibbana* (see Chapter 15).

Southern Buddhism emphasizes the practice of the Noble Eightfold Path. There is another, similar parallel practice teaching, the ten perfections or virtues (*Paramis*), which must be cultivated and developed by a Buddhist in order to progress as a bodhisatta and to become a *Samma Sambuddha*. The practice formulations in Eastern and Northern Buddhism are based on similar principles. The teaching in the Noble Eightfold Path applies. The eight elements are grouped under discipline, meditation and wisdom. The emphasis of practice, however, is on cultivation and development of the ten perfections (*Paramitas*) and progressing on the bodhisattva path to become a *Samma Sambuddha* (see Chapter 17).

Training and Practice

A Buddhist considers these elements not simply with academic or scholarly interest, but as matters that must be put into practice in training to be a Buddhist and for progress as a pilgrim on the Buddhist path. The Buddha's teaching is not only for ordained monks, nuns and priests living in temples and monasteries. It is also for laymen, women and children living at home. This is the Buddhist way of life for all those who choose to follow it, wherever they may be.

A high degree of intellectual or academic attainment is not necessary to begin to understand Buddhism. In Buddhist countries children in Buddhist families are taught, and begin to practise, the religion from a very young age. Many people from Buddhist families may remember being taken to the temple by parents and grand-parents, participating in worship and devotions and listening to chanting and talks, from a very young age. Some concepts are, of course, so complex that you may need a long time to understand and practise them.

The word 'path' may be misleading. It must not be thought that these elements must be practised one after another in the numerical order given above. They are to be developed and practised together and developed in a circular way. According to the order of development there are three cumulative stages; the threefold discipline common to all traditions. The morality of right speech, action and livelihood is the first to be developed. This is followed by the mental development of right effort, mindfulness and concentration. The wisdom of right view and understanding and thoughts and intentions comes last.

Starting with morality, we move to mental development and gain some wisdom. Then morality is made deeper and mental development increased through practice, leading to higher wisdom. In this way the elements of the path are practised with greater concentration until the final realization of *Nibbana*. This may be shown as follows:

(i)   Morality (*Sila*)   Right speech, action and
                                               livelihood
(ii) Mental development (*Samadhi*)   Right effort, mindfulness
                                               and concentration
(iii) Wisdom (*Panna*)   Right view and thought

In Buddhist countries the *Dhamma* is taught under these three headings, which indicate the order in which the pilgrim develops the training. Sometimes the teaching is under the three slightly different headings of generosity, morality and mental development, especially when taught to children.

Morality includes all of the virtues of a good citizen. It signifies the idea of universal loving-kindness and compassion for all living beings and is the foundation of the Buddha's teaching. It promotes a healthy, happy and harmonious life for the individual and society. Without this foundation it is not possible to proceed to the next stage. Mental development is the next stage, when the mind is disciplined and trained so that it can achieve higher stages of consciousness, resulting in a greater capacity for understanding and insight. The final stage is wisdom, which enables a Buddhist to see things as they are in reality.

The elements of the Noble Eightfold Path are interconnected and equally important. They must be practised and developed together. This will depend on the inclination, capacity and stage of development of the individual at any given time. In the end they form one path. Treading the path involves continuous and constant observation and practise, leading to reflection and study. This path is open equally to men and women, for the Buddha did not distinguish between them in their intellectual and spiritual potential. The whole practice has been described in three short statements in *The Dhammapada*, v. 18:

Not to do any wrong (To refrain from all evil);
To cultivate good;
To purify the mind.

This is the teaching of the Buddha.

Venerable Nynatiloka says in the *Buddhist Dictionary* (p. 94) that:

The links of the Path not only do not arise one after another ... But ... they, at least in part, arise simultaneously as inseparably associated mental factors in one and the same state of consciousness. Thus, for instance, under all circumstances at least 4 links are inseparably bound up with any karmically wholesome consciousness, namely 2, 6, 7, and 8, that is Right Thought, Right Effort, Right Mindfulness and Right Concentration [...] so that as soon as any one of these elements arises, the three others also do so. On the other hand, Right View is not necessarily present in every wholesome state of consciousness.

Chapter 6

Three Signs of Being

The Three Signs of Being, or Three Characteristics of Existence, are the Buddha's analysis of all mental and physical things. They are also referred to as the three universal truths or marks of existence. The Buddha said:

> Whether the Buddhas appear or not ... it remains a fact, an established principle, a natural law that all conditioned things are impermanent (*Anicca*), imperfect (*Dukkha*) and that everything is selfless (*Anatta*).
>
> *Anguttara Nikaya*, Part I, p. 286.

The Dhammapada, (vv. 277–9), says:

> Impermanent are all compound things,
> Unsatisfactory (Imperfect, *Dukkha*) are all compound things,
> All *Dhammas* are selfless.

The first two verses refer to compound things while the third verse refers to *Dhammas*. A compound thing is one conditioned by causes. *Dhammas* include conditioned and unconditioned things, therefore impermanence, *Dukkha* and selflessness are the three signs or characteristics of all compound things, all things conditioned by causes. On the other hand, *Nibbana*, not being conditioned, is not impermanent or *Dukkha*, but is included in the meaning of *Dhammas* and is selfless.

The Buddha's last words, recorded in the *Parinibbana Sutta*, were:

> Monks subject to change are all compounded things,
> Strive on with diligence.

The *Saddharma Pundarika Sutra* (p. 70) says:

> The Buddhas, the honoured ones,

Know that nothing has an independent existence ...

The Three Signs or Characteristics of all mental and physical things are therefore:

- Impermanence – *anicca*
- Imperfect, unsatisfactory – *Dukkha*
- Selflessness – *anatta*.

They are interconnected and it is necessary to have a full understanding of these three facts of existence in order to understand the realities of life. There is selflessness because of impermanence. There is *Dukkha* because we do not understand selflessness. In the practice of Buddhism, when the individual progresses in insight meditation, it is the realization of impermanence, *Dukkha* and selflessness that leads to *Nibbana*.[1] This is the teaching in Southern Buddhism.

Eastern Buddhism has the same teaching of the Three Signs of Being. Professor Junjiro Takakusu says in *The Essentials of Buddhist Philosophy* (p. 198):

The time honoured Buddhist principle is threefold:
1. Selflessness of all elements.
2. Impermanence of all component beings and things and elements.
3. All is Dukkha.

   Sometimes a fourth is added,

4. Nirvana is bliss.

These are generally called the Three or Four Signs of Buddhism. (Takakusu)

The teaching is the same in Northern Buddhism. According to Tenzing Gyatso, HH the XIV Dalai Lama, in *The Buddhism of Tibet* (p. 53):

All products are impermanent.
All contaminated things are miserable (Dukkha).
All phenomena are empty and selfless.
Nirvana is peace. (Gyatso)

Anattalakkhana Sutta

The Buddha's teaching on impermanence and selflessness is found in the *Anattalakkhana Sutta*, the second teaching. It was given to the five ascetics a few days after the first teaching (see Chapter 4) on the day of the full moon in July, seven weeks after the Buddha realized *Nibbana*. This *Sutta* may be summarized as follows:

On one occasion the Buddha was living at the Deer Park in Isipatana, near Benares. There he addressed the group of five ascetics saying ...

'This body is not self. If the body were self then this body would not be subject to Dukkha. Since this body is not self it is subject to Dukkha...

'Similarly, feelings, perceptions, volitions and consciousness are not self.

'How do you understand it ascetics, is this body permanent or impermanent?'

'Impermanent, Sir.'

'Is what is impermanent painful or pleasant?'

'Painful, Sir.'

'Now is it fit to regard that which is impermanent and painful since being subject to change as mine, I or myself?'

'Certainly not, Sir.'

'Similarly, ascetics, feelings, perceptions, volitions and consciousness are impermanent and painful.

'Now, is it fit to regard these which are impermanent and painful since being subject to change, as mine, I or myself?'

'Certainly not Sir.'

'Then, ascetics, any kind of body, whether past, present or future, coarse or subtle, internal or external, low or high, far or near, should be understood with right knowledge in its real nature – this is not mine, this is not I, this is not myself.

'Similarly all feelings, perceptions, volitions and conscious-ness ... should be understood as this is not mine, this is not I, this is not myself.

'When a noble disciple sees this he is detached from body, feelings, perceptions, volitions and consciousness.

'When attachment fades, he is liberated and knows that he is liberated. He understands that rebirth is ended, the holy life has been lived out, what should be done is done and there is no more beyond.'[2]

The ascetics were delighted and approved his words. When the Buddha spoke these words the minds of the ascetics were freed of defilements and they all attained *arahatship* and realized *Nibbana*. After hearing the first teaching, only the senior ascetic Venerable Kondanna had progressed, and then only to *sotappana* status, the first stage of *arahatship*.

Impermanence

How do you understand it ascetics, is this body permanent or impermanent?
Impermanent, Sir ...
Similarly ascetics, feelings, perceptions, volitions and conscious-ness are impermanent and painful.

Anattalakkhana Sutta

The totality of existence is impermanent and this is often expressed in terms of the five aggregates. All material, mental, emotional, animate, inanimate, coarse, subtle, organic, inorganic, internal and external things are changing constantly. This process has four stages: arising, gaining strength, fading and passing away. The *Visuddhimagga* (V111. 234) states that the impermanence of things is the arising, changing, and passing away or disappearance of things that have become or arisen. These things are dissolving and vanishing from moment to moment and never stay the same way. This is the law of the universe.

Nothing whatsoever of our ordinary physical, mental or emotional world ever remains the same for two consecutive moments. Continents move. The Himalayas become a little higher each year. World systems are impermanent. Even a specific Buddha and his teaching are impermanent, in that the Buddha's life comes to an end and after a long period his teaching of the *Dhamma* dies out. Subsequently a new bodhisatta is born, attains Enlightenment as a new Buddha and teaches the *Dhamma*. The *Dhamma* is the truth of the natural world; part of it and yet not subject to change. The *Dhamma*, like *Nibbana*, is unconditioned and not dependant on causes and therefore is not liable to change.

Reality is never static but a dynamic process changing all the time. The permanence and stability that appears to us is an illusion because we cannot see the change taking place as it is so subtle. This is a fundamental feature of all conditioned things. Only *Nibbana* and *Dhamma* are unconditioned and permanent. They are also selfless. It is from impermanence that *Dukkha* and selflessness are derived, and these three elements form the foundation of Buddhism.

When the Buddha passed away, Sakra, the chief of the deities, said:

Impermanent are all component things,
They arise and cease, that is their nature,
They come into being and pass away,
Release from them is bliss supreme.

This verse is recited at Buddhist funerals in South Asian countries by the *Sangha* during the service.

Philosophers before the Buddha have mentioned impermanence, but it was the Buddha who connected the three concepts and said that everything impermanent is unsatisfactory and *Dukkha*, and because of impermanence there can be no permanent self.

After the armies of Alexander the Great (356–323 BCE) marched into India and occupied a part of the country, there was much intellectual communication between India and Greece. Some Brahminist and Buddhist ideas are reflected in Greek philosophy. Hereclitus (544–483 BCE) was probably the first Greek philosopher to talk about the ever-changing nature of the living being and the universe; that everything was in a state of continuous flux; and because of the flow of water in a river a person cannot step into the same water twice. The views of Pythagoras (580–500 BCE), who was a contemporary of the Buddha, reflect the same ideas. Medical doctors say that the human body regenerates itself every seven years. Scientists say that atoms and molecules are constantly moving and that there are internal changes taking place in solid rock.

Dukkha

Dukkha the second of the Three Signs of Being is also the First Noble Truth. It has a wide variety of meanings.[3] This poem by Anagarika Sugatananda, (Francis Story), who lived in Sri Lanka for a long time and took novice ordination there, illustrates the range of meanings:

Dukkha is:

Disturbance, irritation, dejection, worry,
despair; fear, dread, anguish, anxiety; vulnerability,
injury, inability, inferiority; sickness,
ageing, decay of body and faculties, senility;

Pain/pleasure; excitement/boredom;
deprivation/excess; desire/frustration, suppression;
longing/aimlessness; hope/hopelessness;
effort, activity, striving/repression;
loss, want, insufficiency/satiety;
love/lovelessness, friendlessness;
dislike, aversion/attraction; parenthood/childlessness;
submission/rebellion; decision/indecisiveness,
vacillation, uncertainty.

> Francis Story in 'Suffering' in Vol. II of *The Three Basic Facts of Existence* (Kandy: BPS, 1983)

Selflessness (No Soul, No I)

This body is not self. If the body were self then this body would not be subject to Dukkha. Since this body is not self it is subject to Dukkha... Similarly, feelings, perceptions, volitions and consciousness are not self... Then, ascetics, any kind of body... should be understood with right knowledge in its real nature – this is not mine, this is not I, this is not myself. Similarly, all feelings, perceptions, volitions and consciousness... should be understood as this is not mine, this is not I, this is not myself.

> *Anattalakkhana Sutta*

Some religions teach of a soul or self, a permanent, everlasting, enduring, absolute entity created by a God or arising from some divine source. It is an unchanging entity in a world where other things are changing. Each individual has a separate soul, which, finally after death, lives eternally either in heaven or hell, depending on the judgment of its creator. According to some religions the soul or atman goes through many rebirths and lives in a process of purification. When completely purified it becomes united with the divine being, God, Brahman, universal soul or atman from which it originally arose. This soul is the spiritual essence of the person, being the thinker of thoughts, feeler of sensations, receiver of rewards and punishments and the creator of a good or a bad life.

According to the teaching of some religions, only human beings have souls. Other living beings, for instance animals, birds and fish, do not have souls and are therefore consigned to a lower order of life. Some religions even go on to explain that these living beings of the lower orders exist simply for the benefit of human beings and for no other purpose. Buddhism, on the other hand, brings all living beings into the one fabric of life.

The Buddhist teaching is uniquely different. All living beings are classed as one, but living in different planes (see Chapter 8). Plants are not considered as living beings on the same level as human beings, animals, birds or fish, because they do not have the capacity to think, have no self-motivation, have no self-mobility, do not have intellectual thoughts and have a limited consciousness.

The second teaching of the Buddha, the *Anattalakkhana Sutta*, which is summarized above, sets out the Buddhist teaching on this subject. It says that a living being consists of five aggregates, groups, heaps or collections (*kandhas skandhas*): the body, feelings, perceptions, volitions and consciousness. The word 'aggregates' is used in the plural because each of the aggregates consists of different elements. These do not individually or collectively constitute a soul or self. The living being consists of these five aggregates. Neither within these aggregates nor outside, in other words neither within the bodily and mental forms of existence nor outside them, can anything be found that could be regarded as a self-existing self, soul or other similar entity. Apart from these aggregates there is no separate entity.

This is the central teaching of Buddhism. Without an understanding of this, a real and complete understanding of Buddhism is not possible. Further, for a Buddhist pilgrim to progress on the path a mere understanding is not enough. There must be experiential realization of this teaching gained by mindfulness and meditation (see Chapter 15).

The whole structure of Buddhist teaching is built around this concept of selflessness. Someone who does not understand the impersonality of all existence and that in reality there exists only this continually changing process of the arising and passing away of bodily and mental elements experiencing *Dukkha*, and that there is no separate self within or outside this process, does not understand Buddhism. Such a person makes the mistake of thinking that there is a self that experiences *Dukkha*, makes good or skilful and bad or unskilful actions, progress on the Noble Eightfold Path and finally realizes *Nibbana*.

The Buddha realized that what we call the being is a process of matter units and mind units. The physical body is a collection of matter units continually arising and vanishing. Similarly, the mind is a collection of different mind units continually arising and vanishing. All of these mental and physical phenomena are occurring of their own accord, due to causes and interdependently of each other, following no-one's will and subject to no-one's control. They constitute no individual or ego-entity. The Buddha realized the true nature of a being – that there is nothing permanent.

The *Visuddhimagga* states, at Chapters XVI 90 and XVII 117, respectively, that:

> Mere Dukkha exists, but none who experiences it;
> Deeds are done but no doer is found;
> Nibbana is but no person realizing it;
> The Path exists but no traveller is found, and
> Who is not clear about conditionally arisen states and does not understand that all actions are conditioned by ignorance... this individual thinks that it is a self that understands or not, that acts or causes to act, that comes into existence at rebirth... that has sense impressions, that feels, desires and becomes attached... is reborn.

In understanding this, we have to distinguish between conventional reality (the understanding of things as they are in everyday life) and absolute reality (the understanding of things as they are in reality). Conventional reality is that in our day-to-day living, as a means of identification, we have to refer to living beings as he, she or an animal. The absolute reality is that there is no such person or living being.

The Buddha has summed up all of the physical and mental phenomena of existence into five aggregates. These are:

- Body
- Feelings
- Perceptions
- Volitions
- Consciousness.

They are classified into body aggregates and mind aggregates. The body consists of the body aggregates and the mind consists of the other aggregates.

In a short classification, the body aggregates are divided into the four primary elements, given below, and the four aggregates forming the mind are each divided into six classes according to the six senses: vision (seeing), sound (hearing), odour (smelling), taste (tasting), body (feeling) and mind (thinking)

There is a more detailed classification. The first, the body aggregates (consisting of the physical aspects of matter), is divided into four primary constituents namely solid (earth), liquid (water), heat (fire) and motion (air). These are also referred to as inertia, cohesion, radiation and vibration. All four aggregates are present in every material object in varying degrees of strength. The *Abhidhamma* divides the body aggregates into 24 secondary qualities, namely: seeing, hearing, smelling, tasting, body, form, sound, odour, taste, femininity, virility, physical base of mind, bodily expression, verbal expression, physical life, space element, physical agility, physical elasticity, physical adaptability, physical growth, physical continuity, decay, impermanence and nutriment.

The second, the feeling aggregates, include all forms of first impression, unprocessed physical and mental feelings and sensations experienced through the senses when an object is first perceived. All feelings may, according to their nature, be classified into five kinds:

- Bodily agreeable
- Bodily painful
- Mentally agreeable
- Mentally painfully
- Neutral or indifferent.

The third, the perception aggregates, include the recognition, interpretation and labelling of first sensations into concepts such as 'friend', 'book' and 'tree'. All perceptions are divided into six classes relating to the six senses.

The fourth, the volition aggregates, includes different types of voluntary positive mental activities and processes, such as: attentiveness, compassion, doubt, desire and determination. This group consists of 50 mental phenomena, of which 11 are general psychological elements, 25 lofty qualities and 14 kammically unwholesome qualities.

The fifth, the consciousness aggregates, includes the five sensory consciousnesses – seeing, hearing, smelling, tasting, touching, with mental consciousness making six in all. Here consciousness means the capacity for experience, and the initial responses and reactions of the sense organs when brought into contact with sense objects. The *Suttas* divide consciousness, according to the six senses, into six classes. The *Abhidhamma* and commentaries give 89 classes of consciousness according to the kammic or moral point of view. The moral quality of feelings, perceptions and consciousness is determined by the volitions.

Individual existence is the continuing process of these mental and physical phenomena. Classification of the aggregates into five groups is an academic and abstract classification by the Buddha to teach this subject and other subjects, such as impermanence and *Dukkha*. Venerable Nynatiloka explains in the *Buddhist Dictionary*, 1972 (p. 83):

What is called individual existence is in reality nothing but a mere process of those mental and physical phenomena, a process that since time immemorial has been going on, and that also after death will still continue for unthinkable long periods of time. These five groups, however, neither singly nor collectively constitute any self-dependent real Ego-entity, or Personality (atta), nor is there to be found any such entity apart from them. Hence the belief in such an Ego-entity or Personality, as real in the ultimate sense, proves a mere illusion.

When all constituent parts are there,
The designation 'cart' is used;
Just so, where the five groups exist,
Of 'living being' do we speak.

The fact ought to be emphasized here that these five groups, correctly speaking, merely form an abstract classification by the Buddha and as such have no real existence, since only a single representative of these groups, mostly variable, can arise with any state of consciousness. For example, with one and the same unit of consciousness only one single kind of feeling – say joy or sorrow – can be associated, and never more than one. Similarly, two different perceptions cannot arise at the same moment. This is also true of the various kinds of sense-cognition or consciousness: only one of them can be used at a time, for example seeing, hearing or inner consciousness, etc. Of the 50 mental formations, however, a smaller or larger number are always associated with every state of consciousness.

Some writers on Buddhism who have not understood that the five *khandas* are just classificatory groupings, have conceived them as compact entities ('heaps' or 'bundles'), while as stated above the groups never exist as such, i.e. they never occur in a simultaneous totality of all their constituents. These single constituents of a group that are present in any given body-and-mind process are of an evanescent nature as are their varying combinations. Feeling, perception and volitions are only different aspects and functions of a single unit of consciousness. They are to consciousness what redness, softness, sweetness, etc., are to an apple and have as little separate existence as these qualities.

The five aggregates may be summarized as follows:

Five Aggregates

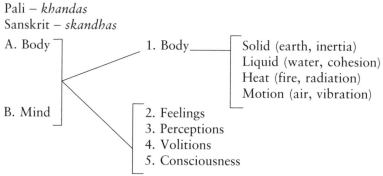

Pali – *khandas*
Sanskrit – *skandhas*

A. Body
B. Mind

1. Body
   - Solid (earth, inertia)
   - Liquid (water, cohesion)
   - Heat (fire, radiation)
   - Motion (air, vibration)
2. Feelings
3. Perceptions
4. Volitions
5. Consciousness

If there is no self, ego or I:

- Who travels in *Samsara*?
- Who creates and experiences *kamma*?
- Who realizes *Nibbana*?

The Buddhist view of life is as follows. Every moment some energies end because their momentum is over and new energies begin. The major parts of the energies continue to the next moment as a stream of energy, changing at the same time. Each unit or strand of consciousness consists of four stages:

- Arising
- Gaining strength
- Losing strength and
- Ending.

Immediately after the end of a thought moment the next arises. Each consciousness transmits its energies to its successor. Each fresh consciousness consists of the transmitted energies of the previous consciousness together with something new. The subsequent thought moment is neither absolutely the same nor entirely different from the previous one, being part of the same stream of life. It is like the flow of a river receiving new water from tributaries with some water evaporating and some being absorbed by the banks, while the water in the river keeps flowing. The energies similarly keep flowing, receiving new energies while some energies end because they lose their momentum. No state once gone ever recurs. These changes are so rapid that it gives a person ignorant of the *Dhamma* the illusion of something permanent – a person.

This stream of energy of consciousness goes through many moments, deaths, lives and rebirths in *Samsara* (the cycle of life, see Chapter 9). The Buddhist Pali term for an individual is *santati* (continuity), which reflects the constantly changing continuity of the physical and mental elements. These have no identifiable source in the past or foreseeable end in the future. Conditioned by *kamma* they keep on flowing until, by following the Noble Eightfold Path, the process is transcended by the realization of *Nibbana*. This process is the Buddhist model of a being corresponding to the model of self, soul or atman in other religions teachings. The selfless (*anatta*) teaching in Buddhism denies the existence of a permanent, unchanging, eternal soul or ego or an abiding self. Buddhism does not, however, deny the continuity of a living being, changing from moment to moment, in *Samsara*. Nor does it deny the unconditioned, only that it is a permanent unchanging self.

In a conventional sense perhaps it may be said that the personality of a living being is the sum total of the mind aggregates and energies at that moment. This is academic, however, as these are constantly changing and there is no permanent, unchanging, eternal self, ego or soul. The living being at any moment is neither the same nor entirely different from the one in the previous moment. An example often given to illustrate this is the flame of a candle. The flame in a given moment is not the same nor different from the flame of the previous moment. Science concedes that there is no actual 'identity' between an atom at one moment and the same atom in the next moment.

Eastern Buddhism developed the idea of emptiness (*sunyata*). It is an extension of the idea of selflessness. This idea of emptiness is extended to cover all things, ideas and concepts. This is an awareness that nothing is self-existent: nothing has an existence of its own. Since there is no self there can be nothing that can belong to a self and this is a means to counter the bonds of attachment. The *Prajna Paramita Sutras* (Wisdom *Sutras*) are a collection of Eastern (Mahayana) Buddhist Sutras, more formally called the *Perfection of Wisdom Sutras*. They explain the concept of emptiness (Sanskrit –

sunyata; Japanese – *ku*). There are several *Prajna Paramita Sutras*. *Prajna* is the wisdom realized by the practice of the *Paramitas* (Pali – Paramis, English – Perfections, Japanese – *Haramita*), see Chapter 17. By practising and perfecting the *Paramitas* a person achieves Enlightenment and realizes *Nibbana*. Therefore *Prajna Paramita* is the wisdom of a person who has realized *Nibbana*. The *Great Sutra on the Heart of the Perfection of Wisdom* is popularly known as the *Heart Sutra* because it expresses the essence of the *Wisdom Sutras*. Here bodhisattva Avalokatisvera, known as Kannon in Japan (Jp: *Kanjizai*), having realized the nature of the five aggregates, perceived that their nature was empty. He then proceeded to share this wisdom with Sariputta (Sanskrit – Sariputra; Japanese – Sharishi).

Prajna Paramita Sutra

MA-KA HAN-NYA HA-RA-MI-TA SHIN-GYO
Kan-ji-zai bo-sa gyo jin han-nya ha-ra-mi-ta ji sho-ken go-un kai ku do is-sai ku-yaku sha-ri-shi shiki fu-i ku ku fu-i shiki shiki soku ze ku ku soku ze shiki ju so gyo shiki yaku bu nyo ze sha-ri-shi ze sho-ho ku-so fu-sho fu-metsu fu-ku fu-jo fu-zo fu-gen ze ko ku-chu mu-shiki mu ju so gyo shiki mu gen ni bi zes-shin-i mu shiki sho ko mi soku ho mu-gen-kai nai-shi mu-i-shiki-kai mu-mu-myo yaku mu-mu-myo-jin nai-shi mu-ro-shi yaku mu-ro shi-jin mu ku shu metsu do mu chi yaku mu toku i mu-sho tok-ko bo-dai-sat-ta e han-nya ha-ra-mi-ta ko shin mu-kei-ge mu-kei-ge ko mu u ku fu on-ri is-sai ten-do mu-so ku-gyo ne-han san-ze sho-butsu e han-nya ha-ra-mi-ta ko toku a-noku-ta-ra sam-myaku sam-bo-dai ko chi han-nya ha-ra-mi-ta ze dai-jin-shu ze dai-myo-shu ze mu-jo-shu ze mu-to-do-shu no jo is-sai ku shin-jitsu fu-ko ko setsu han-nya ha-ra-mi-ta shu soku setsu shu watsu gya-tei gya-tei hara-gya-tei hara-so-gya-tei bo ji so-wa-ka han-nya shingyo.

(Japanese Devotional chant, the Zen temple, Shobo-an, London)

The Heart of the Great Wisdom Sutra

When the bodhisattva Avalokitesvara practised the profound great wisdom gone beyond (*Prajna Paramita*) he clearly saw that the five aggregates (*skandha*) are all empty and thus had passed beyond suffering. Oh Sariputra form is not different from emptiness; emptiness is not different from form. Form is emptiness; emptiness is form. The same also applies to feeling or sensation, perception, mental configurations and consciousness. Oh Sariputra, all things (*Dharmas*) are in themselves empty, neither coming to be nor ceasing to be, pure nor impure, increasing nor decreasing. Thus within emptiness there is no form, no feeling or sensation, no perception, no mental configurations, no consciousness. Within emptiness there is no eye, no ear, no nose, no tongue, no body, no mind; there is no field of seeing, of hearing, of smelling, of tasting, of touching. No field of consciousness. Within emptiness there is no delusion nor extinction of delusion and so on (through the 12 links of the chain of dependent causation) to old age and death, nor extinction of old age and death.

Within emptiness there is no suffering, no cause of suffering, no end of suffering and no way to the end of suffering. Within emptiness there is neither knowledge nor attainment either, and nothing that can be attained. The bodhisattva relies on the great wisdom gone beyond and so his heart is free of hindrances. Because his heart is free of hindrances, he is free of fear. Going beyond all error and delusion, he enters final *Nirvana*. All past, present and future Buddhas rely on the great wisdom gone beyond and so attain to perfect and complete awakening. Know therefore that the great wisdom gone beyond is the great mantra, the wisdom mantra which is supreme and peerless and delivers from all suffering.

> It is true, not vain; therefore I proclaim the Mantra of the Great Wisdom Gone Beyond and I proclaim it thus: GATE GATE PARAGATE PARASAMGATE BODHI SVAHA!' (Gone, Gone, Gone Beyond, Gone altogether Beyond, Enlightenment Fulfilled.)[4]
>
> English translation

In Southern Buddhism selflessness is explained as an analysis in which individual things are minutely analyzed (as explained above), but the Eastern Buddhist explanation is one of synthesis where emptiness is seen by intuition that is called *Prajna Paramita* wisdom.

Dependent Origination

Dependent Origination, *Paticca Samuppada*, is the teaching of the conditionality of all physical and mental phenomena. *Paticca* means 'dependent upon' and *Samuppada* means 'origination'. It is explained in various texts including *Paticcasamuppada Vibhanga Sutta* in Southern Buddhis, and in the *Saddharma Pundarika Sutra* (p. 158) in Eastern and Northern Buddhism.

The teaching shows the conditioned and dependent nature of the stream of life. Together with the teaching on selflessness and impersonality, it forms the foundation of the Buddhist explanation of life and continuity of life. The teaching on selflessness proceeds to analyse the meaning of self and life, while the teaching of Dependent Origination proceeds to synthesize the various elements of life and to demonstrate that they conditionally relate to one another. An understanding of these two teachings is essential for an understanding of Buddhism.

Dependent Origination consists of 12 interdependent causes and effects, and is a statement of the process of birth and death, the causes of rebirth, *Dukkha* and death. It is stated in the form of 12 links in the chain of Dependent Origination or conditioned arising. It is illustrated by the outer circle of the Wheel of Life (see Chapter 9). This is the teaching in Southern Buddhism.

The teaching on Dependent Origination in Eastern Buddhism is the same. Professor Junjiro Takakusu explains in *The Essentials of Buddhist Philosophy* (pp. 29–30) that:

> The creations or becomings of the antecedent causes continue in time series – past. present and future – like a chain. This chain is divided into twelve divisions and is called the Twelve Divisioned Cycle of Causations and Becomings. Since these divisions are inter-dependent, they are called Dependent Production or Chain of Causation. The formula of this theory is as follows: From the existence of *this, that* becomes; from the happening of *this, that* happens. From the non-existence of *this, that* does not become; from the non-existence of *this, that* does not happen.

In Northern Buddhism too we have the same teaching. Tenzing Gyatso, HH the XVI Dalai Lama says in *The Buddhism of Tibet* (p. 32):

> All of these phenomena have some mode of dependence; either they arise, change and cease in dependence on causes, or they are posited in dependence on a continuum, or in dependence on their parts and so forth. No matter what type of dependent phenomena they are, they exist only in dependence on another. Not even one among them is able to stand by itself. Therefore all of them are empty of their own inherent existence...

Geshe Tashi Tsering writes in the *The Four Noble Truths* (p. 93) that:

We can understand how the truth of the origin of suffering works to produce the truth of suffering through the teaching called the *twelve links of Dependent Origination*. This teaching explains the mechanism that produces the two sets of cause and effect (suffering and origin, cessation and path) [...]. Our fundamental ignorance produces the volition to act (karma) that becomes the cause of suffering. A causal state produces a resultant state, which itself is a cause that produces a result – and so it goes on endlessly. The teachings on the twelve links are very helpful to help us to clearly understand how we are circling in endless suffering. As long as we are under the power of karma and delusions in this process, there is no end to the cycle.

The entire body of the *Abhidhamma* texts really examine nothing but these two teachings: the selflessness and conditionality of all existence. The first book of the *Abhidhamma* texts proceeds analytically to explain selflessness. The last book proceeds synthetically, explaining the concept of Dependent Origination to show that all these phenomena are conditionally related to each other. The teaching on Dependent Origination can be set out as follows:

1. **Ignorance** of the truth taught in the Four Noble Truths, that is *Dukkha*, its cause, its end and the way to end it is the chief cause that sets the Wheel of Life in motion.
2. Dependent on ignorance there arise **volitional, conditioned or intentional activities** that constitute *kamma*. Volition is one of the five aggregates. All moral and immoral thoughts, words and deeds are included in volitions.
3. **Relinking or rebirth consciousness** dependent on past volitional, conditioning and intentional activities arises in a subsequent birth. It links the past with the present and is the initial consciousness you experience at the moment of conception.
4. Dependent on and simultaneous with the arising of relinking or rebirth consciousness, **mind and matter** arise.

The second and third links, intentional activities and rebirth consciousness relate to the past and present life. The third and fourth links relate to the present life. This compound of mind and matter should be understood as mind alone, matter alone and mind and matter together. What arises depends on the plane of rebirth (see Chapter 8).

5. Dependent on and conditioned by mind and matter the **six sense bases** – eye (seeing), ear (hearing), nose (smelling), tongue (tasting), body (touch) and mind (consciousness) – arise.

6. External sense objects collide with their respective sense bases or organs giving rise to six types of consciousness. The dependent activation of the sense objects, sense bases and resultant consciousness there gives rise to **contact**.

7. Dependent on contact **feelings** arise. Feelings constitute the second aggregate in the model of the five aggregates (see above). It is this feeling that experiences an object when it comes into contact with the senses. It is this feeling that experiences the desirable or undesirable results of actions done in a previous or the present birth. Feelings or sensations are mental states common to all types of consciousness. There are three kinds of mental feelings, pleasurable, painful and neutral. Together with physical pain and physical happiness they constitute, in total, five kinds of feelings. *Nibbanic* bliss is not associated with any kind of feeling. It is the highest happiness, but it is the happiness of relief from *Dukkha*, not the enjoyment of any pleasurable object.

8. Dependent on feelings **attachment**, thirst and craving arise. Attachment is of three types, attachment to sensual pleasures, attachment to the continuation of life and attachment to desire for the ending of life. It is natural for an individual to develop an attachment to pleasures of the senses. It is through the senses that the mind is in touch with the outside world and it is difficult to resist the intoxicating effect of these pleasures. The most powerful elements in the Wheel of Life (see Chapter 9) are ignorance and attachment. These are the two main causes of Dependent Origination. Ignorance is the past cause that conditions the present, and attachment is the present cause that conditions the future.

9. Dependent on attachment the more intense **grasping** or taking arises. It is this grasping that gives rise to a false sense of self or 'I'. Grasping is of four kinds: sensuality, false views, adherence to rites and ceremonies and belief in a self or soul.

10. Dependent on grasping there arises **becoming**. It includes both moral and immoral actions that constitute *kamma* (the active process of becoming) and the different planes of existence (passive process of becoming).

11. Dependent on becoming arises **birth** and subsequent life. Birth is the arising of the physical and mental elements of the individual.
12. Dependent on birth there is **old age, illness and death**, which is **Dukkha** (see Chapter 4).

When the twelfth link is reached, unless the person has attained Enlightenment and realized *Nibbana*, there is rebirth and the process is repeated again. This process is therefore referred to as cyclic existence. This explains how a living being arises and continues to do so over many births. This explanation of Dependant Origination applies to the different meanings of rebirth, for example from one human life to another, to the arising of a sense of 'I' or self and from moment to moment (see Chapter 8).

The reverse order of Dependent Origination makes the explanation clearer. Old age and death are only possible in relation to a physical and mental being with six senses. Such a being must be born and this presupposes birth or becoming. Birth is the result of past *kamma* or volitions. *Kamma* is due to grasping, which is due to attachment. Such attachment appears when feeling arises and feelings are the outcome of contact between senses and sense objects. This presupposes sense organs, which cannot exist without mind and body. Mind and body originate with rebirth consciousness, conditioned by intentional volitional activities caused by ignorance of things as they are as explained by the Four Noble Truths.

This process may be summarized as follows:

1. **Ignorance** of the truth explained by the Four Noble Truths sets the Wheel of Life in motion
2. Dependent on ignorance, **intentional activities** arise
3. Dependent on intentional activities, **rebirth consciousness** arises
4. Dependent on rebirth consciousness, **mind and matter** arise
5. Dependent on mind and matter, the **six sense bases** arise
6. Dependent on the six sense bases **contact** arises
7. Dependent on contact, **feeling** arises
8. Dependent on feeling, **attachment** arises
9. Dependent on attachment, **grasping** arises
10. Dependent on grasping, **becoming** arises
11. Dependent on becoming, **birth and rebirth** arise
12. Dependent on birth and rebirth, **aging, illness and death** arise, which is *Dukkha*.

When these elements are considered from the point of view of termination or ending, rather that arising starting with ignorance, we have an account of the ending of the process. The process of ending may be summarized as follows:

1. Ending of **ignorance** is the first step
2. Ending of ignorance leads to the ending of **intentional activities**
3. Ending of intentional activities leads to the ending of **rebirth consciousness**
4. Ending of rebirth consciousness leads to the ending of **mind and matter**
5. Ending of mind and matter leads the ending of **six sense bases**
6. Ending of six sense bases leads to the ending of **contact**
7. Ending of contact leads to the ending of **feeling**
8. Ending of feeling leads to the ending of **attachment**
9. Ending of attachment leads to the ending of **grasping**
10. Ending of grasping leads to the ending of **becoming**
11. Ending of becoming leads to the ending of **birth and rebirth**
12. Ending of birth and rebirth leads to the ending of **aging, illness and death** which are *Dukkha*, and the realization of **Nibbana**.

The following table from Venerable Nynatiloka's *Buddhist Dictionary* (p. 129) shows the relationship of dependence between three successive lives.

Past	1. Ignorance 2. Intentional activities	*Kamma* process 5 causes: 1, 2, 8, 9, 10
Present	3. Rebirth consciousness 4. Mind and matter 5. Six sense bases 6. Contact 7. Feeling	Rebirth process 5 results: 3,4,5,6,7
	8. Attachment 9. Grasping 10. Becoming	*Kamma* process 5 causes: 1, 2, 8, 9, 10
Future	11. Rebirth 12. Old Age and Death	Rebirth process 5 results: 3,4,5,6,7

The first two elements or factors relate to the past; the middle eight to the present; and the last two to the future. Intentional activities and becoming, or actions, are regarded as *kamma*. Ignorance, attachment (craving, mental thirst) and grasping (clinging) are regarded as passions or defilements. Rebirth consciousness, mind and matter, six sense bases, contact, feeling, rebirth, old age and death are regarded as effects.

Ignorance, intentional activities, attachment, grasping and *kamma*/becoming, are the five causes of the past that condition the present five effects of rebirth consciousness, mind and matter, six sense bases, contact and feeling of the present.

In the same way, ignorance, intentional activities, attachment, grasping and *kamma*/becoming of the present condition the five effects of rebirth consciousness, mind and matter, six sense bases, contact and feeling of the future.

The teaching of Dependent Origination is a detailed account of the Four Noble Truths. *Dukkha* is found at every stage. In its serial order, starting with ignorance and ending with rebirth and *Dukkha*, Dependent Origination is a detailed analysis of the Second of the Four Noble Truths, the arising of *Dukkha*. In its order of ending the constituent elements in serial order, starting with the ending of ignorance and terminating with the ending of rebirth and *Dukkha*. It is an analysis of the Third of the Four Noble Truths, the ending of *Dukkha*, overcoming the three types of attachment, ill will and ignorance, and realizing impermanence, *Dukkha* and selflessness to realize *Nibbana*. The Noble Eightfold Path shows how this can be done (see Chapter 5).

This process of cause and effect – the rebirth process – continues forever. A beginning of this process cannot be identified as it is impossible to conceive of a time when this life process is not influenced by ignorance. The rebirth process comes to an end only when, through the study and practice of the *Dhamma*, this ignorance is replaced by wisdom and *Nibbana* is realized.

Chapter 7

Actions and Results (Kamma and Vipaka)

Kamma (karma), vipaka and rebirth (or rebecoming), are two fundamental and interrelated elements of Buddhist teaching and practice. Kamma is the law of moral causation and rebirth, the continuation of life, is its associated concept. These two ideas were known in Brahminism, the forerunner of Hinduism, and in Jainism before the time of the current teaching of Buddhism. Gotama Buddha explained and reformulated these concepts in line with his other teachings, all of which went to form Buddhism.

The Five Laws of Nature

Buddhism explains all physical and mental processes that operate in the world with these five laws of nature:

1. Physical inorganic law, e.g. the seasonal changes, causes of wind and rain, nature of heat and cold.
2. Physical organic law, e.g. organic rules relating to plants, human beings, other living beings, heredity and genetic factors, characteristics of fruits and other food stuff.
3. Moral law (kamma-vipaka) of action and result in relation to moral matters.
4. Natural law, e.g. natural events, birth of a Buddha, gravity and other similar laws of nature.
5. Mental law, e.g. the constituents and processes of consciousness, and power and working of the mind.

The moral law of kamma-vipaka is the most immediately important to us in that it explains our status and condition in life and how we can improve this. When we look around us we see great differences among human beings. One person is wealthy and powerful, another is poor and with no authority. One person is attractive in appearance, intelligent and has perfect sense faculties, while another is plain looking, foolish and has impaired sense faculties. One child is born in the midst of plenty and in comfort, has caring parents and a good education, while another is born in circumstances of strife and misery, becomes an orphan and has a poor education. One person is law abiding while another is a criminal. One person is talented and successful; another has poor personal qualities and is unsuccessful. One person is happy and enjoys long life; another is unhappy and has a short life.

Is there a cause for all this or is it pure chance? According to Buddhism these inequalities are not due only to heredity, environment and luck, but also to the operation of the law of *kamma-vipaka*: the results of our inherited past actions and present actions. We are responsible in a great part for our quality of life. When a young man named Subha asked the Buddha the reason for these differences among people, the Buddha's reply was:

> All living beings have actions (Kamma) as their own, their inheritance, their congenital cause, their kinsman, their refuge. It is Kamma that differentiates beings into low and high states.
>
> *Cullakammavibhanga Sutta* (*Majjhima Nikaya*, 135)

The detailed law of *kamma-vipaka* is intricate and operates beyond the range of ordinary human perception. The Buddha said that the working of *kamma* is one of the matters that humans should not try to understand and evaluate intellectually. Only a Buddha can fully understand the working of *kamma*. We can, however, attempt to have a general view of *kamma*.

Nature and Working of Kamma

The first two verses of *The Dhammapada* can be summarized as:

> Mind foreruns all conditions [...] mind made are they; If one speaks or acts with a wicked mind, because of that, pain follows one. If one speaks or acts with a pure mind, because of that, happiness follows one.
>
> *The Dhammapada*, vv. 1–2[1]

Again, a beautiful verse from the *Samyutta Nikaya* states:

According to the seed that's sown
So is the fruit you reap therefrom
Doer of good will gather good
Doer of evil, evil reaps
Sown is the seed, and planted well,
You shall enjoy the fruit therefrom.

Samyutta Nikaya, vol. 1, p. 227

Kamma means action or doing and *vipaka* means result. The law of *kamma-vipaka* states that every intentional action having a moral content has a corresponding result. Therefore:

- Morally good or wholesome intentional actions have good results
- Morally bad or unwholesome intentional actions have bad results
- Morally neutral actions have no such results.

Both *kamma* and *vipaka* are mental qualities or elements of energy. They have no physical form. The law applies automatically to all living beings, in the case of humans whether Buddhists or not, and wherever they may be, in the human world or any other. It is a law of nature, like the law of gravity. There is no lawgiver. The law does not apply to a Buddha or an *Arahat* because they have transcended ignorance and craving and gone beyond the plane at which *kamma* is formed. They may still experience the results of previous *kamma*, however, as when the Buddha's foot was wounded by Devadatta because of a bad past action.

One element of *kamma* may have several results and one result may be due to several elements of *kamma*. Though *kamma* is important, it only one of 24 causal conditions described in Buddhism.

When a situation presents itself to the mind there is a thought moment of choice. We are free to decide from a number of different ways how we are to react. This is our freedom of choice; the exercise of free will. Our reaction may be good or bad. The moral quality of the action is determined by the mental qualities that motivate the action:

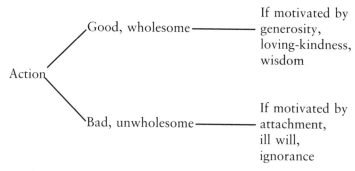

The word action has a wide meaning and includes physical, verbal and mental actions. It is sometimes referred to as actions by the body (deed), speech (word) and mind (thought):

Action ——————⎡ physical – body – deed

⎢ verbal – speech – word

⎣ mental – mind – thought.

Kamma is restricted to intentional actions. Intention is the central element. Unintentional, involuntary and accidental actions do not constitute *kamma*. In its ultimate sense *kamma* means all moral and immoral intentions. The Buddha said:

> Intention (mental volition) is what I call action (Kamma). Having intended (willed), one acts by body, speech and thought.
>
> *Anguttara Nikaya*, vol. III. p. 415

Mechanics

At the time the intention is formed, an element of *kammic* energy comes into being and becomes a part of the consciousness of the individual. The stream of consciousness flows on. The *kammic* energy lies below the consciously accessible level of the mind. When suitable external and internal circumstances arise, the result (*vipaka*) is activated. Different results may be activated in the present life or later lives, from the different *kammic* energies accumulated. This is the understanding in Southern Buddhism. The Eastern Buddhist explanation is similar.

According to Buddhism, human beings and all living things are self-created or self-creating [...]. The creations or becomings of the antecedent causes continue in time series — past, present and future — like a chain... (Takakusu, p. 29)

The Northern Buddhism explains similarly that *kamma* is the function of cause and effect and is a natural law.

When we create an action of body, speech, or mind, the conscious or subconscious volition that causes that action also creates a potential that is deposited in the mental continuum, the stream of consciousness. When the appropriate conditions arise, this potential becomes manifest as a positive or negative result.. (Tsering, p. 74)

Every *kammic* intention has a specific momentum which is reflected in the result (*vipaka*). The *kammic* energy will remain active until the result is fully experienced and the momentum is exhausted. This momentum may remain dormant for some time then suddenly become activated by suitable conditions and change the individual's life for better or worse. This explains the sudden changes in the life patterns of individuals. Once the momentum is exhausted it has no further effect. For example, Venerable Moggallana, one of the Buddha's senior disciples, was clubbed to death by a band of bandits. The Buddha explained that this was because of the bad *kamma* generated by an attempt in a previous birth to harm his parents. Apart from the law of *kamma* it is difficult to understand how a monk who led such an exemplary life came to such a strange and sad end. On the other hand, Angulimala the highway robber and murderer, after hearing the teachings given by the Buddha, became a member of the *Sangha*. With strenuous effort and the help of past good *kamma* was able to progress to become an *Arahat*. This teaches us not to look down on a person in a low status in life, because the person may have a store of good *kamma* which takes effect later that improves his life.

The moral quality of an action will strengthen that quality in the mind. An action motivated by generosity, loving-kindness or wisdom will increase those qualities of the person. An action motivated by attachment, ill will or ignorance will increase those qualities. Further, good actions will increase the tendency to other good actions and *vice versa*. The effect of an element of *kamma* may differ according to the moral nature of the person. The individual's accumulation of good and bad *kamma* and dominating character traits, good or bad, will affect the strength of the *kammic* reaction and time of that reaction. In the case of a good person, a good action may have great effect and a bad action small effect. In the case of a bad person a good action may have small effect and bad action great effect. Diagrammatically:

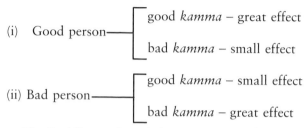

(i)   Good person ── good *kamma* – great effect
                      bad *kamma* – small effect

(ii) Bad person ── good *kamma* – small effect
                    bad *kamma* – great effect

The Buddha explained that it was like a spoonful of salt: if put into a cup of water it makes the water salty, but if thrown into the Ganges its effect cannot be felt. On the other hand, the willingness to transform your general tendencies through mindfulness is important. The *Dhammapada* says:

> Do not ignore the effect of right action, saying it will come to nothing. Just as the fall of raindrops fills the water jar, likewise the wise man gathering merit little by little, fills himself with good Kamma.

Dhammapada, v. 122

The Southern Buddhist teaching explains that *kamma* includes past intentional actions in previous lives and the present life, and present actions. The life situation, mental, moral, intellectual and temperamental condition of a living being at given time is mainly due to the aggregate results of *kammic* actions. By the potentiality of his *kamma* each individual, in the successive stages of life, attracts to himself the situations, environment, contacts and peculiar problems that reflect his own nature. The unexhausted *kammic* forces will be transferred to future lives and will contribute to the pattern of life in the future as the person moves through *Samsara*. In fact it is these *kammic* forces propel the person through *Samsara*. It is as if the person is on a treadmill powered by *kamma*. The process comes to an end on the person attaining *Nibbana* by following the Noble Eightfold Path. The Buddhist aim is to go beyond all *kamma*, good and bad, by transcending attachment, ill will and ignorance.

A person can influence future lives for better or worse by good or bad *kamma*. This is a most important feature of *kamma* that you can, through mindfulness and awareness, to some extent influence the future. There is no room for the concept of predestination in the Buddhist teaching. We move into new births in higher and lower planes or continue in this human plane because of *kamma*. Therefore in living we create ourselves, our life situations in the present and the future and in the world we live in.

Eastern Buddhism gives similar explanations:

> Actions (*karma*) are divided into three groups, i.e. Those by the body, those by speech and those by volition. When one makes up one's mind to do something one is responsible for it [. . .] a living being determines its own nature and existence by its own actions. Therefore we may say the living being is self- created [. . .] According to the nature of the preceding actions, the next Wheel of Life may be of a higher order or of a lower order. (Takakusu, pp. 34–36)

Northern Buddhism also gives a similar explanation. Actions are intentional (prior) or operational (time of deed):

> From the point of view of the effects they impel, actions are of three types: meritorious, non-meritorious and invariable. Meritorious actions impel one to happy migrations, which are the lives of humans, demigods and gods. Non-meritorious actions impel one to bad migrations, which are the lives of animals, hungry ghosts and denizens of hells. Invariable actions impel one to the upper realms, which are those of form and the formless. All of these can be divided into physical, verbal and mental actions [. . .] the effects of an action 'accumulated' in this life may be experienced in this very life, in the next life, or in any life beyond the next. (Gyatso, pp. 26–27)

Is there a collective *kamma*? Each individual has his own *kamma*, which is a part of his own consciousness. There is no sharing of *kamma*. Several people may have created identical *kammas* by similar individual actions. These *kammas* do not coalesce into one collective or joint *kamma*. In a group the people may have similar *kammas* and in a group individuals can reinforce their individual *kammic* tendencies. In the end, however, each individual is responsible for himself. The *kamma* of each person could be activated separately, but at the same time and place as the similar *kammas* of others. We have the example of aeroplane, ship and train disasters, when many people are injured or die at the same time by the same event. It could happen that the *kamma* of several people could be intertwined, for example the members of a family, but there is still a separate *kamma* for each person.

Causes

The main causes of *kamma* are ignorance and attachment. Ignorance as to the real nature of things, as explained by the Buddha in the Four Noble Truths and other teachings, is the chief cause. Dependent on ignorance, *kammic* activities arise. Attachment to worldly things is the other main cause. Some external thing or event activates the mind, working under the delusion of a self or 'I', to attachment or aversion. This results in some action that in turn results in *kamma*. No *kamma* is created by a person who has developed wisdom to an awareness of absolute reality, and who has transcended attachment.

Who is the Doer of the Kamma?

Who is the doer of the *kamma* and who feels the consequences? Venerable Buddhaghosa writes in the *Visuddhi Magga*:[2]

There is no doer of a deed
Or one who reaps the deed's result ...
Intention or consciousness is the doer, and consciousness which feels the result. Buddhism recognises a person in the conventional sense but not in the absolute sense. The element of Kamma energy moves forward in the stream of consciousness. Due to its constantly changing nature, it is not the same consciousness nor one entirely different, but the continuing process of consciousness which feels the results.

The concept of *kamma* is not new to the West. It is reflected in Plato's philosophy. Pythagoras, who was born in the Island of Samos, Greece in about 580 BCE and was therefore a contemporary of the Buddha, travelled to Asia and studied religion and philosophy there. It was he who taught *kamma* and rebirth to the West, explaining it according to the understanding of life at that time: 'All have souls, all is soul, wandering in the organic world and obeying the eternal will or law.' The idea of *kamma* is known to Christianity. The Bible says 'Be not deceived; God is not mocked, for whatsoever a man soweth, that shall he also reap' (Galatians 6:7). The same principle is echoed in the following extract taken from a medieval English source:

> This world is but a thoroughfare and full of woe, and when we depart therefrom, right naught we bear with us but our good deeds and ill. (Hughes 1989, p. 14)

Good, Wholesome and Meritorious Kamma

Intentional actions motivated by one or more good qualities of generosity, loving-kindness and wisdom create good *kamma*. These are:

- Generosity – in money, service, time, material things and so on.
- Morality – observing the ethical principles of Buddhism, these are the Five Precepts for lay persons (see Chapter 11).
- Reverence – paying respect to those worthy of respect.
- Meditation – mindfulness and developing mental culture.
- Service – doing work beneficial to the community.
- Transference of merit – unselfish giving of merit acquired by good deeds.
- Rejoicing in others' merit – being happy about the good fortune of others.
- Hearing the teaching – listening to the teaching.
- Explaining the teaching – teaching the *Dhamma*.
- Understanding the teaching correctly – understanding, correcting and confirming one's view of the *Dhamma*.

Sometimes further actions are added:

- Praising the good actions of others – supporting others in meritorious actions.
- Taking the Three Refuges – confirm one's intention to be guided by the Buddha, *Dhamma* and *Sangha*.
- Avoiding unwholesome actions.

Some of the benefits of good actions are birth in a good and stable family, birth in fortunate circumstances, wealth, happiness, good health, good fortune, wisdom, opportunity to learn and practise the *Dhamma*, birth in higher planes, confidence in the ability to cope with day-to-day life and so on.

Bad, Unwholesome and Unmeritorious Kamma

Intentional actions motivated by one more of the bad qualities of attachment, ill will and ignorance. These are:

- Three caused by deed or body:
  - Killing or harming living beings
  - Stealing, taking what is not your own
  - Unchastity, misuse of the senses.
- Four caused by word or speech:
  - Lying
  - Slander
  - Harsh speech
  - Frivolous talk.
- Three caused by mind or thought:
  - Greed, attachment
  - Ill will
  - Ignorance, incomplete understanding of reality.

The three caused by deed correspond to the first three of the Five Precepts. The four caused by word correspond to the fourth of the Five Precepts. The three caused by mind are the unwholesome motivations referred to as the basis of bad actions, *lobha, dosa* and *moha*, also known in Buddhism as the Three Fires.

Some of the disadvantages of bad actions are birth in unfortunate circumstances, poverty, ill health, unhappiness, misfortune, foolishness, lack of opportunity to learn and practise the *Dhamma*, doubts about the *Dhamma*, birth in lower planes and inability to cope with day-to-day life.

This statement of bad *kamma* is identical with the ten non-virtues of *Dharma* practice in Eastern and Northern Buddhism and is set out in the same way in one of the oldest Chinese texts, *The Sutra of the Forty Two Chapters*[3] and Geshe Tashi Tsering *The Four Noble Truths* (pp. 87–88).

Classification of Kamma

Kamma may be classified in different ways:

- According to the time of operation:
  - Immediately effective *kamma*, having a result in the present life
  - Subsequently effective *kamma*, having a result in the current or next life

- Indefinitely effective *kamma*, having a result in a later life.
- According to function:
  - Reproductive *kamma*, which determines the situation and state of the next life. This is generally understood to be the last thought process of the person
  - Supportive *kamma*, assists, maintains and adds strength to already existing *kamma*,
  - Counteractive *kamma*, which modifies and weakens already existing *kamma*
  - Destructive *kamma* neutralizes and destroys already existing *kamma* and may substitute itself for that *kamma*
- According to the nature, priority of effect and strength:
  - Weighty or serious *kamma* shows results in the current or next life. This may be good *kamma*, such as achieving higher mental states *(jhanas)*, or bad *kamma* such as killing your parents or an *Arahat*, wounding a Buddha, or causing a schism in the *Sangha*
  - Death proximate *kamma*, being an action or thought immediately before passing away, generally influencing rebirth
  - Habitual *kamma*, being actions that are constantly done and remembered and for which the person has a great liking
  - Cumulative *kamma* being all other *kamma* not included in the above, a reserve fund as it were of *kamma*.
- According to the world or plane of existence in which the effects are felt:
  - Sense world, either in the unhappy states or happy states
  - The form world of heavenly beings
  - Formless world where the mind exists without the body.

In general both Eastern and Northern Buddhism have similar classifications.

Conclusion

A beautiful poem included in the advice given by the Buddha to King Pasenadi of Kosala summarizes the nature and working of *kamma*:

> By every deed one performs,
> With body, or with voice, or mind,
> T'is this that one can call one's own,

This one takes as one goes hence.
This is that which follows one
And like a shadow never leaves.

Samyutta Nikaya[4]

The *Dhammapada*, v. 165 says:

By oneself is evil done
By oneself is one defiled
By oneself is no evil done
By oneself is one purified
Both defilement and purity depends on oneself
No one is purified by another.

The law of *kamma-vipaka* removes any responsibility for a person's status and condition in life from fate, predestination or other external cause and places it firmly on the individual. The individual is responsible for his life. Only the present moment exists and the responsibility for using this moment for good or bad lies with each individual. The right effort is of prime importance. In creating good *kamma* the individual can improve the present life and the future, and create a new world.

A Buddhist is not expected to be discouraged by difficulties or failures, but to understand that these are mainly the result of bad *kamma* and to make a continuing effort to maintain a balanced mind and lead a good life in order make good *kamma* and progress on the path. The law of *kamma* gives consolation, hope, self-reliance and courage to a Buddhist, enabling him to understand the present condition of life, avoid unwholesome actions and have hope for the future.

The twin teachings of *kamma* and rebirth show that a moral equilibrium prevails in this world between intentional actions and the quality of our lives. This satisfies the deep instinctive sense in us that there is a principle of moral justice operating in this world. They also relate strongly to the teaching of mindfulness, as it is with mindfulness that a Buddhist cuts through the fetters of attachment, ill will and ignorance. So the teachings of *kamma* point the individual towards the Enlightened mind and the ending of *Dukkha* – the core of Buddha's teaching.

Chapter 8

Rebirth and Rebecoming

A Living Being

A living being is a grouping of constantly changing physical and mental forces that are continuously flowing as a stream. This stream, called *Samsara* or cyclic existence, is powered by ignorance and attachment, is conditioned by *kamma* and comes to an end with *Nibbana*. In this stream there is rebirth, ageing, illness, death, rebirth and so on – one following the other. It is in this context that rebirth has to be understood. It is a universal law that applies to all beings, whether Buddhist or not, in all of the different planes of existence. Rebirth is closely connected to *kamma*. This concept of rebirth has been verified by investigations (see Appendix II).

Gotama Buddha, a *Samma Sambuddha*, developed powers on the night of his Enlightenment that enabled him to see life in the universe without the restriction of time or space. He declared:

> I recalled my varied lot in former existences as follows: first one life, then two lives, then three, four, five ten, twenty, one hundred and more...
>
> *Majjima Nikaya, Mahasaccaka Sutta*, No. 36, i. 248

He developed powers to see not only his own previous lives but also that of others.

In his first exclamation of joy after Enlightenment the Buddha said:

> Through many a birth I wandered in Samsara, seeking but not finding, the builder of this house. Sorrowful is it to be born again and again.
>
> O house-builder! You are seen. You shall build no house again. All your rafters are broken. Your ridge-pole is shattered.

My mind has attained the unconditioned. Achieved is the end of attachment.

The Dhammapada, v. 153–154

Here the Buddha refers to his past lives. The house is his body and the architect was in his mind, namely attachment, a self-created force that was deluded, clinging to experience with the sense of 'I' and mine, a mental element latent in all. The rafters are the ten defilements or unwholesome qualities headed by attachment, ill will and ignorance. The ridge-pole supporting the rafters was ignorance, the cause of all unwholesome qualities. The shattering of the ridge pole of ignorance by wisdom resulted in the complete demolition of the house. With the demolition of the house the mind attained *Nibbana* and there were no more rebirths.

In his very first teaching, the *Dhammacakkappavattana Sutta*, commenting on the Second Noble Truth the Buddha says, 'This very attachment is that which leads to rebirth'. He concludes the teaching with, 'This is my last birth. Now there is no more rebirth'.

In the *Jataka* stories (see Chapter 1), the Buddha relates the details of his previous lives and refers to his disciples, who were associated with him in those lives. In several other texts he refers to beings being born in unhappy states due to bad actions and in happy states due to good actions.

Some individuals display special talents and skills, often at a very early age. Gotama Buddha was lost in meditation at an agricultural festival when a very young child. John Stuart Mill could read Greek at the age of three and wrote a history of Rome at the age of six. Macaulay wrote a world history at the age of six. Beethoven was playing in public at the age of eight and publishing compositions at the age of ten. Mozart was composing minuets before he was four years old. Christian Heinrich Heinecken, born in Lubeck in 1721, was able to speak at the age of ten months, repeat passages from the Bible at the age of one, answer questions on geography at the age of two, speak French and Latin at the age of three, and was a student of philosophy at the age of four. How did these individuals have these special skills at these ages? Heredity and biological reasons do not explain this fully unless supplemented by explanations of *kamma* and rebirth.

Rebirth has been known in the West and has been a part of the teaching of some religions in the past. Nayaka Thera Piyadassi states in *The Buddhist Doctrine of Life After Death* (p. 39) that there is evidence that pre-existence was accepted by the early Christian

Church, but was declared heretical by the Second Council of
Constantinople in the year 553. Pythagoras identified a shield in a
Grecian temple as the one carried by him in a previous birth in the
siege of Troy. *Kamma* and rebirth is a part of Plato's philosophy.
Schopenhauer refers to metempsychosis and the concepts of rebirth
in Buddhism in his philosophy. Some English poets have also written
of rebirth:

> Or if through lower lives I came
> Tho' all experience past became,
> Consolidated in mind and frame,
> I might forget my weaker lot:
> For is not our first year forgot
> The haunts of memory echo not.

Alfred Tennyson

> Our birth is but a sleep and forgetting
> The soul that rises with us, our life's star
> Hath had elsewhere its setting,
> And cometh from after:
> Not in entire forgetfulness,
> And not in utter darkness.

William Wordsworth

It has been found that some children remember their previous
births but forget the facts when they become involved with the
activities of their present life and education. Investigations have been
done in some countries including Myanmar (Burma) and Sri Lanka
where individuals have expressed knowledge of facts about previous
births.[1] Their knowledge has been found to be correct and is
recorded in several books:

- *Twenty Cases Suggestive of Reincarnation* by Dr Ian
  Stephensen in collaboration with Venerable Balangoda Ananda
  Maitreya
- *The Buddhist Doctrine of Life After Death* by Nayake Thera
  Piyadassi
- *The Case for Rebirth* by Anagarika Sugatananda (Francis Story)

Modes of Rebirth and Death

The classical Buddhist explanation about birth is that all beings are
divided into four categories according to mode of rebirth:

- Egg-born beings
- Womb-born beings
- Moisture-born beings
- Beings having spontaneous birth.

The first group consists of birds and oviparous snakes. All human beings, some beings in higher planes inhabiting the Earth, and some animals belong to the second group. The third group comprises some lowly forms of animal life and other beings where the embryo grows in moisture. Some heavenly beings and spirits are included in the fourth group. Beings having a spontaneous birth are invisible to the physical eye and appear spontaneously without passing through the embryonic stage.

Death comes about due to the following four causes:

- Exhaustion of the reproductive *kammic* energy. This *kammic* energy has a certain momentum or potential force. When this is exhausted death occurs. This may happen before the end of the normal lifespan expected in that particular plane of life.
- The end of the normal life span in that plane. Different planes have different life spans. When the maximum age is reached, the life of the being comes to an end even though the reproductive *kamma* is not exhausted.
- Simultaneous exhaustion of the reproductive *kammic* energy and expiration of the lifespan in that plane of life.
- The action of a stronger opposing *kamma* may overwhelm the flow of reproductive *kamma* before the expiration of the lifespan in that plane. The deaths of children and sudden deaths of individuals are explained by this cause.

The first three are called timely deaths. The fourth is known as an untimely death. These processes can be illustrated by a candle going out. The wick may come to an end, all the wax may become liquefied, both may happen at the same time, or a gust of wind may extinguish the flame.

Explanations of Birth and Death

In Relation to Physical Life

After a living being's physical or biological life comes to an end, the life forces continue in another form of psycho-physical life. Death is the end of life in a particular form and rebirth is the beginning of a new life. In the total concept of *Samsara*, the Wheel of Life, death is the end of a single phase of life and the life forces pass on to the next phase of life, which is begun by rebirth. At the moment of death, the conscious mental functions cease and various *kammic* forces begin to operate. The continuing mental thirst or attachment grasps at a new biological base and there is rebirth or rebecoming as a new living being. This may be in any of the planes of existence mentioned below, depending on the *kammic* forces.

For a being to be born somewhere a being must die. The birth is simply the arising of the aggregates, the life forces and energies still conditioned by attachment (also referred to as the psycho-physical forces) in a new life. The stream of life continues in a new form. The parents provide the biological foundation. It is the *kamma* of the previous being that vitalizes the biological base into a new being and conditions its consciousness. It is this invisible *kammik* energy, which has no physical form, and is generated in, and comes from past births, that continues in the new life.

Death is simply the ending of the life forces and energies – the psycho-physical forces – in one form. At the moment of death, when consciousness is about to move on it is confronted with one of three things. First, some *kamma* symbol from the past, appearing as the last thought moment or some habitual good or bad actions. Second, a *kamma* symbol indicating a predominant factor of the past life. Third, a symbol indicating the location of the rebirth. It is common in Buddhist communities when a person is dying for *Dhamma* texts to be read or chanted to influence the end consciousness of the person and move it to a good Buddhist frame of mind. It is understood that the last consciousness determines the new rebirth and the beginning of a new life.

The energies of the previous consciousness move into a new life and continue without any break. This stream of consciousness is unbroken in relation to time or energy. There is no gap. Rebirth takes place immediately, irrespective of the plane of life in which it takes place. Certain Tibetan traditions believe that mental forces can exist for some time – up to seven weeks is mentioned – by themselves without attaching themselves to a group of physical energies. This may correspond to the formless existence in the teaching of other traditions. Death is therefore only the termination of a single phase of life; birth is the beginning of the next phase.

This succession of rebirth and death in the individual life stream is known as *Samsara* or the Wheel of Life. How did all this begin? The Buddha said:

> Without recognizable or identifiable beginning is this Samsara. The earliest point of beings who, obstructed by ignorance and hampered by attachment, wander and fare on, is not to be seen.
> *Kindred Sayings*, part iii, p.118

This life stream continues, powered by ignorance and attachment and conditioned by *kamma* until ended by fully awakened awareness, *Nibbana*. All this is vividly and beautifully illustrated in Tibetan Wheel of Life *mandala* (see Chapter 9).

Eastern Buddhism has the same explanations.

> Buddhism [...] regards time as a circle with no beginning or end. Time is relative [...]. The death of a living being is not the end: at once another life begins to go through a similar process of birth and death, and thus repeats the round of life over and over again.

and

> ... a living being may assume any form of life – human form, or animal form or even the form of a heavenly being (deva) according to the nature of the actions which caused its becoming. This repetition of change from one form of life to another is called Sansara (undulation of life). (Takakasu, pp. 31 and 35)

Northern Buddhism also has the same explanations.

> Cyclic existence is divided into three types by way of different types of abodes; these are a desire realm, a form realm and a formless realm. There are different kinds of afflictions, of these attachment and ill will are the chief.. (Gyatso, pp. 24–26)

Samsara is defined as 'cyclic existence, the state of constantly taking rebirth due to delusions and karma' (Tsering, p. 156)

Moment to Moment

Beings live only for one life moment and always in the present. The life moment of a being is extremely short and lasts for only one thought or conscious moment. From moment to moment the physical and mental energies are changing. They do not remain the same over any two consecutive moments. There is no going back and no permanency.

At the beginning of the conscious moment there is birth, then life for that one moment. At the end of that moment there is death. Therefore from moment to moment there is birth, life and death.

The separate conscious moments follow each other in rapid succession. The living being at any given moment is not the being of the previous moment or the being that will be in the moment to come. The feeling of continuity is a mental illusion. Rebirth occurs through the same conditioned process as described above operating over lifetimes.

Mental Rebirth, the Arising of 'I'

The third explanation of rebirth and death is in connection with the arising and ending of the feeling of 'I', the ego or self in the mind. The feeling that there is such an 'I', ego or self is again a mental illusion (see Chapter 6).

When the incorrect impression of an 'I' arises in the mind due to an attachment or aversion to some physical or mental object there is birth. The mind can only understand this feeling in relation to an 'I' so it immediately relates the feeling to an 'I' or self. Now there is birth of that self. So long as the attachment or aversion continues this feeling of self continues and so this life. There is another rebirth at the next attachment or aversion when the mind again relates it to an 'I', and so the process goes on. Rebirth therefore is purely mental rebirth due to the illusory idea of an 'I'. Life continues so long as this illusion lasts. Death is at the end of this illusion when the attachment or aversion comes to an end.

In a single day or hour there can be many births, lifetimes and deaths. During the time when the idea of 'I' exists there is *Dukkha*. This process is repeated again and again, leading to the cycle of *Samsara*. When *Nibbana* has been attained there can be no such attachment or aversion, only detached awareness, and consequently no continuing rebirth and death. Freedom from rebirth is that state of fully awakened awareness when there is no further arising of 'I'. This is *Nibbana*.

Continuity of Life

A fourth explanation is that there is continuity of life rather than what can be called rebirth, a lifetime and death. A living being is a continuous and ever-changing stream of energies. Death and rebirth are merely changes in the direction of this stream. The stream ends with the end of the life in which *Nibbana* is attained.

Different Planes of Existence

According to Buddhism, the Earth is not the only habitable world and humans are not the only living beings. There are many world systems and many diverse living beings (see Chapter 9). The Buddhist teaching applies in all of these systems. There are two different explanations of the planes of existence, one from the physical point of view and the other from the mental point of view.

Physical Plane Explanation

Rebirth can take place in different planes of existence. There are altogether 31 planes of existence in which beings can be born according to their *kamma*. There are three main planes of existence. At the bottom is the Sentient plane, *Kamaloka*, where the emphasis is on the attractions of the senses. This is divided into unhappy planes and happy planes. The plane above this is the form plane, *Rupaloka*, or Brahma plane. The beings here have renounced sense desires and delight in meditation and *jhanic* bliss. The highest is the formless plane, *Arupaloka*, where the beings do not have physical form or bodies. There are different periods of lifetimes and degrees of happiness and unhappiness in these planes.

The Sentient unhappy plane is divided into four: the planes of spirits, ghosts, animals and those in hell. Those in the spirit, ghost and hell planes are not visible to the human eye. Beings in these planes suffer different degrees of handicaps, unhappiness and misery, both physically and mentally.

The human plane comes at the bottom of the seven Sentient happy planes. This human plane is considered to be the one most advantageous for spiritual development on the Buddhist path. It is a mixture of happiness and unhappiness and provides the widest opportunities for the creation of new *kamma*. The beings have some happiness but are not overwhelmed by it. There is a degree of unhappiness but not so much as to prevent an optimistic view of life according to the Buddhist teaching. So the individual can understand the realities of life and make an effort to improve. The lifespan is neither too short nor too long, so that a being can be aware of birth and death and appreciate the impermanence of life. Also, humans have the mental equipment necessary to understand the *Dhamma*, to evaluate its excellence and practise the teaching.

A being is therefore considered extremely lucky to be born as a human being in circumstances most favourable for progress to *Nibbana*. Bodhisattas prefer to be born in the human plane as it provides the best field in which to serve the world and perfect the requirements for Buddhahood. Those bodhisattas who are to become Enlightened as Buddhas always chose to be born in the human plane. It is understood that Buddhahood can only be attained from this plane.

In the other six Sentient happy planes are the heavenly planes of devas, deities and gods. The beings have all the worldly comforts and luxuries to cater to their senses. Their physical forms are more subtle and refined than those of human beings and they cannot be seen by humans. Their style of life is more pleasurable and they have long lifetimes, but they do not transcend humans in wisdom. Their happy and long lives militate against their understanding *Dukkha* or searching for any explanation of life with any sense of urgency.

Bodhisattas who have perfected to qualities of Buddhahood reside in *Tusita* heaven until they appear in the human world to attain Buddhahood. The next Buddha, bodhisatta Metteyya, now resides in the *Tusita* heaven. Gotama Buddha's mother was reborn in the *Tusita* heaven and later in the *Tavatimsa* heaven where the Buddha went to teach her the *Dhamma*.

It is understood that humans can communicate with these deities, and that the deities have the power to help humans. They are dependent on the help and merit offered by humans for their progress. In their daily worship and at special ceremonies held for various reasons Buddhists generally offer blessings to the deities.

Beyond the Sentient plane are the 16 form planes (*Rupaloka* or Brahma planes). Those who have attained *jhanas* and high stages of mental development are born in these planes according to the levels of development cultivated. In some of the higher planes, by the power of meditation it is possible to separate matter from mind. Here beings who have renounced sense pleasures lead very high-quality lives, engage in meditation and higher mental training and enjoy progressively increasing states of mental bliss.

Beyond this are the four formless planes (*Arupaloka*). Here the beings have a purely mental existence without matter or bodies.

In the form and formless planes there is no gender distinction between beings. The Buddhist teaching applies in all of these planes

or worlds. After their lifetimes these beings are reborn according to
their operative *kamma*. They are within the cycle of *Samsara* or
cyclic existence until they attain *Nibbana*.

Table of planes of Existence

Plane		Manifestation	Number of planes
Formless plane (*Arupaloka*)		Existence of mind only	4
Form plane (*Rupaloka Brahmaloka*)		Existence of mind and matter or form	16
Sentient plane (*Kamaloka*)	Sentient happy plane	Deities, gods, heavenly beings	6
		Human beings	1
	Sentient unhappy plane	Beings in hell	1
		Animals	1
		Ghosts	1
		Spirits	1
			31

Similar teachings are found in all the Buddhist traditions. In *The
Essentials of Buddhist Philosophy* (pp. 137–139), Professor Junjiro
Takakusu explains that Eastern Buddhism describes a world system
of ten realms or planes. The higher four are saintly and the lower six
ordinary. The Buddha plane is included. The realms or planes are:

A. Saintly realms
   1. Buddhas
   2. Bodhisattva – a would-be Buddha
   3. *Prateyeka* Buddha – a Buddha for himself and not
       establishing a Buddha *Sasana*
   4. *Sravaka* – a direct disciple of the Buddha.

B. Ordinary realms
   5. Heavenly beings – superhuman but not Enlightened without the teaching of a Buddha
   6. *Asuras* – fighting spirits
   7. Human beings – neutral in nature
   8. *Pretas* – departed beings and hungry spirits
   9. Beasts – innocent in nature. Includes the whole animal kingdom
   10. Depraved beings – beings in hell. The lowest stage.

These ten realms are mutually exclusive and inclusive, each one having the remaining nine realms within it. For example, the realm of humans will include the other nine, from Buddhas to beings in hell. So will each of the other nine. This idea exemplifies the mental plane explanation given below.

Northern Buddhism has similar classifications and explanations. Tenzing Gyatso, HH XIV Dalai Lama writes in *The Buddhism of Tibet* (pp. 24–25) that cyclic existence is divided into three types abodes, realms or planes:

- Desire realm, where beings experience the pleasures of the five senses: forms, sounds, odours, tastes and tangible objects.
- Form realm divided into two parts. A lower realm of beings not attracted to external pleasures but experiencing the pleasures of inner contemplation; and a higher realm of beings that have transcended pleasurable feelings altogether and now experience neutral feelings.
- Formless realm where all sense matters are absent and there is only mental existence.

There are six types of Sentient beings who migrate in cyclic existence:

- Gods, including beings in the form and formless realms as well as the six types of gods in the desire realm
- Demigods
- Human beings
- Hungry ghosts
- Animals
- Beings living in hell.

This relates to the Table of Planes of Existence set out above. The

Tibetan Wheel of Life *mandala* shows these worlds in a most vivid and beautiful way (see Chapter 9).

Mental Plane Explanation

A second explanation of the planes of existence is that the different planes are purely mental states. They refer to the mental attitude of the individual at any given time. If the being is restless, he is in the spirit world. If the being has greed, strong attachments and hunger, he is in the world of hungry ghosts. If he cannot understand things, he is in the animal world. If the being is afraid, angry and anxious, the life is in the hell plane. A mental attitude of hard work, fatigue and sensual pleasure indicates the human world. A mind free of fatigue and intent on luxuries and sensual pleasure indicates the outlook of the deities. A mind bored with sensual pleasure and wishing to lead a pure life spending time on meditation is the mentality of the Form plane. A mind that considers the material body an impediment and prefers to exist in a purely mental form indicates a life in the Formless plane.

The length of time of the mental state can vary from one full physical lifetime to just one moment. A being could be reborn in several planes of mental existence in any one day. Here again, all Buddhist teaching governs each life. The constant change of mental birth, life and death is *Samsara* or cyclic existence and the way out is by attaining *Nibbana*.

Chapter 9

The Wheel of Life

The Wheel of Life, sometimes called the wheel or cycle of change or existence (Sanskrit – *bhavachakra*; Tibetan – *srid-pai-khor-ho*), is a circular picture consisting of concentric circles showing the cycle of life called *Samsara*, the world we live in. *Samsara*, also described as the Wheel of birth and death, is the world of all conditioned phenomena, which has the threefold characteristics of:

- Impermanence
- *Dukkha* or imperfection and
- Selflessness.

It is a visual aid for teaching Buddhism and shows how living beings are caught up in this cycle or wheel, in a life of *Dukkha*. What the Buddhist strives for is a release from the cycle by realizing *Nibbana*. It is a map of life and summarizes most of the fundamental Buddhist teachings. In most temples in Asia it is displayed prominently and a senior member of the *Sangha* is at hand to explain the meaning to visitors. The depiction of the Wheel differs from country to country. Some are simple and diagrammatic. Those from the countries in the Himalayan region are elaborate and colourful. What is explained here is the line diagram below of a Wheel in the Tibetan style.

It is held by Mara, sometimes called Yama. Mara is the personification of evil, temptation, desire, attachment, fear and death. Sometimes Mara, or Yama, is described as a non-human person, the Lord of Death. When Gotama Buddha was progressing in his final meditation, the distractions he encountered are described as being presented by Mara (see Chapter 2). Mara is a terrifying person one wishes to avoid. Mara is shown devouring the Wheel with its fangs, leaving us in no doubt that to be caught in this cycle is a supremely wretched situation.

Three Fires

In the circle at the very centre of the Wheel is a cockerel, a snake and a pig are shown. They represent the teaching known as the Three Fires, also called afflictions, defilements, passions, poisons and unwholesome roots in the different traditions. They symbolize the three fundamental vices or negative factors that provide the power that keeps the Wheel turning. These animals represent:

- Cockerel – attachment, greed, desire, craving (*lobha*)
- Snake – ill will, anger, hatred, jealousy, aggression, aversion (*dosa*)
- Pig – ignorance, delusion, wilful blindness (*moha*).

These three are shown whirling around, chasing one another, illustrating the endless cycles of blind compulsion in which those under their power are caught. These three, attachment and desire, ill will and ignorance, power the Wheel. They are inter-connected. Ignorance of the *Dhamma* leads a person to a false sense of self and consequent attachment and desire. We believe that obtaining some worldly object or wish will bring lasting satisfaction and entail no significant *kammic* result. We cannot have everything we wish for, so unfulfilled or unhappy attachment and desire leads a person to ill will and anger, and sometimes violence. Actions motivated by attachment, ill will and ignorance create bad, unwholesome *kamma* (see Chapter 7).

The Buddhist view of the mind and the mental world, made up of the mental aggregates of feelings, perceptions, volitions and consciousness, consists of both intellectual and emotional elements and processes. Sometimes these forces are described as the elements of mind and heart. We normally associate the mind with intellectual matters, but irrational emotions also arise in the mind.

The intellectual elements and processes are thoughts. These are ideas or pieces of reasoning are produced by thinking. They are rational energies and are based on reason and reasoning. Thoughts are neutral in nature. They are neither good nor bad, however, a thought may become good or bad by association with an emotion.

The emotional elements and processes, often irrational, are called mental or instinctive feelings. They are energies. All emotions are feelings, but not all feelings are emotions. A feeling becomes an emotion if it is based on the association of the illusion of self to an external person or thing. For example, feeling cold is simply a feeling; but a feeling of anger is an emotion because it is based on the association of the illusion of self to an external person. They arise automatically.

Emotions are not neutral in nature. They are either good or bad. Some emotions, for example loving-kindness, compassion and not wanting to take things belonging to others, are good, positive and wholesome. These good emotions arise when the mind is developed and controlled through the knowledge and practice of the *Dhamma*. As a result, the person does not have a strong sense of a self and is less influenced by the Three Fires of attachment, ill will and ignorance. Other emotions, for example, anger, jealousy and wanting to take things belonging to others, are bad, negative and unwholesome. These bad emotions arise when the mind is not developed and controlled by the knowledge and practice of the *Dhamma* because such a mind has a strong false sense of a self and is greatly influenced by the operation of the Three Fires of attachment, ill will and ignorance. It is possible for the same mind to be controlled, positive and wholesome at certain times; and uncontrolled, negative and unwholesome, at other times.

These emotional energies may give rise to volitional intentions (the fourth aggregate, see Chapter 6), which move the person to actions in response to contact with the outer or inner world. These actions create *kamma* (see Chapter 7). The Zen Buddhists call this the uprush of passions. The Zen meditation of Daily Life Practice and the similar Southern Buddhist practice of *Sila*, or morality, enable a person to control and transcend these negative emotions. Northern Buddhism explains that the causes of cyclic existence are contaminated actions and afflictions, also referred to as defilements. The training is to understand and let go of attachment to these defilements. In fact, the moral teaching of all Buddhist traditions is directed to this end.

Sometimes, as explained above, the intellectual and emotional elements are interconnected. For instance, in the Three Fires, attachment and ill will are emotions, while ignorance is intellectual.

Life Cycles

Moving outwards, in the second circle we see beings climbing up and then falling down. Some paintings show only humans; others show changes to other forms of life. The beings climb up and have good births. Then due to the operation of the Three Fires, which they have not yet brought under control, they have negative or bad volitional intentions. These result in actions that create bad or unwholesome *kamma* and they fall down and are born in lower planes (see Chapter 8). After life in the lower plane, due to previous good volitional intentions having caused good *kamma* they climb up into good births in higher planes. So this cycle or process goes on until a being is able to transcend this cycle by realizing *Nibbana*.

Six Planes of Existence

The third circle shows the six planes, sometimes called worlds or realms, of existence of living beings in the Sentient plane. The walls of temples in Asian countries have colourful paintings of these worlds that show the nature of life there in graphic detail.[1] These planes relate both to the physical plane and the mental plane explanations.

Clockwise, at 5 o'clock (some paintings have a different order), is the plane of hungry ghosts and spirits, which are generally invisible to human beings. They are forever hungry and thirsty. Some have small mouths, needle thin throats and large stomachs, and cannot consume sufficient food or drink to satisfy their hunger and thirst. Some have deformed bodies and some have mental defects. Their understanding is very limited and they are not capable of any rational thinking. They are evil smelling and if wearing any clothes these will be dirty, torn and tattered. They have no homes as such and live in dirty places or forests. They feed on scraps of food thrown away by others. Some cannot walk but have to crawl on all fours.

At 6 o'clock is the miserable plane, sometimes called hell. Here beings have constant pain and suffering, both physical and mental. They have no peace or comfort. Wall murals and life-sized images in Buddhurajamaha Vihara in Dickwella, Sri Lanka and other temples in Asia show people who have been born in this plane due to bad *kamma* queuing up for punishments meted out by the Demon King of hell. They are constantly at loggerheads with one another. There are special punishment sheds. Wall murals in temples in Sri Lanka show some of these unfortunate beings being sawn in two by devils and having stakes driven through their bodies. Some are shown being boiled in vats of oil.

At 7 o'clock is the plane of animals. We think of animals as having a free and good life, either in the wild or when domesticated. In reality the animal plane is an unhappy plane. In the wild they are subject to cold, thirst, hunger, the weather, illness, wounds and attack by other animals. They may become food for other animals or be shot with guns by human beings for sport. Some are kept in zoological gardens in poor conditions. Some are caught and made to work for human beings or are killed for food. Some are used for painful medical experiments and some have their body parts taken for food or to prepare medicines. Few die a natural death of old age. Domesticated animals are strictly controlled by humans. Some are treated well but many suffer ill treatment of various sorts and many end up being food for human beings.

These three are unhappy planes where the birth is due to bad or unwholesome *kamma*. They entail much suffering. Also those living in these planes are unable to understand their situation and have a limited perception of the world. They live in such harsh conditions that they may not be able to generate any good *kamma*. The *Saddharma Pundarika Sutra* (pp. 104–105) gives a graphic description of life in these planes.

The next three planes are considered happy, where beings are born due to their good or wholesome *kamma*.

The human plane is at 11 o'clock. It is fortunate to be born as a human being at a time when the *Dhamma* is extant in the world, at a place where the *Dhamma* is known and have the opportunity to learn and practise it.[2] In these circumstances the person may, due to good *kamma*, decide to follow the Buddhist path. All human qualities that we associate with the heart – friendliness, selflessness, warmth of heart, creativity, kindliness, joy, benevolence, sense of beauty, gratitude, generosity, loving-kindness, tolerance and wishing to help other beings – are sourced in this plane.

The plane of fighters and demons is at 2 o'clock. They spend their time fighting and participating in aggressive activities. Their lives are not totally happy and they waste their energy and lives in unprofitable activities. They are also known as jealous gods.

Twelve o'clock is the plane of deities, devas and gods. There are many of these heavenly planes.[3] Here the beings lead very pleasant lives.

Southern Buddhist teaching does not say that they have the power to intervene in human affairs or that they wish to do so. The teaching does not state that they help humans. According to Eastern and Northern Buddhism, however, some of these deities, being the higher-level bodhisattvas, wish to help other beings on the Buddhist path. They occasionally help beings to lead happy lives without stress in order to practise the *Dhamma*. They are able and do respond to requests for help and support from humans. For example in the *Saddharma Pundarika Sutra* bodhisattva Avalokatisvera is referred to as the cry regarder, the one who pays regard, and responds to cries for help from human beings. This help is given in the form of blessings fashioned to meet the specific situation.

The *Dhamma* applies in all of these planes of existence. The beings are born in these planes according to their good or bad *kamma*. The law of impermanence applies and their lives there are temporary. When their lives come to an end they move on and are reborn according to their operative *kamma*. The deities and devas may achieve Enlightenment and realize *Nibbana* from these planes. The human plane is the most fortunate plane to be born into because it is here that the conditions are most suitable for developing good *kamma*. Buddhahood can only be attained from the human plane.

Dependant Origination

The various links in the chain of Dependent Origination are symbolically represented by 12 small images shown on the outer circle of the Wheel of Life. There are slight variations in the images in different paintings.[4] Moving in a clockwise direction from the top, and starting at 1 o'clock, they are:

1.   A *blind man* – Ignorance. The inability to see the truth.
2.   A *potter* – Action. Volitional, conditioned and intentional activities. With the raw materials of clay and water the potter creates a new pot on his particular kind of wheel.
3.   A *monkey* – Conditioned consciousness. A monkey is restless and virtually impossible to control. It blindly grasps one branch after another as it swings through the trees. Similarly, consciousness is restless with *kammic* urges.
4.   *Men in a boat* – The boat carries the men across the stream. Similarly, the mind carries a person's *kammic* inheritance from life to life.
5.   *Houses with doors and windows* – The doors and windows are the openings through which external stimuli and sense data pass into the mind.
6.   *Lovers* – They signify the contact of external stimuli and sense data with the sense organs, giving rise to the sense impressions or consciousness.
7.   A *man whose eye is pierced by an arrow* – The feelings that arise from sense impressions are so strong that they partially blind us. We cannot therefore see the true way but stumble on into desire.
8.   A *man drinking* – Feelings give rise to attachment and desire. This is a kind of insatiable thirst. Satisfying this attachment, desire and thirst leads a person to greater attachment, desire and thirst, and reduces the resistance to worldly things and pleasures.
9.   A *monkey clinging to a tree* – The monkey, a symbol of the uncontrolled mind, gripped by attachment and desire has found a suitable object to desire and has grasped it. This makes it conscious of itself and generates a feeling of safety

and permanence. The monkey does not look happy, nor is it enjoying the fruit. It is just clinging on.

10. *A pregnant woman* – The grasping and the sense of self has created a new life.
11. *A woman giving birth* – A new life arrives. The birth is the visible arising of the physical and mental elements of the individual.
12. *An old man* – He carries a burden, which is the weight of all the ills that beset human life: old age, illness and death, which is *Dukkha*. He is walking towards a lake, which signifies death and dissolution. It is from this lake that the blind man in the first picture has emerged.

And so the chain of events goes on.

Breaking this chain results in deliverance from *Dukkha* and transcending the Wheel of Life (*Samsara*). This breaking may be achieved at any link but is done most effectively and decisively at the first link (ignorance). It is ignorance that gives rise to the links in the chain of Dependent Origination. If ignorance can be transcended then the links are broken one by one. The links of feeling and attachment are further links at which this chain may be expediently and effectively broken. This leads to the ending of *Dukkha* and the realizing of *Nibbana*.

The teaching of the chain of Dependent Origination is a detailed account of the Four Noble Truths. *Dukkha* is found at every stage. In its serial order, Dependent Origination explains the Second Noble Truth, the origin of *Dukkha*. If considered in the order of ending, the constituent elements of Dependent Origination explain the transcending and ending of *Dukkha* by realizing *Nibbana*. The Noble Eightfold Path shows how this can be done.

So the world goes on without a beginning or an end, governed by its own rules and under no one's control. Is a Buddhist to simply accept all this and do nothing to escape from this Wheel of Life that causes continuous *Dukkha*? There is a way out. There is a circled image of Gotama (Sakyamuni) Buddha. In some paintings this image is in each of the sections showing the planes of life, and in other paintings he is outside the circle in the top right-hand corner. The Buddha is outside and free from this Wheel of Life. He teaches us that the power of attachment, ill will and ignorance can be broken by following the Noble Eightfold Path, perfecting the *Paramitas* and achieving fully developed awareness, attaining Enlightenment and realizing *Nibbana*.

Chapter 10

Dhammapada

One of the meanings of the word *Dhamma* is the teachings of the Buddha. *Pada* means sections or portions, so *dhamapada* can be translated as 'sections or portions of the *Dhamma*'. It is often referred to as the 'way of truth' or 'sayings' of the Buddha. The monks who participated in the First Council, three months after the Buddha passed away, arranged and clarified the text, naming it *Dhammapada*. It consists of about 423 melodious Pali verses spoken by the Buddha on many different occasions. The verses cover various subjects and illustrate the moral and philosophical teachings of Buddhism. The circumstances that led the Buddha to recite these verses are presented as stories attached to the respective verses. The *Dhammapada* was one of the earliest portions of the Pali texts to become known in the West. Buddhists often have a copy at hand and dip into it for a quick refreshment of the *Dhamma*.

This chapter presents a selection of verses from the *Dhammapada*. Some verses are also quoted in other chapters.

General

All conditions have mind as their originator. Mind is their chief and they are mind-made. If one speaks or acts with a wicked mind unhappiness follows him, even as the wheel follows the hoof of the draught-ox.   v. 1

Similarly if one speaks or acts with a pure mind, happiness follows him like the shadow that never leaves.   v. 2

In those who harbour such thoughts as, he abused me, he beat me, he defeated me, he robbed me, hatred never ceases.   v. 3

In those who do not harbour such thoughts hatred will cease. v. 4

Hatreds never cease by hatred in this world. By loving-kindness alone they cease. This is an ancient law.   v. 5

Those who know the real as real and unreal as unreal, they develop correct thoughts and achieve the goal.   v. 12

Even as rain enters an ill thatched house, so does attachment enter an undeveloped mind.   v. 13

Even as rain does not enter a well thatched house, so does attachment not enter a well developed mind.   v. 14

Heedfulness

Mindfulness (heedfulness) is the path to Nibbana, negligence is the path to rebirth. The mindful are not reborn, the negligent are reborn.   v. 21

The Mind

The unsteady mind is difficult to guard and difficult to control. The wise person steadies the mind, as a fletcher straightens the arrow.   v. 33

The mind is hard to check, swift, moves to any attraction. The control of the mind is good. A controlled mind is conducive to happiness.   v. 35

The mind travels far, with a succession of thoughts, formless in the body. Those who restrain the mind are freed from attachment and rebirth.   v. 37

Before long this body will lie in the ground, cast aside, without consciousness, even as a useless log.   v. 41

Whatever harm an enemy can do, an ill directed mind can do one greater harm (bad intentional acts give rise to bad Kamma). v. 42

What neither mother, nor father nor any other relative can do, a well directed mind can improve one's condition (good intentional actions give rise to good Kamma).   v. 43

Flowers

As a bee without harming the flower, its colour or scent, flies

away collecting only the honey, even so should a wise person live.
                                                                 v. 49

One should not consider the faults of others, things done and left undone by others, but one's own deeds done and undone.   v. 50

As from a heap of flowers many a garland is made, even so many good deeds should be done by a human being.   v. 53

Fools

Long is the night to the wakeful, long is the mile to the weary; long is repeated lives to the foolish, who do not know the truth.
                                                                 v. 60

If as he lives, the individual does not meet a companion who is better or equal, let him journey alone. There is no companionship with the foolish (those who do not seek the truth).   v. 61

A fool who thinks he is a fool is for that very reason a wise person. A fool who thinks he is wise is called a fool indeed.   v. 63

The Wise

As a solid rock is not shaken by the wind, even so the wise are not shaken by praise or blame.   v. 81

Just as a lake, deep, clear and still, even so on hearing the teachings the wise become exceedingly peaceful.   v. 82

There are only a few who realize Nibbana. The rest of mankind continue with rebirth.   v. 85

The Arahat

The one who has completed the journey (the Noble Eightfold Path), who is sorrowless (who has attained the third stage of Sainthood, *anagami,* and will not be born again in this world), who is wholly free from everything (attachment), who has ended all ties (greed, ill will, indulgence in rites, adherence to dogma), he does not have the fever of passion.[1]   v. 90

Thousands

Self-conquest is, indeed far greater than the conquest of all other folk.'   v. 104

For one who frequently honours and respects elders, four things increase: age, beauty, happiness and energy.   v. 109

Though one should live a hundred years without seeing Nibbana, yet better, indeed, is the single day's life of one who sees Nibbana.
                                                                        v. 114

Punishment

All tremble at punishment. Life is dear to all; comparing others with oneself, one should neither harm (kill) nor cause others to harm (kill).   v. 130

Old Age

Through many a birth I wandered in Samsara (existence),
Seeking, but not finding, the builder (attachment) of this house (body).
Sorrowful is birth again and again.
O' attachment, you are seen. You shall build no house (body) again
All your defilements (passions) are ended. Your ignorance is gone.
My mind has attained Nibbana,
Achieved is the end of attachment.   vv. 153–154

The Self

One is the guardian of oneself. What other guardian could there be? With oneself fully controlled one obtains a guardian difficult to better.   v. 160

By oneself is evil done
By oneself is one defiled
By oneself is no evil done
By oneself is one purified
Both defilement and purity depends on oneself
No one is purified by another.   v. 165

The Buddha

Not to do any wrong,
To cultivate good,
To purify the mind.
This is the teaching of the Buddhas.   v. 183

He who has gone for refuge to the Buddha, the Dhamma and the
Sangha, sees with right knowledge the Four Noble Truths,
Dukkha, the Cause of Dukkha, the Transcending of Dukkha and
the Noble Eightfold Path which leads to the ending of Dukkha.
                                                         vv. 190–192

Happiness

Victory breeds ill will; the defeated live in pain. The peaceful live
happily, giving up victory and defeat.   v. 201

Health is the highest gain; contentment the greatest wealth; the
trustful are the best friends; Nibbana is the highest happiness.
                                                              v. 204

Affections

Hold nothing dear, for separation from those that are dear is
sorrowful: bonds do not exist for those to whom nothing is dear
or not dear.   v. 211

From affection or attachment comes grief and fear; for one who is
wholly free from affection or attachment there is no grief or fear.
                                                         vv. 213–214

Anger

One should give up anger; one should abandon pride; one
should overcome all that ties one to rebirth. Difficulties do not
come to one who does not cling to mind and body, and is
without passion.   v. 221

Conquer anger by loving-kindness: conquer evil by good; conquer
stinginess by giving; conquer lies by truth.   v. 223

One should guard against wrongs caused by the body.
One should guard against wrongs caused by speech.

One should guard against wrongs caused by the mind.
The wise are restrained in deed, speech and mind.   vv. 231–234

Taints

Whosoever, harms living beings, indulges in wrong speech, takes
what is not one's own, misuses the senses, takes intoxicating drinks,
such one interferes with his or her own progress in this world.
vv. 246–247

The Way

Of paths the Eightfold is the best. Of truths the Four Noble ones
are the best. Non-attachment is the best of states, and of beings
the Buddha is the best.   v. 273

This is the only Way, there is none other for understanding Reality.
v. 274

You yourselves must make the effort; The Buddhas are only
teachers. The meditative ones who enter the Way are delivered
from the bonds of attachment.   v. 276

Impermanent are all compound things;
Unsatisfactory (imperfect, Dukkha) are all compound things;
All Dhammas are selfless.
One who perceives this with wisdom is tired of attachment. This
is the path to realizing Nibbana.   vv. 277–279

Indeed from meditation wisdom arises, without meditation
wisdom decreases; knowing this twofold path of gain and loss,
let a person conduct himself so that wisdom grows.   v. 282

Miscellaneous

If by giving up a slight happiness one may gain a greater one, let
the wise person give up the lesser happiness in consideration of
the greater happiness.   v. 290

He who wishes his own happiness by causing pain to others is not
released from ill will, being himself entangled in the web of ill will.
v. 291

Craving

The gift of truth excels all gifts; the flavour of truth excels all flavours; the pleasure of truth excels all pleasures; he who has overcome attachment overcomes all Dukkha.   v. 354

The Bhikkhu

He who is controlled in hand, foot, speech and mind, he who delights in meditation, and is composed, he who is alone and contented, him they call a Bhikkhu (monk).   v. 362

The Brahmana

He that does no evil through body, speech or mind, who is restrained in these three respects, him I call a brahmana.[2]   v. 391

He who, in every way, knows the death and rebirth of beings, who is detached, realized Nibbana, and Enlightened, him I call a brahmana.   v. 419

Part III

Practice

Chapter 11

Lay Person's Morality

More than 98 per cent of Buddhists are lay persons and the moral guidelines that apply to them are an important aspect of *Living Buddhism*. The *Oxford English Dictionary* gives several definitions of ethics, including '. . . moral principles, especially those of a specified religion', and 'A set of moral principles by which any particular person is guided'. The definitions of moral include '. . . pertaining to human character or behaviour considered as good or bad', and '. . . pertaining to the distinction between right and wrong, or good and evil, in relation to the actions, volitions, or character of responsible beings'.

Moral principles regulate human conduct so that human beings can live together in communities for mutual protection, solidarity, economic prosperity, peace, happiness and social stability. The law performs a similar function of maintaining peace and order in society. Lawyers explain the relationship between law and morality as being like two coins, one placed on the other, and the upper coin not completely covering the lower. Whereas law is enforced with sanctions by the courts of law, moral rules apply by general acceptance and have no worldly sanctions.

In some religions moral guidelines are the mandate of a divine being and are the foundation of social harmony. In Buddhism moral guidelines are related to the philosophical and wisdom teachings, and in addition to being the foundation of social harmony set out the first steps of the Buddhist path to *Nibbana (Nirvana)*.

The moral guidelines are a part of the practice teachings of the *Dhamma*. The practice of morality is summarized in this verse from *The Dhammapada* (v. 183), and the *Parinirvana Sutra*:

Not to do any wrong (To refrain from all evil),
To cultivate good,

To purify the mind.
This is the teaching of the Buddhas.

Dhammapada, v. 183

The first two lines refer to moral guidelines and the third to mental training. Actions motivated by generosity, goodwill, loving-kindness and wisdom are good, skilful, wholesome and profitable. Actions motivated by attachment, ill will and ignorance are bad, unskilful, unwholesome and unprofitable. The importance attached to morality in Buddhist practice is indicated from these words of the Bodhisatta Gotama in *Silavimansa Jataka* (No. 362): 'Apart from virtue wisdom has no worth'. The teaching in morality is related to that in *kamma* and rebirth. Good, skilful actions have good results and bad, unskilful actions have bad results, either in this life or in future lives (see Chapter 7).

The foundation of Buddhist life is morality. The three elements of right speech, action and livelihood in the Noble Eightfold Path set out the teaching on good morality. This is also explained in the Five Precepts. Generosity and morality are the first two elements of the *Paramis* of the Southern school, and the *Paramitas* and bodhisattva path of the Eastern and Northern schools. These are the first two elements a lay person has to cultivate to progress on the path to becoming a Buddha.

Generosity

It is the spirit of *dana*, freely offered generosity, that has kept the entire Buddhist tradition alive for over 2,550 years. Generosity is not specifically mentioned in the Noble Eightfold Path, but is the first element in the bodhisatta perfections in all traditions and first element of good *kamma* or meritorious actions. When Buddhism is taught to young children in Buddhist communities it is generosity that is taught first. It is the giving of money, food, clothes, books, time, work and help for the benefit of others and it is an important aspect of a good Buddhist life. The *Jataka* stories give many examples of Bodhisatta Gotama practising generosity in being ready to give away his wealth and possessions, his wife and children, and even his own body for the benefit of others.

The main focus of generosity is the monastic *Sangha* who depend on the lay people for alms food, robes, medicines and other necessities of life. The Buddha established this reciprocal relationship to be of mutual benefit to monastics and lay people. One of its important functions is to ensure the continuity of the Buddha *Sasana* (teaching). The temples of the Southern Buddhist traditions generally have a list of supporters providing daily alms food. The monks, nuns and priests return a greater gift by teaching and example.

The gift of Truth excels all gifts

The Dhammapada, v. 354.

Lay people contribute money for publishing books on Buddhism and for festival celebrations, ordinations, building projects and other requirements of temples and monasteries. Some donate their time and do work, such as cleaning in the temple. In the Southern Buddhist traditions there is a special *kathina* celebration at the end of the rainy season retreat *(Vassa)*, which extends from about July to October. During this time lay people make special contributions of towards the necessities of the temple for the coming year. Help in various forms is also given at all times to people in need. Generosity extends to all living beings and Buddhists give what help is needed.

The mind of the giver is the most important aspect of generosity. Giving is with compassion and loving kindness with no expectation of return. Generosity generates good merit for the giver, but this is not so important. The blessing of generosity is the joy of giving. It is not an investment in merit. It can be said that the recipient of generosity provides an opportunity for the giver to be generous and create good merit. Sometimes the merit of generosity is given to others, for instance when children arrange an alms giving for departed parents or other relatives.

Precepts

Five Precepts

The Five Precepts are the fundamental moral guidelines for all Buddhists in all traditions. They apply automatically, whether formally taken or not. In South Asian Buddhist communities they are a part of daily worship and are applied during festival days, almsgivings, special ceremonies and Buddhist meetings. In some traditions a request has to be made for the Precept, phrased in a special way. They are 'taken' by lay people reciting them, generally after a monk or nun, but it may be after a senior lay person. This is done with concentration and the motivation to live accordingly. In some traditions the formal taking of the Five Precepts is considered to be an initiation, confirmation, or reconfirmation as a Buddhist. In some Eastern traditions a lay person may take the Three Refuges and Five Precepts at a *jukai* ceremony conducted by a priest in a temple. This is considered to be a lay ordination so that the person is now recognized as a Buddhist. Two verses in *The Dhammapada* summarize the Five Precepts and indicate their importance:

> Whosoever, harms living beings, indulges in wrong speech, takes what is not one's own, misuses the senses, takes intoxicating drinks, such one interferes with his or her own progress in this world.
>
> *The Dhammapada*, vv. 246–247

The Five Precepts (see Chapter 12) are to avoid:

1. Intentionally harming living beings
2. Taking what is not given
3. Misuse of the senses
4. Wrong speech, and
5. Intoxicating drinks and drugs.

They are normally set out in the negative, but the positive view indicates the correct action to be followed by a person. There is no concept of 'sin' in Buddhism, as in some religions. An action contrary to a Precept is not considered a 'sin', but a negative action that is a hindrance and a retrograde step to the person's progress on the Buddhist path. If a Precept is broken it still continues to apply to the person.

In the Eastern and Northern schools the substance of the Precepts is set out as the '10 non-virtues of *Dharma* practice' causing bad, unwholesome and unmeritorious *kamma* (see Chapter 7).

Avoid Intentionally Harming Living Beings

This involves not just killing but any sort of intentional physical, mental or spiritual harm to living beings, which includes animals, birds, fish, insects and human beings and yourself. It covers helping or encouraging others to act contrary to this Precept and creating the circumstances when this can be done. The extent of moral guilt seems to depend on the identity of the victim, but the moral character of the victim is not relevant.

Habitual harming of other beings coarsens the moral character of the person and renders the person insensitive to his mental condition. Situations such as shooting animals and birds for sport, fishing, killing insects, vivisection, abortion and euthanasia need to be understood in the context of this Precept. So does the position of members of the armed forces and the giving of support to governments at war.

In relation to mercy killings it has to be understood that every living being has the results of his own *kamma* to work out. Interference with the consequence of that *kamma* does not end the *kamma* and the unexhausted portion is carried over to the next life.

This Precept has a positive meaning. It means to have loving-kindness towards all beings and to work for their benefit.

Avoid Taking What is Not Your Own

This means more than taking what is not given to you, because that implies someone giving. It includes taking property the owner of which is unknown. It means taking property that does not rightfully belong to you and includes encouraging or helping others or creating the circumstances in which others can act contrary to this Precept.

This property has a wide meaning and includes physical property, intellectual property and identity. Direct taking, indirect taking, such as by fraud or deception, and any form of dishonest dealing will be against this Precept. So is taking from a thief or from someone who has possession but not full ownership as recognized by the law.

Acting contrary to this Precept creates attachment and promotes the idea of the self. The positive view of this Precept is to respect others' ownership of property, to look after and be content with your own possessions and to be generous in helping others with material things.

Avoid Misusing the Senses

This Precept is often explained as avoiding improper sexual activities. Since the word '*kamesu*' in the Pali text is plural, however, the wider explanation is to avoid improper activities relating to all the senses.

For householders the first meaning is of prime importance. Many parts of the teaching give advice about the correct relationship between the sexes, the avoidance of improper sexual activity and the importance of a good family life for householders. The Precept also means not to encourage or help others in, or create the circumstances for, actions against this Precept.

In its wider meaning the Precept means to avoid misuse of the body by stimulating the senses because excessive sensual indulgence again creates attachment and promotes the idea of the self. The positive side of this Precept is to be restrained in sensual activities and to avoid excessive indulgence.

Avoid Wrong Speech

This Precept has a much wider meaning than just lying. It covers defamatory, divisive, harsh, abusive and frivolous speech, and any other form of speech that creates disharmony in the community. You should not encourage others to speak in such a way, praise them for it or create the circumstances for such speech. Anagarika Sugatananda (Francis Story) writes about truthfulness in *The Buddhist Outlook*:[1]

> Constant untruthfulness has a strong psychological effect; it is a habit formation destructive to character. Man's whole ability to reason and form his judgments comes from the power to distinguish between the true and the false. If this [...] faculty of being able to recognize the truth, and moral instinct to respect it, are continually perverted, the reasoning power degenerates and disintegration of the personality sets in. When this occurs, the karmic law of cause and effect can only produce a rebirth in some inferior state after death.
>
> (Sugatananda, 1973)

Speech includes printing, publishing, radio broadcasting, television and all forms of communication.

The positive side of this Precept is to always to speak the truth and be of gentle speech that does not hurt anyone or cause disharmony in the community. It also means to use your judgment and remain silent at times.

Avoid Intoxicating Drinks or Drugs that Cloud the Mind

The mind is the focal point of Buddhist practice and unless the mind is kept clear and alert the result is heedlessness and actions contrary to the other Precepts and moral guidelines. This Precept also means helping or encouraging others to act against the Precept or praising them for doing so.

Dealing in intoxicants or drugs is a wrong way of life under the Noble Eightfold Path. A mind affected by intoxicants will lack the alertness required for meditative training and will not be able to make the fine distinctions between good and bad mental qualities needed to develop wisdom. Taking intoxicants or drugs as medicine prescribed by a doctor is obviously not against this Precept since the intention is for your well being.

The positive aspect of this Precept is to maintain a clear and alert mind at all times and to develop mindfulness in all activities. This Precept of avoiding intoxicants creates a boundary through which you are less likely to lose mindfulness and transgress the other Precepts.

Eight and Ten Precepts

Whereas the Five Precepts are moral guidelines, the Eight and Ten Precepts are the rules of mildly ascetic nature. In the Eight Precepts, one, two, four and five are the same as in the Five Precepts. The Third Precept changes to 'avoid unchaste conduct'.

There are three additional Precepts to avoid:

6. Food after mid-day
7. Dancing, singing, music, entertainments, garlands, perfumes, cosmetics and adornments
8. High and luxurious seats and beds.

The Ten Precepts are developed from the Eight Precepts and the rules relating to novice or temporary ordination. The Seventh Precept divides into two, the Eighth becomes the Ninth and there is a new Ten Precept to avoid: dealing in gold, silver and money. This last Precept is significant in that it forms the basis of the alms mendicant life.

The Precepts can be summarized as follows:

Precept number	Five Precepts	Eight Precepts	Ten Precepts
		Avoid	
1	Harming	Harming	Harming
2	Taking	Taking	Taking
3	Senses	Unchaste conduct	Unchaste conduct
4	Wrong speech	Wrong speech	Wrong speech
5	Intoxicants	Intoxicants	Intoxicants
6	–	Food	Food
7	–	Entertainments and adornments	Entertainments
8	–	Luxurious seats	Adornments
9	–	–	Luxurious seats
10	–	–	Dealing in money

The *Brahmajala Sutra* sets out the disciplinary Precepts of Eastern traditions accepted by all of the traditions in Japan (which are especially prized by the Tendai and Shingon traditions) in a slightly different way. The ten grave rules are to avoid:

- Harming living beings
- Taking what is not your own
- Being unchaste or misusing the senses
- Wrong speech
- Taking or dealing in alcoholic drinks or drugs
- Talking of the faults of others
- Praising yourself
- Being envious
- Cherish the gratitude of others
- Praise the three treasures (the Buddha, *Dhamma* and *Sangha*).

The Eight Precepts are generally taken as a special training when the people, often dressed in white, in the Southern traditions spend time at the temple on a special day, such as the day of the full moon. It amounts to a temporary renunciation of family life. On these days the temples arrange a programme of *Dhamma* talks, meditation, worship and discussions for the full day. In the evening the people take the Five Precepts and are released from the Eight Precepts.

Meditation retreats are normally conducted under the Eight or Ten Precepts. In countries such as Myanmar and Thailand, a person may take temporary ordination as a novice under the Ten Precepts and live in the temple for some time (see Chapter 16). In circumstances where full ordination is not possible, or where a person has completed family obligations and wishes to become detached from family life, the person may take the Ten Precepts and live in a temple or holy place permanently.

In Northern Buddhist practice there are a similar Eight Vows or Precepts taken for 24 hours or longer by lay people staying at a monastery.

General Moral Values

On one occasion the people could not agree on what the blessings of life were and this disagreement extended to the deities. Sakra, the chief of the deities, sent one of the deities to the Buddha, who was then living in the Jetavanarama monastery where he spent the greater part of his life, to ask his opinion. In the *Maha Mangala*

Sutta, mangala means that which is conducive to happiness and prosperity. It is a text that is frequently chanted at Buddhist ceremonies. The Buddha explained the blessings of life as follows:

- Not to associate with the foolish, but associate with the wise and to honour those worthy of honour;
- To reside in a locality where the people live according to the *Dhamma*, to have made meritorious actions in the past and to set yourself on the right course;
- Much learning, skilled livelihood, disciplined life and of pleasant speech;
- To support your parents, cherish your wife and children and engage in peaceful occupations;
- Generosity, good conduct, helping relatives and blameless actions;
- To avoid unskilful actions and intoxicating drinks, and be steady in virtue;
- Reverence, humility, contentment, gratitude and hearing the *Dhamma;*
- Patience, obedience, the company of holy persons and religious discussions;
- Self-control, moral life, understanding the *Dhamma* and realization of *Nibbana;*
- Having a steady mind unaffected by worldly matters, freed from sorrow, negative mental states and wrong views.

This opinion was given 2,550 years ago in North India. I asked three friends of mine living in modern cities, with all the amenities of a comfortable life, what their opinions were on this subject. This is what they said:

Friend 1
'To be born into this world as a human being is a great blessing. To be able to live one's life free of worry and in good health is an added blessing.
To be able to forgive and show compassion to others is a blessing.
To be happy and content throughout one's life, is something we all strive for, and the teachings of the Buddha show us the way to achieve this.
May all beings be well and happy and free of suffering.'

Friend 2
'As much as I pray for all we know and do not know – which

covers all beings in this world, my special daily prayers are to have a loving, kind and caring family, and for all to lead happy, peaceful, healthy, prosperous and contented lives. For my children and theirs to have lives filled with every happiness, good health, love, laughter, good fortune and loving-kindness. I consider these to be my highest blessings.'

Friend 3
'To be born as a human being with the potential to become truly human, at a time when the Buddha's teachings are known, at a place where they are known, be fortunate to come into contact with them and have the aspiration to follow the teachings. To be happy and content with one's circumstances, to have good family and friends. To have opportunity to help others. These are the blessings of life.'

We see that these sentiments are the same, though separated by over 2,550 years, and that the *Dhamma*, being the law of nature, is not differentiated by time, place or society and that it alive in the community.

After hearing the *Maha Mangala Sutta* about the Buddha's views on the blessings of life, the deities now wanted to hear the Buddha's views on the causes of a person's downfall. They sent one of their number to the Jetavana monastery, where the Buddha was residing, to enquire about this matter. While the *Maha Mangala Sutta* deals with the way of life conducive to progress and happiness, the *Parabhava Sutta* supplements it by pointing out the causes of downfall. Here the Buddha says that one who loves the *Dhamma* progresses while one who is indifferent to it declines. The Buddha continues with the other causes that lead to a person's downfall.

These include:

- Keeping the company of bad people while avoiding the company of good people
- Bad actions
- Being fond of sleep and constant companionship
- Idleness
- Laziness
- Irritability
- Not supporting and looking after elderly parents
- Deceiving a holy person
- Being selfish with one's wealth and material benefits

- Being conceited and looking down on others
- Being an immoral person, drunkard or gambler
- One who squanders his wealth
- Sexual misconduct
- One who places unsuitable persons in positions of authority
- Being ambitious beyond one's means.

In India at the time of the Buddha the Brahmins were understood to be the highest caste (social class) of people. Other castes had lower status in declining order. Scheduled classes, known as the outcastes, were right at the bottom. People inherited their caste from their parents and it was not possible to move from one caste to another during life. The Buddha explained that a person should be judged not by birth but by his actions:

Not by birth is one an outcaste
Not by birth is one a Brahmin
By deed one becomes an outcaste
By deed one becomes a Brahmin.

Vasala Sutta

One Dhigajanu asked the Buddha to explain the conditions that lead to progress and happiness in this life and in future lives. The conditions leading to worldly progress and happiness in this life, the Buddha explained, are persistent effort, watchfulness of earnings, good friendship with people of high moral standing and a balanced livelihood. The conditions of spiritual progress that lead to progress and happiness in future lives were explained as being confidence in the Buddha, morality, generosity and wisdom.

Vyagghapajja Sutta

Loving-kindness is an important quality in Buddhist life. It is a subject of meditation and helps to break down the barriers in a person's thinking between himself and the rest of humanity. In *Karaniya Metta Sutta* (the teaching on loving-kindness), a beautiful text that also includes words of loving-kindness meditation and is often chanted at Buddhist ceremonies, the Buddha explained the essence of loving-kindness. The first three verses set out the standard of moral conduct required:

Be honest with one self, upright, conscientious, of good speech, gentle, humble, contented, live simply, peaceful, with few requirements, senses calmed, prudent, modest, independent and avoid unskilful actions.

Karaniya Metta Sutta, vv. 1–3

Verses four and five give the actual meditation:

May all beings be happy and secure, may their hearts be wholesome. Whatever living beings there be – those mentally feeble or strong, physically long, stout or medium, short, small or large, those seen or unseen, living far or near, those who are born and those who are to be born, may all beings, without exception, be happy minded.

Karaniya Metta Sutta, vv. 4–5

The last five verses set out the things to be avoided:

Not deceive nor despise any person, not wish in anger or ill will to harm another, to have compassion to all beings just as a mother would protect her only child at the risk of her own life, have thoughts of loving kindness without limit, without ill will, without enmity, develop mindfulness at all times, avoid wrong views, be virtuous and endowed with insight and give up sensual attachments.

Karaniya Metta Sutta, vv. 6–10

Living such a life is considered to be living in the Brahma *viharas* or divine abodes (see Chapter 15). As explained in the right livelihood element of the Noble Eightfold Path, five kinds of trade are expressly prohibited, namely: dealing in arms and weapons, human beings, animal flesh, intoxicating substances and poison.

Conclusion

The human world is one of the worlds of desires of the senses. Living beings are connected to the outside world through the six senses. There is a natural bias towards satisfying the senses and people are intoxicated by attachment to sensual pleasures. Complete freedom to live as you like is to become a slave to the senses. *The Dhammapada*, (v. 166) says, 'One's spiritual welfare should not be neglected for the sake of others'. So each person has a duty to himself to work for his own welfare and in that way he can benefit others also. The Three Fires or three unwholesome roots of attachment, ill will and ignorance (called afflictions, defilements and passions in the Eastern and Northern schools, see Chapter 9) mean that good does not come naturally but has to be cultivated with effort. Some people have good moral qualities from birth due to good tendencies developed in past lives.

Buddhist moral guidelines are not divine rules given by a God. They are a natural morality formulated by the Buddha's investigation, analysis and understanding of the results of a person's actions. These guidelines are willingly undertaken and apply, and continue to apply, automatically even though a person may act against them. Acting contrary to them is not a 'sin' but hinders a person's progress on the Buddhist path.

The Five Precepts have been carefully formulated by the Buddha and are timeless universal moral guidelines. The first four have been accepted as guidelines for all people by the Parliament of World Religions and have the same content as numbers six to ten of the Christian Ten Commandments. Observing them strengthens the moral fibre of the person.

In Buddhism the moral guidelines are important for two reasons. First, as in other religions, they show the way to establish a civilized community where we can live happily. Second, they are the foundation of the spiritual journey on the Buddhist path. The moral guidelines help us to avoid unwholesome mental impulses, afflictions, defilements and passions as they are called in the Eastern and Northern schools, and wrong deeds. They are a necessary purification to clear the way for progress on the path to wisdom, a sense of no 'I' and *Nibbana*.

Morality is closely connected to *kamma* and rebirth. A breach of the moral rules has negative results in the current life as well as in future lives. Bad habits are carried over and reflected in future lives. Morality, or *Sila*, is the foundation for cultivating awareness. It is also the basis of calming the mind and of developing wisdom, the two elements that weave together to support the realization of *Nibbana*. Although of prime importance, good morality is only the foundation. Good morality alone cannot achieve *Nibbana*; however, it is impossible to achieve *Nibbana* without good morality.

Chapter 12

Worship and Veneration

According to the *Oxford English Dictionary*, veneration is 'The action or fact of showing respect or reverence'. Reverence is 'Deep respect and veneration for some thing, place, or person regarded as having a sacred or exalted character' and 'to worship in some manner'. Worship is 'To honour or revere as a supernatural being or power, or as a holy thing' or 'to treat with signs of honour and respect'.

Gotama Buddha's advice on worship was to understand the *Dhamma* and live accordingly. Shortly before he passed away, he was honoured, as the successor of the Buddhas of old, by flowers from the sala trees falling on him and by heavenly music. He turned to venerable Ananda and said:

> Now it is not thus, Ananda, that the Buddha is rightly honoured, reverenced, venerated, held sacred or revered. But the monk or nun, devout man or devout woman, who continually fulfils all the greater and lesser duties, who is correct in life, walking according to the Precepts – it is he who rightly honours, reverences, venerates, holds sacred, and reveres the Buddha with the worthiest homage.[1]

Over the years, however, many Buddhists have felt that some visible external activity was helpful to reinforce their commitment to the *Dhamma*. They have developed activities and ceremonies to pay respect and honour to a teacher and the teaching (*Dhamma*, *Dharma*) in a way that reminds them of the Buddha, affirms their commitment to the *Dhamma*, and contributes to their progress on the path of a Buddhist pilgrim. Worship is an integral part of the practice of Buddhism in all schools and traditions. Nynaponika Thera writes:

One who is incapable of any reverential attitude will also be incapable of any spiritual progress beyond the narrow limits of his present mental condition [...]. It is by recognizing and honouring someone or something higher, one honours and enhances one's own inner potentialities.

(Devotion in Buddhism, vol. 1, no. 18,
The Wheel Publications, BPS 1960, p. 7)

The Triple Gem

The Triple Gem consisting of the **Buddha**, the **Dhamma**, and the **Sangha** is the foundation of Buddhism and worship is focussed directly or indirectly on this. The answer to the question 'Who is a Buddhist?' is often given as a person who accepts the Triple Gem, the Buddha, *Dhamma* and the *Sangha* as guides, has a present and continuing intention to live according to the *Dhamma* as a religion, and makes an immediate and ongoing effort to do so (see Chapter 16).

The current Buddhist teaching is that of Gotama (Sakyamuni) Buddha. However, the word **Buddha** in this context has a meaning wider than reference to one historical Buddha. It includes all *Samma Sambuddhas* (Universal Buddhas), that is Buddhas of the past and the future who have attained *Samma Sambodhi* (universal or perfect self-Enlightenment). The Buddha is referred to here as the personification of Enlightenment, *Nibbana*, wisdom and absolute reality. Eastern and Northern Buddhism teach the *Trikaya* doctrine. This explains that the Buddha has three bodies (see Chapter 18):

- *Dharmakaya* – one immortal *Dharma* (teaching) body
- *Sambhogakaya* – many manifestations of the *Dharmakaya* for the benefit of the bodhisattvas
- *Nirmanakaya* – earthly manifestations of the *Dharmakaya*, for example, Gotama Buddha, for the benefit of ordinary living beings.

The *Dhamma* (*Dharma*) is the teaching of the Buddha, and all Buddhas teach the same *Dhamma*. The word has four meanings, namely:

- The written texts
- The teachings (also known as the wisdom teachings)
- The practice
- What is realized by the practice.

The written texts consist of the Pali Canon, Chinese, Korean, Japanese and Tibetan texts and their various translations. The teachings are based on the Four Noble Truths. The practice is the Noble Eightfold Path and the ten perfections in Southern Buddhism, and correspondingly, the practice of compassion, Ten Perfections and bodhisattva path in the Eastern and Northern Buddhism. What is realized by practice is Enlightenment or *Nibbana* (*Nirvana*), also referred to as wisdom, fully-awakened awareness, realization of the *Dhamma*, and realization of the absolute truth. Many Buddhists end private communications and greetings with the words 'Blessings of The Triple Gem'.

General Formalities of Worship

All traditions use a shrine as the focal point of worship and meditation. Some shrines are very simple and may consist only of one Buddha image, while others may be quite elaborate. There may be a special shrine room, or a shrine may be set up at one end of a hall or room. The shrine consists of platforms at different levels on which articles used in worship are placed. The Buddha image is kept at the highest level. At the lower levels are flowers, oil lamps or candle holders, incense holders and any other offerings. Wall hangings, pictures, images and other artefacts may also be used in worship.

Some Buddhists worship at home once or twice a day, either or both in the morning and evening. In temples and monasteries there is generally worship morning and evening, at the time of the mid-day meal and before an evening meal, if there is one. Worship is an integral part of celebrations of all kinds including special days, alms giving, memorial services, blessing services and special events.

Often called worship by body, speech and mind, it is a combination of physical, vocal and mental activity. It is customary to take one's shoes off as a mark of respect when entering the temple premises, a shrine room or when at worship. In Asian countries, temple premises usually include a residence for the *Sangha*, a shrine room, a *dagoba*, a Bodhi tree and a hall for talks, discussions and *Dhamma* classes.

Element of Physical Activity

'Physical activity' is considered first. Worship is normally at the shrine, facing a Buddha image that is always kept in a prominent position. This helps to concentrate the mind of the devotee on the

Devotees preparing to offer flowers in worship at the Ruvanvalisaya Dagoba, Anuradhapura, Sr Lanka.

activity at hand. Some Buddhists have a shrine room at home, arrange a corner of a room as a shrine, or place a Buddha image at a respectfully high position on a shelf as a shrine. At a temple or monastery, worship normally takes place in a specially decorated shrine room or hall. First there is the offering of flowers, lights and incense, and sometimes food, water and soft drinks, at the Buddha image. The devotee pays homage by kneeling and then bowing with the hands placed palms together in front of them (called *anjali* in South Asia and *gossho* in Japan). Sometimes worshipers lower their forehead to touch the floor, and in some cases they do this three times in honour of the Triple Gem. Generally the devotee is seated on a cushion placed on the floor or on a low chair.

In countries such as Sri Lanka there is a Bodhi tree in the temple premises. Devotees place flowers and light oil lamps on a table in front of the tree, pour water for its roots and worship there. In some traditions devotees worship at the images of other Buddhas and bodhisattavas placed at the head of the shrine room of temples. Some worship at the *dagobas* and *cetiyas* in the temple premises. A number of Buddhists do work in the temple, such as cleaning, sweeping, gardening, polishing brass, arranging flowers, cooking and washing.

In Thailand circumambulation of the *dagoba* or shrine is a part of the activity, and some people paste gold leaves on the Buddha image.

In some traditions, for example Northern Buddhism (Tibetan), devotees perform full-length prostrations on the floor of the temple or ground outside. Again, in Tibet they turn prayer wheels that contain transcripts of Buddhist texts. Some devotees hang multicoloured flags at the temple, *dagoba* or Bodhi tree.

All of these activities are considered worship of the Triple Gem.

Element of Vocal Activity

'Vocal activity' is the second element. The devotee or group of devotees recite the text of the worship by memory or read from a book or worship sheet, aloud or silently. If a monk or nun conducts the worship, the devotees follow in reciting the words of the text, often phrase by phrase. In some traditions the whole group chant the text together. Sometimes devotees read or chant Buddhist texts seated near the Buddha image or the Bodhi tree, and some listen to the chanting or simply sit and watch the activities going on.

Mental Element

The 'mental element' is the third and most important part of worship. It involves focussing the mind on the activity and appreciating that one is involved in an important element of Buddhist practice. The words are recited with concentration, understanding and reflection on their meaning. The devotee concentrates on the whole of the worship, reflects on the Triple Gem, tries to understand how worship contributes to his progress as a Buddhist pilgrim and begins to think less of the self.

Formal Worship

In all traditions there is diversity in the form of worship. The Sri Lankan Southern Buddhism form of worship is set out in detail first, followed by the worship in selected traditions in Eastern and Northern Buddhism to show the similarities and interesting differences.

Worship in Southern Buddhism

The text is taken from the worship sheet of the London Buddhist Vihara. The worship starts with paying homage to the fully Enlightened one:

A devotee worships at a temple in Chau Doc, Vietnam.

'*Namo tassa bhagavato Arahato samma sambuddha*' (Homage to the blessed one, the exalted one, the fully Enlightened one) is recited thrice.

The devotee takes the Three Refuges.

'*Buddham saranam gacchami* (I go to the Buddha as my refuge)

Dhammam saranam gacchami (I go to the *Dhamma* as my refuge)

Sangham saranam gacchami (I go to the *Sangha* as my Refuge).' (For a second time.)

'*Dutiyam pi Buddham saranam gacchami*

Dutiyam pi Dhammam saranam gacchami

Dutiyam pi Sangham saranam gacchami.'
(For a third time.)
'*Tatiyam pi Buddham saranam gacchami,*
Tatiyam pi Dhammam saranam gacchami
Tatiyam pi Sangham saranam gacchami.'

The Dhammapada says:

> He who has gone for refuge to the Buddha, the Dhamma, and the Sangha, sees with right knowledge the Four Noble Truths: Dukkha, the Cause of Dukkha, the Transcending of Dukkha, and the Noble Path which leads to the End of Dukkha.
>
> *The Dhammapada*, v.190–192

A refuge is a place of protection, safety and sanctuary. The devotee takes refuge in the Triple Gem. Refuge is taken in the Buddha as the teacher of the path to *Nibbana*, in the *Dhamma* that shows the way and supports the pilgrim, and the *Sangha*, as the teachers and living evidence of the *Dhamma*. 'Refuge' here is a state of mind in which the elements of the Triple Gem are accepted as guides, and where the person has an intention to live according to the *Dhamma* and make an immediate ongoing effort to do so. This state of mind is referred to as true Buddhist *saddha* (faith), consisting of will, understanding and confidence. One formally becomes a Buddhist by taking the Three Refuges. It is a refuge in oneself and one's effort to live according to the teaching. Gotama Buddha's last words were:

> Decay is inherent in all compounded things! Work out your salvation with diligence!
>
> *Maha Parinibbana Sutta* (p. 173)

Next the devotee takes the Five Precepts. In the traditions of some countries, such as in Thailand, they are only given on formal request.

> *Panatipata veramani sikkhapadam samadiyami*
> (I take the Precept of not harming living beings (I shall help all living beings).)

> *Adinnadana veramani sikkhapadam samadiyyami*
> (I take the Precept of not taking what is not rightfully mine (I shall be content with what I have).)

> *Kamesu micchacara veramani sikkhapadam samadiyami*
> (I take the Precept of not misusing the senses (I shall reduce my attachment to worldly things).)

Musavada veramani sikkhapadam samadiyami
(I take the Precept of not indulging in wrong speech (I shall speak correctly and properly).)

Sura-meraya-majja-pamadatthana veramai sikkhapadam sa-madiyami
(I take the Precept of not taking drugs or intoxicants (I shall take wholesome food and drink only).)[2]

These Five Precepts have been carefully thought out and formulated and were offered by Gotama Buddha as guidelines to a profitable, skilful, and good Buddhist life contributing to peace and harmony with oneself and others. They are mirrors to reflect on wholesome and unwholesome ways of living one's life. Used well they are tools to deepen awareness, responsibility and wisdom in one's everyday life. It is not a 'sin' to break a Precept but it hinders one's progress as a Buddhist pilgrim.

These Precepts are incorporated in the three elements, right speech, right actions and right livelihood, of the Noble Eightfold Path constituting *Sila* in Southern Buddhism and compassion elements in Eastern and Northern Buddhism (meaning morality, loving-kindness and true respect for oneself and others). They have to be developed in Buddhist practice as the foundation for mindfulness, meditation and wisdom. There are further Precepts, adding up to eight and ten, undertaken on special occasions (see Chapter 11).

Before worship commences, flowers, lights and incense are placed at the Buddha image as offerings. These are not rituals or token gestures. The words recited have a direct reference to the *Dhamma*.

Pupphapuja

I offer these fresh, fragrant, colourful flowers at the lotus-like feet of the noble one. With these flowers I worship the Buddha, *Dhamma* and the *Sangha* and by this merit may I have release (from *Samsara*). Even as these flowers must fade, so does my body pass to decay (reminding the devotee of impermanence of all compounded things).[3]

Padipapuja

With these lights I worship the Enlightened one. Just as the lights disperse the gloom, that light of the three worlds disperses the darkness (of ignorance).

Dhupapuja

With perfumed incense I worship the Enlightened one, worthy of reverence and offerings (the *Dhamma* being like the perfume that spreads in the world and enhances its quality).

Here follows the recitation of the qualities of the Buddha, *Dhamma* and *Sangha*. The nine qualities of the Buddha:

1. *Araham* – has four meanings: most worthy person, one who has broken the wheel of *Samsara*, one who has destroyed the enemies of mental defilements, and one without secrets.
2. *Samma Sambuddha* – *means* one who has realized the Four Noble Truths through direct personal experience and achieved universal and perfect Enlightment.
3. *Vijja-carana sampanno* – *vijja* means supreme knowledge and clear vision of the past, present and future, and a perfect vision of the nature of life. *Carana* refers to the elements of spiritual practice, 15 altogether including perfect moral conduct, control of the senses, self-confidence, endeavour and mindfulness.
4. *Sugato* – meaning gone in the right manner perfecting the *Paramis* on the journey of a bodhisatta.
5. *Lokavidu* – means one who knows the nature of all the different worlds of the universe, that space is infinite and that there is no beginning or end
6. *Anuttaro purisadhamma sarathi* – incomparable teacher for training people's minds.
7. *Satta devamanussam* – teacher of the perfect way of self-development (consisting of *Sila, samadhi* and *panna*, i.e. moral conduct, mental culture and wisdom) to deities and living beings.
8. *Buddha* – is one who has awakened himself and realized the Four Noble Truths. He has realized that what we call the 'self' is a process of mind units and matter units proceeding interdependently. The physical body is a collection of matter units continually arising and vanishing. Similarly, the mind is a collection of different units continually arising and vanishing. Within the so-called 'I' there is nothing permanent. A Buddha has realized this true nature of self.
9. *Bhagava* – is the blessed and fortunate one. He is fortunate in six ways: he has the supreme capacity to control himself and lead others; high moral, mental and spiritual development; immense glory; fine physical body; has succeeded in every wish he has entertained; and has inexhaustible energy and courage.

The six qualities of the *Dhamma* are well explained by the Buddha:

1. *Sanditthiko* – relating to the present
2. *Akaliko* – timeless, with immediate benefit
3. *Ehipassiko* – inviting investigation
4. *Opanayiko* – leading to *Nibbana*
5. *Paccattam veditabbo* – to be realized
6. *Vinnuhi'ti* – by the wise, each for oneself.

The nine qualities of the *Sangha*, meaning the *Ariya Sangha* (noble disciples), consist of ordained and lay persons who have reached one of the eight spiritual attainments. The first four refer to their personal qualities and the others to their worthiness:

1. *Supatipanno* – of good conduct
2. *Ujupatipanno* – of upright conduct
3. *Nayapatipanno* – of wise conduct
4. *Samicipatipanno* – of gentle conduct.

The words then refer to the four pairs of persons or eight individuals who are the disciples of the Buddha. The 'four' refers to the four stages of:

(a)   Stream winner (*sotapanna*)
(b)   Once returner (*sakadagami*)
(c)   Never returner (*anagami*)
(d)   *Arahat*.

Each stage has a pair, one realizing the stage and one perfecting the stage, making up the eight. Eastern and Northern Buddhism, in comparison, have the ten stages of the bodhisattva path (see Chapter 17).

These disciples are worthy of:

5. *Ahuneyyo* – offerings
6. *Pahuneyyo* – hospitality
7. *Dakkhineyyo* – gifts
8. *Anjalikaraniyo* – reverential greeting
9. *Punnakkhettam lokassaa'ti* – they form the finest field of merit in the world (generating goodwill, loving-kindness and friendly concern).

Chanting of the Buddhists texts by the *Sangha*, with lay people sometimes joining in, is the next part of the worship. This is known as *pirith*. The *Suttas* most commonly chanted are the *Mangala Sutta, Karaniya Metta Sutta,* and *Ratana Sutta.* One end of the sacred thread is kept dipped in a jug of water. The thread is then unrolled and passed around the devotees so that each person holds a part of the thread between the fingers during chanting. The thread has three strands, representing the Buddha, *Dhamma* and *Sangha.* This generates a feeling of group worship. After chanting each person is given a few drops of water from the jug to drink. A portion of this *pirith* thread, now a consecrated sacred thread, is tied around the wrist as a blessing. Some devotees request that extra sections of the thread to be given or posted to relatives and friends. The sound of chanting has a calming effect on the mind. Many devotees find it a meditative and devotional experience that produces a sense of mental well being.

If worship is at the temple on a festival day, formal meditation led by a member of the *Sangha* is often a part of the proceedings. At certain times the chanting may be relayed through audio tapes. The proceedings may also include talks on Buddhist subjects and a discussion forum. On festival days, such as *Vesak* (Buddha Day), some devotees take the Eight Precepts and spend the whole day at the temple, where a full programme is arranged (see Chapter 14). Many temple complexes in Sri Lanka have a separate *devale* or shrine room where devotees may worship the deities.

Worship in Eastern Buddhism

Most Buddhists of the Eastern Buddhist traditions have a shrine at home called a *butsudan.* It will have an image of Sakyamuni (Gotama) Buddha or another Buddha or bodhisattva of an Eastern Buddhist tradition. It will also have *Sutra* texts and ancestral mortuary tablets dedicated to departed relatives. The family worship here regularly, often daily.

Throughout Japan daily services are held in Buddhist monasteries and temples. They are conducted by members of the *Sangha,* and involve worship of the Triple Gem and the chanting of Sutras and mantras revered by the particular tradition. On festival days there are special programmes. In Japan there is considerable overlap between Shinto and Buddhism, with Buddhist temple complexes often containing Shinto shrines for worship. Again, in Japan lay practice does not differ in essence from the spiritual practices of ordained members of the *Sangha.*

Homage to the threefold refuge of the Buddha, the *Dhamma* and the *Sangha* begins worship in most traditions. Some traditions also chant the title of the Lotus Sutra, the words 'Namu myoho renge kyo'.

Worship at the Three Wheels Temple in London is in the Jodo Shin, Pure Land tradition that emphasizes devotional practice. Worship takes place facing a Buddha image placed at the shrine. Offerings of flowers, lights and incense are made. Refuge is taken in Amida Buddha, who represents and includes the Triple Gem at the daily service. When special meetings take place, refuge is taken in the Triple Gem.

Pure Land Buddhists have a ritual chant called the *nembutsu*, 'Namu Amida Butsu' (Praise the Amida Buddha). Chanting is from the *Larger Sutra of Eternal Life, Meditation Sutra* and *Amida Sutra*. Formal silent meditation is not the main part of worship in this tradition. In other traditions silent meditation is a more prominent part of worship. In this there is an interesting connection between worship and meditation. If worship is honouring the Triple Gem, in the practice of formal and informal meditation one is aiming to cultivate the ultimate honour – to embody the qualities of awareness and liberation pointed to by the Triple Gem (see the Meaning of Worship, later in this chapter).

In the Tendai tradition the priest may sometimes have his home consecrated as a Yakushi–do, a Tendai temple dedicated to Bhaisajyaguru worship. The priest will worship twice a day in the shrine room, facing the image of the healing Buddha placed prominently on the shrine. Offerings of flowers, lights, incense and food are placed regularly at the shrine. A priest writes:

> ... for an Eastern Buddhist such as myself, the 'Triple Gem' means the three basic elements of Buddhism to which we all attest and take refuge in, namely the Buddha, the Dharma, and the Sangha. The formula I use every morning and evening during my service, with the accompanying prostrations, is as follows,
>
> *Isshin chorai* – I prostrate with the highest respect (head touching the floor)
> *Jippo Hokai* – In the ten directions of the Dharma World
> *Jyoju Butsu* – to the Buddha,
> *Isshin chorai and Jippo Hokai* is repeated in relation to,
> *Jyoju ho* – to the Dharma
> *Jyoju So* – to the Sangha.'

He continues:

... prior to commencing meditation with my Group (the Sangha) on Wednesday evenings, we all chant the following formula together three times:

'I take refuge in the Buddhas, the Dharma, and the Sangha
With the merit I create by practising giving and the other perfections
May I attain Enlightenment for the sake of all living beings.'

This formula, to my mind, constitutes, publicly, a declaration to one's commitment to Eastern Buddhism and is one which I expect all participants to make.

Personal letter from Ganshin Rock, 2007

Chanting from the Lotus and Heart Sutras (see Chapter 6) is a part of worship. There is silent, formal meditation, together with visualization of, for example, Sakyamuni Buddha or Buddha Vairocana, or other Enlightened beings such as Fudo-Myo when the group conduct tantric meditation.

Worship in the Zen tradition is at a shrine where an image of Sakyamuni (Gotama) Buddha is placed in a prominent position. Offerings of flowers, lights, incense and tea are placed at the shrine each morning. Zen worship takes the form of chanting and is done twice a day, morning and evening. In the morning the repentance is chanted first, followed by the going for refuge text, which is similar to the Southern Buddhism but with minor modifications:

I take refuge in the Buddha. I take refuge in the Dharma. I take refuge in the Sangha.
I take refuge in the Buddha, the most venerable one. I take refuge in the Dharma, venerable in its purity. I take refuge in the Sangha, venerable in its harmony.
I have taken refuge in the Buddha. I have taken refuge in the Dharma. I have taken refuge in the Sangha.
In the true Tathagata of complete and perfect Enlightenment I put my faith. He is my great master. I will rely on him as my teacher and not follow evil demons or other ways.
Out of compassion, out of compassion, out of great compassion.

The four great vows are chanted at least two times a day in every Zen monastery. They are always repeated three times and are chanted with folded hands, for in them the whole of the bodhisattva path is outlined. In chanting them we remind ourselves again and again of what one's work is along the way:

Sentient beings are numberless; I vow to help all to awaken.
The defiling passions are countless; I vow to work them all out.
The Dharma Gates are manifold; I vow to learn them all.
The Buddha's Way is supreme; I vow to walk it to the end.

Chanting next of the Heart Sutra (see Chapter 6) is followed by
the two *dharanis*, (mantras, devotional chants), *shosai-shu*, the
dharani of removing disasters, and *daihi-shu*, the *dharani* of great
compassion. Next the transmission is chanted as a reminder of the
handing down of the Dharma from the Buddhas of old to
Sakyamuni Buddha, and from him to the disciples in India, China
and Japan. Following the transmission an admonition by Daito
Kokushi is chanted.[4] Finally, merit is turned over by chanting of the
four bodhisattva vows for the benefit of all beings.

Formal, silent meditation is an important element of Zen practice.
Meditation *(zazen),* is practised by ordained and laity alike. Once
proficiency is gained in Daily Life Practice, *zazen* (quietening the
heart) and *samatha* meditation, insight meditation, is taken up in the
form of *koans* that may be formally given to the student or may arise
from Daily Life Practice.

Worship in Northern Buddhism

Buddhists of the Tibetan traditions perform individual and family
worship at shrines set-up in the home. Services and worship are held in
the shrine rooms of temples and monasteries daily and more
elaborately on festival days. An image of Sakyamuni Buddha is placed
in a prominent place at the shrine. Other Buddhas and bodhisattvas
are also important in these traditions and may have their own shrines.
Offerings of flowers, lights, incense and food are placed at the shrine.

Details of worship are quite complex and what appears below are
simplified selections taken from texts on worship and private letters.

Taking refuge in the Triple Gem is the:
Basis of all paths to liberation,
Foundations of all vows,
Source of all good qualities, and
Differentiator of Buddhists and non-Buddhists.

The Triple Gem is the Buddha, the *Dharma* and the *Sangha*. The
words of the formula for taking refuge are similar to those in the
other traditions and are similarly recited thrice.

A teacher at the Jamyang Buddhist Centre in London, a centre for Mahayana teaching, writes:

> In Tibetan Buddhism we recognize four motivations for going for Refuge in The Triple Gem, only three of which are considered Dharma in the Lam-rim (gradual path) tradition of practice. The four are – going for Refuge to achieve:
> - the unEnlightened purposes of this life – happiness etc.
> - the unEnlightened purposes of future lives – happiness etc.
> - freedom from being under the control of ignorance, attachment and anger.
> - full Enlightment so as to be the best vehicle for helping others on the path.

Only the last three are seen as religious motivations in the Lam-rim tradition.

In Tibetan Buddhism we take Refuge in both 'external' and 'internal' Triple Gems. The external Triple Gem is:

- Buddha – the historical Shakyamuni and the principle of Enlightenment
- Dharma – the teaching of Shakyamuni and the realizations up to and including full Enlightenment
- Sangha – the disciples of the Buddha, and the four Sangha's of practitioners (male and female renunciates, lay men and women – with primacy to the renunciates), the community of practitioners.

The internal Triple Gem is:

- Buddha – one's own future full Enlightenment as a Samyak Sambuddha
- Dharma – one's own realizations of the understanding along the path up to and including full Enlightenment
- Sangha – one's own living embodiment of those realizations as a support for practice both oneself and the community.

A commentary explains:

> When you say, 'I take refuge in the Buddha', you should regard the Buddha as the Teacher who shows you the Path to Liberation and ask him to show the Path to you and other Sentient beings. When you say, 'I take refuge in the Dharma', you should regard the Dharma as the actual path and ask it to be the Actual Path

and Vehicle to your and others' Liberation. When you say, 'I take refuge in the Sangha', you should regard the Sangha as your Assistants and Guides for you and others on the Path of Liberation and to help you remove negative circumstances and bring forth auspicious conditions.

Devotees in the Vajrayana tradition take refuge in the guru as spiritual master and embodiment of the Buddha, *Dharma* and *Sangha*. The guru is the teacher and the source of all *Dharma* and spiritual guidance on the path to Enlightenment.

The concept of the Buddha is explained according to the Eastern Buddhist doctrine of the Trikaya (see Chapter 18). The *Dharma* consists of the scriptures and realization. Scriptural *Dharma* is the *Tripitaka* (three baskets): the *Vinaya*, or discipline, that tames the negative emotions; the Sutras that summarize the teachings in words and categorizes them by meaning; and the *Abhidharma* that generates wisdom to understand the nature of reality directly. The *Dharma* of realization consists of the three Precepts: the *Vinaya* dealing with the Precept of morality; the Sutras dealing with the Precept of concentration; and the *Abhidharma* dealing with the Precept of wisdom (compare this with the Noble Eightfold Path of *Sila*, *Samadhi* and *Panna* in Southern Buddhism).

The *Sangha* is the community of monks and nuns who have embarked on the noble path. It is also the community of bodhisattvas who have reached the irreversible stage (see Chapter 17).

Chanting is an important element of worship and the Heart Sutra, which describes the essence of the Perfection of Wisdom Sutras (see Chapter 6), is a favoured text. Devotees chant mantras, phrases that are repeated in order to progress spiritually. The mantra of Bodhisattva Avalokatisvera, '*om mani padme hum*' (blessings of the jewel in the lotus) is chanted frequently. Mantras are written down and placed in prayer wheels after being consecrated by rituals performed by Lamas. Turning the wheel mindfully brings the same benefits as reciting the mantra.

There are special dance ceremonies in Eastern Buddhism not found in other Buddhist traditions. The dancers wear masks and elaborate costumes and act out sacred historical stories. These dances are performed by monks at religious festivals. They are a moving and powerful emotional, devotional and spiritual experience for both dancers and spectators.

The Northern Buddhist traditions have developed complex meditation techniques and these form an important element of worship. Formal meditation is often accompanied by visualization of Buddhas and bodhisattvas.

Meaning of Worship in Buddhism

Formal worship has developed over the years in different communities, countries and traditions. It is essentially *worship of the Triple Gem* and the different forms are very similar, although there are variations in detail. Buddhists generally worship facing a Buddha image, the purpose of which is to remind the devotee of the Triple Gem. The historical Buddha, Gotama (Sakyamuni) Buddha, is no longer alive. The worship is therefore not a communication with a Buddha, seeking and expecting a response, but *a reflection on the Triple Gem, the Buddha, Dhamma and Sangha* and a reminder to live according to the teaching. Worship is an act of mental purification and a *meditation on the Triple Gem*. Gotama Buddha said:

> You yourselves must make the effort; the Tathagatas are only teachers. The meditative ones who enter the way are delivered from the bonds of Mara.
>
> *The Dhammapada*, v. 276

It is understood that worship generates blessings that benefit all beings.

Some Buddhists focus their worship on Buddhist deities, bodhisattvas and deities of other religions, seeking help of one sort or another. It is possible for these deities to give help, not of a material kind but in the form of guidance, comfort and confidence. In fact it is understood in the Eastern and Northern Buddhist traditions that bodhisattvas who have reached a certain stage of development can help people.

Since worship is a meditation, and meditation leads the pilgrim to Enlightment and realization of the absolute truth (including *anatta* or non-self) it is appropriate to refer to an anecdote related by Francis Story.[5]

A Christian missionary touring China came across a Chinese Buddhist monk chanting in a temple. When the monk had finished the missionary asked him, 'To whom were you praying?' The monk looked surprised and replied, 'To no one'. 'Well, what were you praying for?' the missionary asked. 'Nothing' the monk replied. The missionary turned away, baffled. As he was leaving the temple, the monk added kindly, 'And there was no one praying, you know.'

Benefits of Worship

Buddhist worship uplifts one from the routine of daily life. It generates energy to cope with daily tasks and provides a focus for life. The perceivable benefit in one's daily life of reflecting on the Triple Gem is a greater energy to engage in life's difficulties in a supportive and open-hearted way, using them as part of one's practice to see through attachment, ill will and ignorance. Worship develops the five spiritual mental factors, namely, faith, energy, mindfulness, concentration and wisdom.

Consciousness of the Triple Gem helps one to control negative mental impulses and to move away from the sense of 'I' or self. Worship provides one with inspiration from the Triple Gem in order to develop a balanced view of life and to understand that:

> The inevitable difficulties that belong to human life are then looked on not as calamities that happen to me, but as the ordinary ups and downs of life, to be dealt with as good as possible, borne to the extent that they must be without the usual complaints and taken as good practice.[6] (*Ven. Myokyo-Ni, 2003*)

Nyanaponika Thera writes, in *Devotion In Buddhism*, (Wheel Publications, BPS, Vol. I, 1960 p. 11):

> The Recollection of the Buddha, being productive of joy (*piti*), is an effective way of *invigorating the mind*, of lifting it up from states of listlessness, tension, fatigue, and frustration, which occur during meditation as well as in ordinary life.

Repetitive acts of worship have a beneficial, cumulative effect as one progresses along the path of the Buddhist pilgrim. Worship in a group generates confidence in the understanding that one is acting with fellow Buddhist pilgrims treading the same path. Some Buddhists engage in worship to generate merit for the benefit of others, namely various deities, departed relatives, friends and those currently living. They believe that the merit or blessing will benefit those others. The Buddha has said that mindfulness of the qualities of the Buddha, *Dhamma* and *Sangha*, the 32 component parts of the body, meditation on compassion and meditation on loving-kindness will give protection to one from danger.

Chapter 13

Art, Architecture, Artefacts and Symbols

The artistic talents of many Buddhists have been directed towards Buddhist subjects. Creating a Buddhist work of art is considered to be an important devotional work, a practice of mindfulness and contemplation in itself. It enables Buddhists to express their reverence for the Buddha, *Dhamma* and *Sangha*. The art conveys and reminds people of the various elements of the *Dhamma* more effectively and immediately than words and it reinforces the view that Buddhism is not simply a religion but a way of life and civilization. Many Buddhists consider art to be as important as oral and written teaching.

Art

The walls and ceilings of temples often have paintings and murals illustrating scenes from the *Jataka* stories, Buddha's life and the history of Buddhism. Some temples have life-sized figures depicted in these scenes. The artwork reflects the style of the country. In Japanese temples there are beautiful paintings done in Japanese style. The Horyu-ji monastery has painted lacquer panels showing scenes from various Buddhas' past lives as well as other subjects. Tibetan monasteries have elaborate and colourful paintings of Buddhas, bodhisattvas, deities and demons on the walls and also on canvas, paper and silk wall hangings (*tankhas*).

Architecture

Buddhist temples and monasteries have decorative and dignified architecture. Temples are sometimes carved inside huge rocks, for instance the Dambulla rock temple in Sri Lanka and the cave

The author and Venerable Vicitta, a Burmese friend, on the highest level platform of the Shwe Dagon Pagoda, Yangon, Myanmar.

monastery of a Thousand Buddhas in China. In Japan the Zen temples and gardens are simple, reflecting the character of Zen training. Emperor Asoka erected pillars in India with inscriptions from the *Dhamma* on them to make the teaching better known. The famous pillar erected around 250 BCE at Sarnath by Emperor Asoka was surmounted by the figure of four lions facing the four directions on a circular base showing a horse on the left and a bull on the right of the Asokan chakra wheel. This has been adopted as the national emblem of India. The 'Asoka chakra' wheel from the base of the figure is depicted in the centre of the Indian flag.

A *stupa*, *caitya*, *dagoba*, pagoda or *chorten*, depending on the country, is the name given to a bell-shaped structure. It is usually a part of a temple complex. These structures are built to enshrine Buddhist relics and are objects of worship, devotions and meditation.

The Shwe Dagon Pagoda in Yangon in Myanmar dates originally from the time of the Buddha and is understood to enshrine eight hairs from his head. It is built on a hill and now has an electric lift to reach the base of the higher level. *Dagobas* have one or more built-in shrines where people can offer flowers, lights and incense. They have a paved area around the base for people to walk around and attend to devotional activities. Many devotees can be seen reading or reciting Buddhist texts or meditating, seated around the bases of the Ruvanvalisaya *Dagoba* in Anuradhapura, Sri Lanka, and the Shwe Dagon Pagoda.

The *dagobas* differ in size and shape from country to country. The Ruvanvalisaya *Dagoba* is about 51 metres high. Even higher is the Jetavanarama *Dagoba* in Anuradhapura, which is about 122 metres high with a base diameter of more than 113 metres, putting it on a par with some of the Egyptian pyramids and making it one of the largest Buddhist buildings in South Asia.

The Abhayagiri *Dagoba* now standing at 110 metres was built by King Abhaya in the first century BCE. Around it stood a temple complex with a community of over 5,000 monks. South of the *dagoba* is the Abhayagiri Museum, a gift to the people of Sri Lanka from Buddhists in China, which contains relics and archaeological finds illustrating the ancient friendship between China and Sri Lanka. In the year 412, the Chinese pilgrim Fa Hien visited Anuradhapura and references to these religious sites are found in the account he wrote of his travels.

Dagobas are generally built with money contributed by the temple's supporters and wealthy families as an act of devotion. The larger ones have been built with public money by rulers of kingdoms. Some cities have large numbers of *dagobas*. Anuradhapura has many *dagobas* and Buddhist sites. Bagan, formerly Pagan, once the capital of Myanmar, one of the richest archaeological sites Asia stands on the banks of the Ayeyarwaddy River. At one time it had over 13,000 temples, pagodas and religious structures dating from the eleventh–thirteenth centuries. Today it has over 2,000 well-preserved pagodas and temples.

Some traditions have a ceremonial circumambulation of the *stupa*. Different explanations are given as to what the various parts of the *stupa* represent. For instance, it is said that the ground on which the *stupa* stands represents generosity; the base represents moral restraint; the bell-shaped body the different worlds; and the spire *Nibbana*.

Artefacts and Symbols

Images of the Buddha

At first the Buddha was represented by a symbol such as a flower, tree, wheel or *stupa* (mentioned above). The first images of the Buddha in human form date from about the first century BCE. The images are made from plaster, wood, metal or similar substance. Generally those outdoors are carved from rock. Images are generally of Gotama (Sakyamuni) Buddha, the historical Buddha of our time, and the different styles reflect the tradition, period of history and country they are in. The facial features reflect those of the people of the country in which the image was made. Buddhists treat these images with great devotion and respect. For instance, it is considered disrespectful to sit on the ground with one's feet towards the image.

Some images are small enough to be held by hand and are suitable to be kept at home. They are handled with great care and arranged with other Buddhist materials in a respectful position, some height from the floor, often at a small home shrine – on a shelf or in a special shrine room. Those in temples and monasteries, often in a special shrine room, are larger in size. Those out of doors are much larger again, some being more than 100 feet in height.

Buddhists worship facing a Buddha image. The Buddha is understood to have 32 special marks and images often reflect many of these. The long earlobes signify spiritual wealth. The extension on the top of the head indicates that the Buddha has attained higher levels of consciousness. The round mark on the forehead, called the *Dharma* eye, indicates that he was aware of things unknown to ordinary people. The hair is generally shown as being curly, a sign that he was a very holy person.

The Buddha is shown seated, standing, walking or reclining on his right side. Often he is shown seated in the lotus position, with his legs crossed and each foot resting on the upper part of the other leg. This is the traditional meditation position. The body is kept stable and balanced.

There are a number of positions of the hands, called *mudras*, and these have different meanings:

- If the ends of the fingers of the right hand are touching the ground means that the Buddha is calling the world to witness his achievement and take notice of his teaching.
- The palm of the right hand facing the front is the position that shows fearlessness.
- The thumb and first finger of both hands forming circles is in reference to the first teaching.
- The right hand held facing the front at face level with the thumb and first finger forming a circle with the three other fingers straightened indicates great compassion.
- An open palm placed on the other in front of the seated Buddha image is the classic meditation or *samadhi* position.

Images of the Buddha reclining on the right side usually show him at the end of his life before passing away. In the Himalayan traditions, the seated Buddha is often shown holding a small metal object, called a *vajra*, in his hand. The word *vajra* has two meanings – something hard and unbreakable like a diamond, and something sudden and powerful like a thunderbolt. It is understood to represent all that is unbreakable and powerful about the Buddhist path. Parts of the Northern Buddhist tradition involve special teachings, practices and meditational exercises and called *Vajrayana*.

Sometimes there may be an image of Bodhisatta Metteyya, the Buddha to come. Some traditions have images of other Buddhas, such as Amida and Mahavairochana, in addition to those of Sakyamuni Buddha. They may also have bodhisattvas such as Avalokatisvera, Manjushri and Tara.

Alms Bowl

The monks and nuns, the ordained *Sangha*, do not undertake paid employment (see Chapter 16). The lay supporters supply their material needs, including alms food. In South Asian countries it is the custom for the *Sangha* to go on an alms round. They go from house to house or walk in single file through the village. Many a South Asian will remember seeing a monk standing silently in the front garden of the house holding an alms bowl. This is an opportunity for lay people to donate alms food, which is placed in the bowl. After the round the monks return to the temple. The food is consumed from the alms bowl at a set time, generally before mid-day. Sometimes lay people cook the food at home and take it to the temple or cook the food in the temple. If the *Sangha* are invited home for an alms giving they bring the bowls with them. The food is then served into the alms bowls and consumed. Ordinary plates may be used in homes or at the temple instead of alms bowls.

The alms bowl is sometimes incorrectly referred to as a 'begging bowl'. The *Sangha* do not beg for food, but collect their alms food according to established practice, and provide an opportunity for lay people to show their generosity and gain merit by providing the *Sangha* with alms food. This reinforces the special relationship between the *Sangha* and lay people.

Bodhi Tree

The Bodhi tree, a tree of the same kind under which the Buddha attained Enlightenment, is an object of worship and devotion for Buddhists. In South Asian countries a temple complex will generally have a Bodhi tree. Anuradhapura in Sri Lanka has the *Sri Maha Bodhi*, the oldest historically authenticated tree in the world. It was grown from a branch taken from the tree under which the Buddha attained Enlightenment. The *Sri Maha Bodhi* is held with the greatest reverence by all Buddhists since it provides a direct relationship with Gotama Buddha. There is a constant stream of devotees coming to worship at the tree at all times of day. Buddhists offer flowers, lights and incense, pour water around the roots and perform worship and devotions at the Bodhi tree.

Where a Bodhi tree is at the side of a road people often break their journey to worship and make donations for the upkeep of the complex.

Bowls and Dishes for Offerings

Seven things are traditionally offered to an honoured guest in India. Following this custom, in some traditions seven bowls are placed every morning at the shrine as symbolic offerings to the Buddha image, treating the Buddha as an honoured guest. The seven items offered are water for washing the hands, water for bathing the face, flowers, incense, drinking water, perfume and food. The light offering is represented by a candle or a butter lamp.

The offerings are often symbolic and water is offered in the seven bowls.

Flags

Sometimes Buddhists decorate shrines, temples and Bodhi trees with small multicoloured flags strung together, making them very attractive to the eye. In Himalayan Buddhist countries there are prayer flags that have auspicious mantras, syllables and prayers printed on them wishing happiness and giving blessings to all living beings. The movement of these flags in the wind is understood to generate and carry these good wishes to all.

A Buddhist flag was designed in the year 1880 by Mr J R de Silva and Col. Olcott to mark the revival of Buddhism in Sri Lanka. It was accepted as the international Buddhist flag in 1952 at the World Buddhist Congress. It signifies the unity of Buddhists and is used in nearly 60 countries during festive Buddhist celebrations. It is understood that the colours of the flag were the colours of the rays that came from the Buddha's body, showing the purity of his mind and body. The colours in the flag relate to certain Buddhist qualities: blue (universal compassion), yellow (the Middle Way), red (blessings), white (purity and liberation), orange (wisdom) and the sixth is a mixture of these colours.

Flowers, Lights and Incense

In most traditions Buddhists make offerings of flowers, lights (candles or lamps) and incense at the Buddha image in the shrine room as an integral part of worship or devotions (see Chapter 12). In temples and sometimes in homes there is a daily offering. Flowers signify the impermanence of life and lights and incense signify the *Dhamma* that illuminates the world.

The lotus flower is popular for use as an offering. Buddhists consider the lotus an image of Enlightenment as it grows in the mud, through the water and then opens into the sunlight. This is understood to be the path of the human mind, which grows out of the mud of attachment, ill will and ignorance into the clean air of Enlightenment.

Gongs, Bells and Singing Bowls

These are used in some traditions in Buddhist worship and meditation. Their precise use differs from tradition to tradition and depending on the occasion. They may be used to attract the attention of the worshipper or meditator, or to mark the beginning and end of periods of worship or meditation. Sometimes they are used to provide a rhythmic accompaniment to chanting at worship. In the Northern tradition, the bell and *Vajra* represent the union of wisdom and compassion in Tantric symbolism. Bells are used in certain rituals to call the deities.

Mandalas

A *mandala* is a specially designed pattern made up of circles, squares and triangles. Some *mandalas* show pictures of the Buddha and bodhisattvas as well. It is understood to be a picture of the Buddhist world of deities and beings, and at the same time a map of a human being.

Mandalas are generally found in Himalayan countries and are used for meditation. They are very colourful works of art made up of different coloured grains, often sand. The grains are put together one by one and the monks create the picture as a devotional exercise, working two or three at a time and taking enormous, painstaking effort.

This may take several days. When completed, devotions and worship follow. At the end, the whole *mandala* is thrown away, often into flowing water. This is understood to signify the Buddhist idea of emptiness. The Kalachakra *mandala* represents the universe as described by the Kalachakra *Tantra*, an important text in the Northern tradition.

Prayer Beads

A string of beads, usually 108 in number, is used in Buddhist worship, devotions and meditation. Beads are used in other Asian religions too.

The beads are made of various materials such as seeds, bones and wood. The number 108 comes from the South Asian tradition and is older than current Buddhist teaching. Different explanations are given for this number; the number of times the diameter of the Sun exceeds that of the earth, the number of *Arahats* or holy beings and the number of passions or defilements of human beings.

Prayer Wheels

These are found in the Buddhist countries of the Himalayas. Each consists of a rotating cylinder with a handle or on a stand. Small ones can be held in the hand, while the bigger ones can be a meter or more in diameter and are constructed in temple premises, normally at the entrance. Mantras, Buddhist words of blessings, are written down and placed in the prayer wheel after being consecrated by acts of worship by the monks. Sometimes the words are written or carved on the larger prayer wheels and then consecrated. Turning the wheel mindfully is considered by Buddhists to activate the blessings.

Wheel

The wheel is the symbol of the *Dhamma*. It is one of the oldest symbols in Buddhism. The Buddha's first teaching is known as the 'turning of the Wheel of Truth'. It is shown with eight spokes that represent the eight elements of Noble Eightfold Path (see Chapter 5).

Wheel of Life

The Wheel of Life is a circular picture divided into several sections. It shows the Buddhist view of life in this and other worlds, and how human beings are part of this cycle. Some are diagrammatic. Those from the Himalayan regions have elaborate and colourful paintings (see Chapter 9).

Chapter 14

Pilgrimage, Festivals and Celebrations

Pilgrimage

In Buddhist communities, going on a pilgrimage is considered a devotional activity and is quite popular among people in Asian countries. The devotees visit places of importance in Buddhist history, special shrines, temples and monasteries. Buddhist relics have been enshrined in some of them. They like to recall past events and to pay homage to these places that are visible evidence of Buddhist life. People from Western countries also go on pilgrimage to Buddhist sites in Asia.

Pilgrims may be individuals, small family groups or bigger groups from a Buddhist organization in a town or village. Sometimes groups of devotees arrange a coach, take foodstuffs and go on a pilgrimage over several days, visiting a number of temples and shrines. Some of the temples have simple accommodation and cooking facilities for use by pilgrims. Some pilgrim groups take cooking utensils and cook by the wayside.

Shortly before he passed away, Gotama Buddha spoke to venerable Ananda of four places made sacred by his association that devotees should visit with reverence. They are:

- Lumbini, in the Indian borders of Nepal, which is the birthplace of the Buddha
- Buddha Gaya, where he attained Enlightenment
- Isipatana, near Benares, where he gave the first teaching
- Kusinara, where he attained *Parinibbana* and passed away.

'And they Ananda', the Buddha went on, 'who shall die with a believing heart while on pilgrimage shall be reborn in heavenly states'.

Mahaparinibbana Sutta

There are temples and shrines at all of these places. At Buddha Gaya there stands a Bodhi tree descended from the one under which Gotama Buddha attained Enlightenment. In Sri Lanka a Bodhi tree that grew from a branch from the original tree is still alive in the ancient city of Anuradhapura, the capital of Sri Lanka from about the third century BCE to the tenth century. This Bodhi tree is within the area designated as the cultural triangle by UNESCO.

There are many other sacred sites popular with pilgrims in Anuradhapura. Pilgrims also visit:

- The historical and Buddhist sites in Polonnaruwa, the capital of Sri Lanka in the eleventh and twelfth centuries
- Mihintale where Buddhism was first introduced to Sri Lanka in about 240 BCE
- The famous Dambulla Rock Temple.

All of these sites are within the cultural triangle. In the Sri Dalada Maligawa, the temple of the Tooth in Kandy, Sri Lanka, there is enshrined a tooth of Gotama Buddha. On the top of Sri Pada, a mountain in Sri Lanka, there is a footprint understood to be that of the Buddha that came there to teach. Two other temples, the ones at Kelaniya and Nagadipa, also mark places in Sri Lanka visited by the Buddha. Apart from these temples there are many others of great importance visited by pilgrims.

Two strands of the Buddha's hair are enshrined in the Shwe Dagon Pagoda in Yangon, Myanmar, and the site is understood to be one visited by the Buddha (see Chapter 2). The Temple of the Emerald Buddha in Bangkok and Phra Pathom Chedi in Nakhon Pathon are popular with pilgrims in Thailand. So are the remains of Borobudur temple in Indonesia.

In Japan, many pilgrims visit the Tendai temples on Mount Hiei, the Shingon temples on Mount Koya and the temples around Kyoto. The Asakusa Kwanon (Sensoji) temple in Tokyo is a great attraction. On Shikoku Island there is a special pilgrim route with numerous temples and shrines. In Tibet, pilgrims visit the important monasteries, especially Potala Palace, the home of the Dalai Lama.

Festivals and Celebrations

Devotees consider participation in Buddhist festivals and celebrations an important part of Buddhist practice. In addition to the religious background, some festivals have social and cultural features. They are forms of community activities enjoyed by devotees, young and old.

Some festivals, such as those marking the birth, enlightenment and passing away of the Buddha are common to all traditions. At the same time we see variations in the nature, form and dates of festivals between different traditions and countries. Some festivals are specific to a particular tradition, some are national, some local. There are numerous festivals but only the important ones are mentioned here.

South Asia

In countries where Southern Buddhism prevails, festivals are generally on the days of the full moon. The more devout Buddhists visit the temple full and half moon days. Some formally undertake the Eight Precepts and spend the whole day at the temple. A special programme is arranged, generally including:

- a formal undertaking of the Eight Precepts
- worship
- offerings at the Buddha image in the shrine room
- talks on the *Dhamma*
- offering alms food (the midday meal) to the monks
- chanting
- meditation
- discussions on the *Dhamma*.

Many devotees visit the temple at some time during the day bringing gifts and contributions of food. There is often a communal midday meal. A special feature of the festivals in Sri Lanka is the *perahara* or a procession of musicians, dancers, jugglers, acrobats and decorated elephants sometimes carrying Buddhist relics. This starts at the temple, winds its way through the town or village and then returns to where it started.

One of the most colourful *peraharas* is the *Esala perahara*, which takes place in July/August in the ancient capital of Kandy in Sri Lanka. The festival takes place at night over a period of ten days and the last night is that of the full moon in August. The *kandyan* dancers swirl to the pulsating rhythms of the highland drummers, other dancers dance in unison, some people carry items of historical importance, torchbearers twirl their lights and over 100 elephants wearing decorative coverings escort the Maligawa temple elephant, who carries a token relic of the Buddha's tooth enshrined in the temple.

The new year is celebrated in the middle of April. Houses are cleaned, people wear new clothes, start cooking at the auspicious time, prepare special foods such as milk-rice, visit relatives and friends and entertain visitors.

In Thailand the new year (*Songkran*) festivities include a special water festival when people splash each other with water, engage in water fights in the streets and hold boat races. Caged birds are released and fish in tanks returned to rivers and ponds.

Gotama Buddha's birth, Enlightenment and passing away are celebrated on the day of the full moon in May, called *Vesak* or Buddha day. This is perhaps the most important festival. In addition to the normal programme, temples and houses are decorated with flags and lanterns, there are various entertainments and pageants, including the acting out of some *Jataka* stories, huge decorated paintings of scenes from the Buddha's life are constructed from wood, and food and soft drinks are distributed from wayside stalls. In Thailand scented water is poured on Buddha images and monks lead devotees in a threefold circumambulation of the *stupa* in the temple.

In Sri Lanka, the day of the full moon in June (*Poson*) is celebrated. *Poson* is the anniversary of venerable Mahinda bringing Buddhist teaching to the island. The day of the full moon in July is celebrated as *Esala* or *Dhammacakka* day, to remember Gotama Buddha's first teaching to the five ascetics in the deer park in Benares. This marks the beginning of the three-month retreat, *Vassa*, during which the *Sangha* remain in the temple and do not travel.

Kathina is celebrated in October or November at the end of the monks' and nuns' three-month retreat. It is a special thanksgiving ceremony when lay people express their warm gratitude to the *Sangha*. Devotees give robes, money, foodstuffs and other things needed in the temple.

Japan

In Japan festivals are celebrated at temples by making offerings, worship, reading prayers from the Sutras and chanting to honour Sakyamuni Buddha, other Buddhas and bodhisattvas. Devotees make a point of visiting temples and shrines on these days.

The most important festival is *Hanamatsuri*, the flower festival in

April to celebrate Sakyamuni Buddha's birth. Images of the infant Buddha are decorated with flowers and scented water and sweet tea is poured over them. The Enlightenment is celebrated in December by *Jodo-e* festivities, and *Nehan-e* festivities celebrate the Buddha's passing away (*Parinirvana*) in February.

The festival of *Obon* is celebrated in July to pay respects to ancestors. Graves are cleaned and decorated with flowers. Offerings of flowers and incense are made at family shrines at home. The ancestors are invited to return to their families, lamps are lit to show the way and food is set out for them. The *bon-odori* or 'bon dance' is an attraction in many towns and villages. Visitors often participate in this dance.

Higan is celebrated in March and September at the equinox, again to remember and honour dead friends and relatives and to remind people of impermanence. Graves are decorated and cleaned and ceremonies are held to give blessings to departed ones.

In addition to this, the Japan's different traditions hold festivals to celebrate teachers, especially those related to that particular tradition.

Tibet

Tibetan Buddhists celebrate the Buddha's birth, Enlightenment and passing away at the festival of *Saka Dawa* on the day of the full moon in June. The first teaching is celebrated at *Chor Khor Duchen* festival on the day of the full moon in July. Traditional celebrations include a service, worship, Sutra recitation, chanting, fasting and meditation. Two other important festivals are *Cho Trul Duchen*, to celebrate the display of miracles, and *Lha Bab Duchen*, to celebrate Gotama Buddha teaching his mother and other deities in the realm of heavenly beings. These festivals are held on the days of the full moon in March and November respectively.

In Tibet the new year is celebrated in an elaborate way by the *Losar* festival in February. Houses are cleaned and special food is cooked. Devotees visit monasteries with offerings. The monks perform various religious ceremonies aimed at driving away evil spirits. Wearing masks and exotic robes they carry out dances and plays depicting the struggle between good and evil. The dancing is accompanied by music from horns, drums and cymbals and is a deeply moving religious experience for lay people and *Sangha* alike. During *Losar* festivities Buddhists wear new clothes, prepare special food and drink, visit friends and relatives, entertain and take part in feasts and dances. *Losar* is immediately followed by the great prayer festival celebrations to ensure a prosperous year.

There are numerous other festivals, some celebrating Buddhist events, some to make offerings for local deities and others to remember important teachers.

Western Countries

Festivals are celebrated in Western countries, although not in exactly the same way. The temples and monasteries of the different traditions arrange celebrations of festival days that are generally held on a Sunday. There is often a full day's celebration involving worship, talks, discussion, chanting, meditation and a midday meal.

An example of a full day *Vesak* programme might be:

9.00	Hoisting the Buddhist Flag
9.05	Lighting of the traditional oil lamp
9.10	Administering the Eight Precepts and admonition (*anusasana*)
9.20	Worship – paying homage to the Buddha
9.30	Meditation – instruction and practice
10.00	Tea served
10.15	Talk on the Four Noble Truths
11.15	*Buddhapuja* – offering flowers, light, incense and a share of alms food at the Buddha image
11.30	*Dana* – Offering alms food to the *Sangha* and lay people observing the Eight Precepts
12.15	Lunch for the community
1.15	Reading of the *Anattalakkhana Sutta*
2.00	Discussion – questions and answers
3.00	Talk on *kamma*
3.45	Tea served
4.00	Talk 'Challenge of the *Dhamma*'
5.00	Talk 'The *Dhamma* looks to the future'
5.45	*Paritta* chanting and *Punyanumodana*
6.00	Administering the Five Precepts.

Main Buddhist Festivals

In addition to the religious background, some festivals have social and cultural features. Since these celebrations have developed in different countries and over long periods of time, they vary. In some countries the dates relate to the lunar calendar, in other countries they relate to the Gregorian calendar. The same event may be celebrated on different dates in different countries. Some festivals, such as those marking the birth, Enlightenment and passing away of Gotama (Sakyamuni) Buddha are common to all traditions, while others are specific to certain traditions or countries. There are numerous festivals, and those in this list are the more important national festivals in South Asia (S), Japan (J) and Tibet (T).

Date	Celebration	What happens or is celebrated
1 January	New Year's Day (J)	Pilgrimage to temples and shrines
15 February	*Nehan-e* (J)	Buddha's passing away
March Full moon	*Cho Trul Duchen* (T)	Display of Miracles
21 March	*Higan-e* (J)	Reminder of impermanence
8 April	*Hanamatsuri* (J)	Buddha's birth
13/14 April	New Year's Day (S)	Visiting temples
May Full moon	*Vesak*, Buddha Day (S)	Buddha's birth Enlightenment and passing away (*Parinirvana*)
June full moon	*Saka Dawa* (T)	Buddha's birth Enlightenment and passing away (*Parinirvana*)
July Full moon	*Dhammacakka* Day (S)	First teaching
July Full moon	*Chor Khor Duchen* (T)	First teaching
15 July	*O-bon* (J)	Ancestor memorial day
21 September	*Higen-e* (J)	Reminder of impermanence
A summer day	*Segaki-e* (J)	Thanksgiving day – food and money given to temple
October full moon	*Kathina* (S)	Offerings made to the *Sangha* at the end of the retreat
November full moon	*Lha Bab Duchen* (T)	Teaching his mother and other deities in the realm of deities
8 December	*Jodo-e* (J)	Buddha's Enlightenment

Chapter 15

Meditation, Mindfulness and Retreats

The Buddhist teaching, *Dhamma* (*Dharma*) consists of the wisdom teachings and guidelines to practise. The wisdom teaching is an intellectual statement of the *Dhamma*. It comes from and points towards the realization of the *Dhamma*. The practice is what a Buddhist has to do to progress on the Buddhist path. The teaching considers the living being in terms of the five *khandhas*, or aggregates of attachment or clinging. These are divided into two: the body and the mind. The body (*rupa*) is analysed further into extension (earth), cohesion (water), heat (fire), and motion (air), and is part of nature. It arises, develops and then disintegrates according to biological rules. The mind consists of four aggregates: feelings (*vedana*), perceptions (*sanna*), thoughts (*sankhara*) and consciousness (*vinnana*) (see Chapter 6). The *Oxford English Dictionary* defines the mind in similar terms, as the seat of consciousness, thought, volition and feeling.

It is the changing aggregates of the mind that move from one life to another in rebirth or rebecoming, giving the illusion of a person. The mind is the focal point of Buddhist practice. It is in the mind that the pilgrim perceives *Dukkha*, grapples with the forces of attachment and craving, struggles along the path of Buddhist practice and finally achieves *Nibbana*. All of Buddhist practice is directed towards understanding, managing, guarding and developing the mind. The first two verses of *The Dhammapada* can be summarized as:

> Mind foreruns all conditions. Mind is chief; mind made are they. If one speaks or acts with a wicked mind, because of that, suffering follows one. If one speaks or acts with a pure mind, because of that, happiness follows one.
>
> *The Dhammapada*, vv.1–2

Santideva was an Indian Buddhist monk who lived between the years 685 and 763 at the Buddhist University of Nalanda and followed the Mahayana tradition. In his classic, *The Bodhicaryavatara* (*The Path of the Bodhisattva*) about 725, he writes, in Chapter 5, verse 1 that:

> One who wishes to guard his training must scrupulously guard his mind. It is impossible to guard one's training without guarding the wandering mind.

Buddhist Practice

In Southern Buddhism, practice is set out as the Noble Eightfold Path and development of the 10 *Paramis* or perfections. In Eastern and Northern Buddhism, it is the bodhisattva path and development of the 10 *Paramitas* or perfections. Practices in Southern, Eastern and Northern Buddhism are comparable and similar (see Chapter 17).

Practice consists of morality (*sila*), mindfulness (*samadhi*) and wisdom (*panna*). Morality is the foundation and mindfulness is the way of achieving wisdom. *The Dhammapada* states:

> Indeed from meditation arises wisdom. Without meditation wisdom wanes. Knowing this twofold path of gain and loss, let one so conduct oneself that wisdom increases.
>
> *The Dhammapada*, v. 282

Wisdom is the ability to differentiate between skilful and unskilful actions and the awareness of absolute reality. Mind training in Buddhism can be explained by looking at the sixth, seventh and eighth elements of the Noble Eightfold Path. Right effort, right mindfulness and right concentration or meditation make up the Buddhist mental development, mindfulness and meditation. Here the word 'right' means according to Buddhist teaching. The word meditation is a vague and general translation of the Pali word *bhavana*, which means mental culture, training and development. The purpose of this training is to cleanse the mind of impurities and attachments, to develop tranquillity and awareness, to realize *Nibbana*, Enlightenment, the *Dhamma*, to develop fully awakened awareness and perceive absolute reality. These all refer to the same state of consciousness. Meditation is not an escape from daily life, but rather a confrontation with life resulting in increased awareness, ending of ignorance and attachment, and realization of impermanence, *Dukkha* and selflessness, non-self, or no 'I'.

Hindrances

The *Satipatthana Sutta* refers to the awareness of five kinds of hindrances to progress in this practice.

- Attachment to pleasant sense objects, such as form, sound, odour, taste and contact
- Ill will or aversion towards undesirable persons, things or situations
- A morbid or lazy state of mind lacking in energy
- Mental restlessness, excitement or worry, as these prevent the development of tranquillity
- Doubt, indecision and unsteadiness in what is being done.

Development of the mind includes full control over the mind and the development of mental independence: 'It is contrary to the principles of Buddhism to surrender one's personality completely to another, even to obtain help in meditation.' (Anagarika Sugatananda (Francis Story), *The Buddhist Outlook*, vol. I, BPS, 1973, p. 152.)

A few ill informed people have argued that taking drugs is similar to meditation. There is one common element – they both lead to altered states of consciousness. There are, however, significant differences. Meditation is a natural activity, while taking drugs is unnatural. Meditation is within the framework of the Noble Eightfold Path as explained by Gotama Buddha, while taking drugs has no foundation. Meditation is not harmful if done correctly and under proper guidance, while taking drugs has harmful effects. Lastly, meditation leads to freedom from attachment, while taking drugs leads to attachment, dependence and addiction. Indeed morality (*Sila*) is the foundation of Buddhist practice and mental training and taking drugs is a breach of the Fifth Precept – not to take intoxicants or drugs that adversely affect the mind.

Satipatthana Sutta

The foundation of teaching on meditation and mindfulness given by Gotama Buddha is in the *Satipatthana Sutta*, and this teaching also appears in other texts. *Sati* is awareness or mindfulness and *patthana* is to establish. This teaching sets out the way to establish the person in mindfulness. The *sutta*, a clear, precise and comprehensive treatment of the subject, is one of the finest pieces of literature published on any subject, in any language and at any time. The text is treated with great respect and reverence by Buddhists and the *sutta* is frequently recited or listened by a person who is ill or dying.

At the beginning and end of the text there appears this statement:

> This is the sole way, monks, for the purification of beings, for overcoming sorrow and lamentation, for the destroying of pain and grief, for reaching the right path, for the realization of Nibbana, namely the four Foundations of Mindfulness.
>
> *Satipatthana Sutta*

What are these four? The *sutta* goes on: contemplation of the body, feelings, mind and mind-objects. These four subjects equate to the five aggregates, the five groups of existence (*khandas*) (see Chapter 6) and hence this exercise amounts to the contemplation of a living being, oneself. It is not an escape from life, but a direct awareness of the daily activities of life, feelings and mental attitudes. Here is a summary of the *Satipatthana Sutta*:

- Contemplation of the body:
  - Mindfulness of breathing and contemplation of the body and originating and dissolution factors of the body;
  - Postures of the body. Awareness of going, standing, sitting and lying down;
  - Mindfulness with clear comprehension. Awareness of bending, stretching, eating, drinking, walking and other such activities;
  - Reflection on the repulsiveness of the body. From the soles of the feet upwards and from the crown of the head downwards, enclosed by the skin and full of impurities. The 32 elements of the body;
  - Reflection on the material elements. In this body there are earth, water, fire and air elements;
  - Nine cemetery contemplations. Bodies in the cemetery in varying stages of disintegration.
- Contemplation of feelings: An awareness of experiencing pleasant, painful and neutral feelings, worldly and unworldly, and their physical and mental origin. The originating factors or dissolution factors or both.
- Contemplation of the mind: an awareness of the presence or absence of attachment, ill will, delusion, mental rigidity, distraction, development, level of existence, concentration and defilements.

- Contemplation of mind-objects (*Dhammas*, reality of things and intellectual topics):
  - Five hindrances, their presence, absence, arising and abandonment;
  - Five aggregates of clinging. Material form, feeling, perceptions, mental formations and consciousness. The five elements of the so-called personality, their arising and passing away;
  - Six internal and six external sense bases. The eye and visible form, ear and sounds, nose and smells, tongue and flavours, body and tactile objects, mind and mind objects. Their origination and dissolution factors;
  - The seven factors of Enlightenment. Mindfulness, investigation of reality, energy, joy, tranquillity, concentration and equanimity. Their originating and dissolution factors and absence or presence;
  - Four Noble Truths. *Dukkha* (stress, imperfection, dissatisfaction, suffering), origin of *Dukkha*, cessation of *Dukkha* and the path leading to the cessation of *Dukkha* (the Noble Eightfold Path)'
  - Contemplation of these subjects relating to oneself, others and both, and the originating and dissolution factors.

The results of the practice of the four foundations of mindfulness are realization of *Nibbana*, and non-return to the world of sense existence. Nynaponika Thera states in *The Heart of Buddhist Meditation*, 1962, that:

The whole Discourse on the Foundations of Mindfulness may be regarded as a comprehensive theoretical and practical instruction for the realization of that liberating truth of Anatta (selflessness, no-self, or No-I), having the two aspects of egolessness and voidness of substance. (p. 75)

Formal Meditation

The different aspects of meditation and mindfulness are interconnected and complementary. For explanatory purposes, however, it is convenient to consider the subject in different sections. The main division is into formal or intensive meditation and informal or general meditation or mindfulness.

Formal meditation is specifically arranged and organized and is carried out over a pre-determined period of time, alone or in a group. When done in a group it is still individual meditation however it is practised by several people at the same time and place. The meditation by individuals does not coalesce into some form of corporate or joint meditation. Meditation can be done at home, in a temple or similar place, or in the forest or some outdoor place. A suitable calm and quiet environment is essential. The postures used are sitting, standing, walking and lying down. A daily session of formal meditation is recommended for all Buddhists. Although explained separately, in practice the meditator may move between these different forms of meditation in one session. The Southern Buddhist, Tibetan and Zen styles of meditation illustrate the different aspects of formal meditation.

Southern Buddhism

Anapanasati – Breathing Meditation
This is done in a sitting position. The meditator concentrates on the in and out breaths. Concentration is on the point of the nostrils, following the in and out movement of the air, or in the Burmese method, the rising and falling movement of the abdomen when breathing. This meditation is the starting point of other forms of meditation.

Metta Bhavana – Meditation on Loving-kindness
Here the meditator generates, develops and projects loving-kindness, compassion and benevolence towards the self, parents, family, relatives, friends, neutral and hostile persons. Then to all living beings. The focus may on living beings in different directions in the world, or to groups such as females, males, noble ones, imperfect ones, *devas*, human beings, living beings and so on. The discourse on loving-kindness, *Karaniya Metta Sutta* (see Chapter 11), states:

> Whatever living beings there be – those mentally feeble or strong, physically long, stout or medium, short, small, or large, those seen or unseen; dwelling far or near; those who are born and those who are to be born – may all beings, without exception, be happy minded.
>
> *Karaniya Metta Sutta*

When the level of loving-kindness is the same to all groups then the meditation is successful.

Metta bhavana leads to tranquillity, calmness and the *jhanas* or meditative states. The meditator may attain the four states of mind that represent the highest levels of ordinary consciousness. These are the *Brahma viharas, metta* or loving-kindness, *karuna* or compassion, *mudita* or sympathetic joy, and upekkha or detachment (see later in this chapter).

Samatha – Tranquillity Meditation

The mind receives external signals through the six sense doors, namely the eye, ear, tongue, touch, nose and mind. It is constantly dealing with these signals and reacting to them. As a result the mind is flickering and not steady or concentrated. In s*amatha* meditation the meditator concentrates on one subject, such as a colour, shape or object. The texts enumerate 40 subjects for meditation. This calms and concentrates the mind and leads to *samadhi* and *jhanas*, which are higher planes of consciousness. This form of meditation existed before the time of Gotama Buddha and is practised in other religions. It is not a purely Buddhist meditation.

Vipassana – Insight Meditation

This is a purely Buddhist form of meditation and is only expounded by a Buddha. Starting with breathing meditation, the meditator concentrates on anything that comes to his awareness through the six sense doors. The meditator experiences truths and insights unknown to the rational intellectual mind, which can only be perceived by experience. One of the best short accounts is that given by the famous Burmese meditation teacher Venerable Mahasi Sayadaw Agga Mahapandita U Sobhana to his disciples on their induction into meditation at the Sasana Yeiktha Meditation Centre in Yangon, Myanmar (Practical Vipassana Meditational Exercises, 1978, p. 17):

> The practice of *Vipassana* or Insight meditation is the effort made by the meditator to understand correctly the nature of the psycho-physical phenomena taking place in his own body. Physical phenomena are the things or objects which one clearly perceives around one. The whole of one's body that one clearly perceives constitutes a group of material qualities (*rupa*). Psychical or mental phenomena are acts of consciousness or awareness (*nama*). These (*nama – rupas*) are clearly perceived to be happening whenever they are seen, heard, smelt, tasted, touched,

or thought of. We must make ourselves aware of them by observing them and noting thus: 'seeing, seeing', 'hearing, hearing', 'smelling, smelling', 'tasting, tasting', 'touching, touching', or 'thinking, thinking'.

(Mahasi Sayadaw Agga Mahapandita U Sobhana)

There are other ways of practising *vipassana* than this noting method. Many teachings point out that awareness is our natural state. The affiliations are like clouds that defile and blind the mind. The effort to recognize and cultivate this awareness is natural to a human being. The key point is that the meditator gains direct experience of impermanence (*anicca*); stress, imperfection, dissatisfaction and suffering (*Dukkha*); and selflessness (*anatta*), and realizes *Nibbana* and Enlightment.

Tibetan

The Tibetan tradition emphasizes the necessity of *samatha* and *vipassana* meditation for the attainment of liberation, complete Enlightment and of gaining some facility in *samatha* before starting *vipassana* practice. It emphasizes supra-mundane (*lokuttara*) types of practice, i.e. those focused on understanding the selfless (*anatta*) nature of all experience, more than mundane (*laukika*) types of practices, i.e. those focused on *anicca* and *Dukkha* natures. Like other Buddhist traditions, the Tibetan tradition uses imagination to bring about understanding of the *Dukkha* nature of *samsaric* existence, i.e. that the world is filled with skeletons, 32 impure substances and the sufferings of other realms. The practice of Buddha *anusmati*, recollection of the Buddha, can be done with a visualized image of the Tathagata with the 32 major marks and 80 minor signs. Such an image can also be used to gain *samatha* or to conduct mundane *vipassana* meditation (by noting the characteristics on the physical body of the Buddha and their causes).

Buddhist *tantra* practice uses visual images and the creation of imagery in a different way. It teaches that a visual image can be used to develop both *samatha* and *vipassana* meditation at the same time: *samatha* by using it as an object to settle and focus the mind and *vipassana* in a mundane sense by noting the characteristics on the physical body of the Buddha. It can be used in a supra-mundane sense by being aware of both the appearance and its selfless (*anatta*) nature at one and the same time rather than alternating or sequentially. The

Buddhist *tantra* practice known as 'self-generation' uses both the appearance of the practitioner as a divine being in a divine place with untainted enjoyment and behaviour and the knowledge of the selfless (*anatta*) nature of all that appears to counteract any tendency to inappropriate clinging to unreal images of self. Thus it comes back to the central liberating message of the Buddha – selflessness (*anatta*).

Zen

Japanese Zen meditation tradition developed from the Chinese Chan tradition. First the student has to grasp the fundamental Buddhist wisdom teachings, including the Four Noble Truths, Three Signs of Being, *skandas*, *kamma*, rebirth, the elements (*dhatus*) and the 12 linked chain of Dependent Origination. In addition, some knowledge of Eastern Buddhist developments, such as *sunyata*, suchness and emptiness as well as something of the Zen patriarchs. The student is then given instruction in Daily Life Practice (*Sila*) and will be expected to apply it to his own daily life. The student is expected to cultivate awareness (mindfulness) in all his daily activities, physical, mental and emotional.

This is the practical application of the principles laid down in the *Satipatthana Sutta*. Central to this practice is the giving of oneself into what is being done at this moment. This learning to give oneself into the doing instead of always trying to be the 'doer' is essential, as awareness (*sati*) cannot arise if the notion of 'I' the 'doer' is present.

Along with this there is working with the passions (*klesas*), which consists not only of becoming aware of the passions as they arise by practising restraint, but also the willing endurance of the fiery onslaught of their effect on full consciousness. This is the practice of restraint is awareness of *citta* (heart/mind) and mental objects (*Dharma ayatana*). This is not possible if the passions are being acted out and the person is being carried away by them.

Once the person is used to this practice, instruction in the practice of *zazen* (sitting meditation) is given and the student is expected to sit for at least one hour a day. With the Daily Life Practice settling attention span, the student's level of awareness allows for this practice to be undertaken in earnest. Without Daily Life Practice, *zazen* does not yield much fruit as it can easily become a chase after blissful states, health and relaxation. In other words, 'my' conception of happiness by getting what I want.

On the other hand, without *zazen*, Daily Life Practice can become superficial and the insights cannot fully ripen into consciousness. As *zazen* can open the student up to the elements of the unconscious, the ability to withstand the uprushes of passion is important otherwise the practitioner continues to employ the usual defence mechanisms against such elements (either a screen of thoughts or falling asleep) or gives up the practice altogether. *Zazen* is the natural extension of Daily Life Practice and brings clarity to the insights that have arisen from the practice of awareness (mindfulness).

Once this too is settled in the mind, the student may begin insight meditation, either by using material arising directly from daily life or by a formal set of themes and *koans*. These are used to bring the student to a clear understanding of different aspects of the Buddha's teaching, particularly the Three Signs of Being – impermanence, *Dukkha* and selflessness (see Chapter 6). *Koans* are sayings of the Buddha or Zen masters, designed to take the mind beyond the intellectual level to a high spiritual level in meditation. They are used to bring a person to a realization of his true Buddha nature.

Informal Meditation and Right Mindfulness

Meditation or mindfulness is the training and development of the mind and the increasing of awareness. Performing daily activities with mindfulness, especially activities relating to Buddhist practice, is informal or general meditation, or right mindfulness. This is the application of the Zen Daily Life Practice to one's life. Mindfulness merges into formal meditation.

Buddhist worship or devotional activities, whether done at home, at a temple or shrine is informal meditation. Taking refuge in the Triple Gem, offering flowers, incense and light, reciting the qualities of the Buddha, *Dhamma* and *Sangha*, and reading, reciting or chanting the Buddhists texts are all forms of informal meditation or right mindfulness. 'Right' means done according to the *Dhamma*. Mental attitude is important. Activities must be done with full awareness of their place in the context of *Dhamma* practice. The texts most frequently chanted are the *Heart Sutra, Karaniya Metta Sitta, Saddharma Pundarika* (Lotus) *Sutra,* especially Chapter 25, and the *Mangala Sutta.* Words that have a special meaning in Buddhism, for example '*Buddho*', and mantras such as *namu myoho renge kyo* (I seek refuge in the lotus Sutra), *om mani padme hum* (blessings of the jewel in the lotus), and *namu Amida Buddha* (praise to Amida Buddha), are repeated as the sound can awaken the qualities of what is being chanted within one's own mind. This constitutes informal meditation. Devotees chant the names of the different Buddhas and bodhisattvas and sometimes use beads for counting. In some traditions devotees repeat *koans*.

Visiting a temple or monastery, listening to talks, participating in ceremonies, offering alms and working in the temple are all forms of informal meditation, right mindfulness and cultivating awareness, provided they are done with the correct Buddhist attitude and with concentration. In this way, normal daily activities such as cooking, cleaning, walking, gardening, and living in the present moment are also forms of meditation. Many teachings point out that awareness is our natural state. The passions, defilements or afflictions are like clouds that defile and blind the mind. The effort of meditation and mindfulness is to recognize and cultivate that awareness natural to one's being.

Brahmavihara

Brahma means 'sublime' or 'noble' and *vihara* means 'state of conduct' or 'style of living'. *Brahmavihara* means 'noble style of living'. Various thoughts and emotions arise in the mind and sometimes these are described as the elements of the mind and heart (which are explained in Chapter 9).

All good human qualities that we associate with the heart, such as selflessness, warmth of heart, creativity, kindliness, joy, benevolence, sense of beauty, gratitude, generosity and tolerance are classified into four virtues. They are:

- Loving-kindness – *metta*
- Compassion – *karuna*
- Sympathetic joy – *mudita*
- Equanimity – *upekkha*.

These four sterling virtues are collectively termed *brahmavihara* – modes of sublime conduct, noble living, sublime states or divine abodes. An individual who lives in accordance with these qualities is deemed to live a noble and divine life.

These four outstanding qualities are known as illimitable because they extend equally to all living beings without any distinction – human beings, animals and deities. They are all-embracing, non-exclusive, impartial and not bound by selective preferences and prejudices. Irrespective of religious beliefs, an individual could cultivate these fine qualities as a blessing to oneself and others. Although some of these virtues are focussed on others, in the end their practice is a purification and development of the individual's own mind.

Loving-kindness – Metta

Metta means loving-kindness, goodwill, benevolence and friendliness. It is the wish for the welfare and happiness of all beings without exception and includes loving-kindness to oneself as well as all other beings. The Buddha exercised loving-kindness equally towards his son Rahula, his adversary Devadatta, his personal attendant Ananda, his disciples, supporters and opponents. It is this loving-kindness for others that moves a bodhisattva to postpone Nibbana and continue to be born in Samsara for the benefit of others. The Karaniya Metta Sutta[1] sets out the wide meaning of loving-kindness.

> Hatreds never cease by hatred in this world: by love alone they cease. This is the ancient law.
>
> The Dhammapada, v. 5

Loving-kindness leads to compassion (karuna) and sympathetic joy (mudita). This quality of loving-kindness should be differentiated from personal affection or sexual love. Buddhism recognizes, however, that personal affection between parents and children, husband and wife, members of a family, relatives and friends is a natural and good aspect of human life. The opposite of loving-kindness is anger, ill will, jealousy, hatred and aversion – qualities that very few individuals will own up as having.

Loving-kindness or metta is not only a way of life, but is also as metta bhavana, an aspect of formal meditation (see above). In the practice and meditation of loving-kindness one develops less consciousness of the self, the distinction between the self and others disappears and finally the individual begins to identify the self with all beings.

Loving-kindness is the ninth and most important Parami to be developed by a bodhisatta (see Chapter 17). The next Buddha is Buddha Metteyya (Maitriya), the Buddha of loving-kindness. He currently lives in the Tusita heaven as Bodhisatta Metteyya where he will remain until it is the correct time for him to be born in the human world and the deities invite him to do so in order to practise the *Dhamma* and become Enlightened as the next *Samma Sambuddha.*

It is said in the *Anguttara Nikaya* that the Buddha has declared that if loving-kindness is cultivated, developed and firmly established, the individual may expect 11 blessings: have peaceful sleep, peaceful awakening, freedom from bad dreams, freedom from harm from fire, poison and weapons, a quickly concentrated mind, a happy and serene countenance, be dear to the spirits, have the protection of heavenly beings, have an untroubled death, and birth in the heavenly Brahma world if not born as an *Arahat.*

Compassion – Karuna

Compassion is the next of the virtues that makes an individual noble. Its chief characteristics are the wish to help others, remove their difficulties and suffering and work for their welfare. Compassion moves an individual to help and serve others simply for their benefit, expecting nothing in return, not even gratitude.

The decision of the bodhisatta, then living as the ascetic Sumedha, not to realize *Nibbana* at the time of Buddha Dipankara but continuing in *Samsara* with all its unsatisfactory features in order to strive to become a *Samma Sambuddha*, was due to his compassion for living beings. The *Vyaghri Jataka* relates how the bodhisatta sacrificed his life to save a starving tigress and her cubs. When a sick monk was being neglected by other monks the Buddha himself attended on him. Again, the Buddha showed great compassion towards the courtesan Ambapali and the murderer Angulimala, both of whom became his disciples and changed their respective characters.

Many people need compassion: the poor, needy, physically and mentally ill, helpless, lonely, destitute and the spiritually poor. It is said in Buddhism that the vicious, wicked and ignorant also need compassion because they are mentally and spiritually ill. For these reasons, all living beings – humans, animals and deities – deserve compassion. A Buddhist should have compassion for someone who harms him. We suffer harm because of bad *kamma* and the person who does the harm does not have a balanced mind.

Sympathetic Joy – Mudita

This virtue of sympathetic or appreciative joy flows naturally from loving-kindness. It means to be happy at the happiness, good fortune, prosperity and success of others. Sympathetic joy is more difficult to practise than the first two virtues of loving-kindness and compassion because it demands greater personal effort and strong willpower. Although focussed on others, the practice of sympathetic joy is very much concerned with purifying oneself, since it destroys ill will, jealousy and envy, one of the Three Fires driving the individual through *Samsara*. It makes the individual's life much happier.

It is very easy to be happy at one's own success or the success of those near and dear to us, but more difficult to be happy at the success of others, including those not well disposed towards us. The chief characteristic of sympathetic joy is to be happy about the prosperity and success of others. One has to develop this virtue to the extent that one is as happy at the success of others as if it were one's own success. There is a chain reaction in that such thoughts encourage the growth of other noble virtues such as tolerance, generosity, friendliness and compassion and reduce the bad negative emotions of ill will, jealousy and selfishness. It generates the important idea in Eastern and Southern Buddhism that one begins to think less of oneself, and the idea emphasized in Northern Buddhism that it reduces the distinction between oneself and others.

One should extend sympathetic joy to oneself also and be happy at one's own effort, success, good fortune and situation in life, compared to millions of others in less fortunate circumstances. This should be done even if one is aware that one's good fortune is due to the operation of good *kamma*. If one is constantly discontented with life there is no tranquillity, no peace of mind.

Equanimity – Upekkha

This last virtue in the *brahmavihara* means to see and view things impartially with equanimity, balance of mind and mental equilibrium. It advises a middle path avoiding attachment, favour and attraction on one hand, and aversion, disfavour and repulsion on the other. It advocates the avoidance of either excitement or indifference, to consider the pleasant and unpleasant with the same mental balance and not get angry, depressed or anxious about what has to be encountered in life.

Equanimity deals with self control. It is especially important and difficult to develop for lay people who have to live in a changing world amid fluctuating circumstances. It encourages the individual to treat the eight worldly conditions of loss and gain, fame and ill-repute, praise and blame, pleasure and pain with equanimity and a balanced mind. The Buddhist teaching explains that all these changing conditions of life, the successes and gains, the failures and losses are temporary and impermanent. They are the results of past good and bad *kamma*, and once the momentum of the *kamma* is exhausted the condition passes.

Contentment and mindfulness are important for developing equanimity. *The Dhammapada* (see Chapter 17) says:

> As a solid rock is not shaken by the wind, even so the wise are not ruffled by praise or blame [...] whether affected by happiness or by pain, the wise show neither elation nor depression. Equanimity is the tenth in the list of *Paramis* to be developed by the bodhisatta.
>
> *The Dhammapada*, vv. 81 – 83

Loving-kindness embraces all living beings; compassion embraces those in distress, need and want; sympathetic joy embraces the successful and prosperous; and equanimity embraces oneself amid all the changing conditions of life. These four qualities or states of mind represent the highest levels of ordinary human consciousness. Living such a life is considered to be living in the *brahmavihara* or divine abodes.

Benefits of Buddhist Meditation

Medical conditions such as high blood pressure, increased heart rate, increased cholesterol, excessive fatigue, depression, stress and sleep-lessness are benefited by regular meditation. Evidence points to an enhancement of the autoimmune system and benefits relating to the reduction of drug and alcohol addiction, unnecessary tendencies to self-blame and emphasis on negative personality qualities.

Metta meditation brings about an increase in the sense of peace, as one is not in conflict with oneself or others, a positive friendly attitude, friendship towards all beings including animals, birds, and fish and a caring awareness towards the environment. Some Buddhists believe that this meditation can end the feeling of being harassed by ghosts and spirits.

Samatha meditation contributes to concentration, tranquillity, calmness, patience, self-confidence, a general sense of well being, a present happy life and favourable rebirths.

Vipassana or insight meditation is the true Buddhist meditation, discovered by a Buddha and taught only by a Buddha. This meditation enables the individual to understand the present moment, the process of life and to realize by direct meditative experience the impermanence (*anicca*), imperfections (*Dukkha*), and selflessness (*anatta*) of all material and mental elements of existence. The individual then realizes *Nibbana*, Enlightment, fully awakened awareness, the *Dhamma* and absolute reality.

All aspects of the Buddhist teachings on meditation and mindfulness are based on the teaching in the *Satipatthana Sutta*. The content of this teaching appears in other texts as well, for example the *Mahaparinibbana Sutta*. There is meditation in other religions also, but this is discursive or general meditation. *Vipassana* or insight meditation is found only in Buddhism. Where a religion recognizes a God as creator and the existence of a soul, there cannot be anything similar to insight meditation. Formal and informal meditations do not fall into separate compartments, but go hand in hand comprising Buddhist meditation and right mindfulness.

Nynaponika Thera says in *The Heart of Buddhist Meditation*, 1962, that:

> ... the systematic cultivation of Right Mindfulness, as taught by the Buddha in his discourse on Satipatthana, still provides the most simple and direct, the most thorough and effective, method for training and developing the mind for its daily tasks and problems as well as for its highest aim: mind's own unshakable deliverance from Greed, Hatred, and Delusion [...] from the very first stages of that road, the method of Right Mindfulness will show immediate and visible results of its efficacy [...] Step by step the practice of Right Mindfulness should absorb all activities of body, speech, and mind, so that ultimately the subject of meditation will never be abandoned.[2]

Retreats

Meditation is at the centre of Buddhist practice. Many Buddhists, members of the *Sangha* and lay people meditate at home or at the temple regularly. Some attend meditation workshops and retreats. A retreat is so-called because it involves getting away from the normal day-to-day life. A member of the monastic *Sangha* or a lay person may arrange to go to a monastery specializing in meditation, to attend a retreat organized by the monastery or for a personal retreat. In addition to retreats, many temples and monasteries arrange meditation workshops during the day or evening.

Retreats are generally conducted in strict silence and the programme timetable is strictly adhered to. There is no talking, reading (even books on Buddhism), telephone, radio or television. The only intellectual activity is listening to the teacher and, when the timetable permits, asking questions, obtaining advice and discussing progress in meditation. It is understood that any intellectual activity interferes with mindfulness and meditation. In this way Buddhists are encouraged to not just listen to the rational mind, but to go beyond. Ajahn Cha used to say, 'Listen with your heart'. The teachers explain that no one has realized *Nibbana* by reading, listening to, talking or thinking about the *Dhamma*. All the Buddhas and *Arahats* have realized *Nibbana* by practise, i.e. leading an ethical and moral life (*Sila*), together with mindfulness and meditation leading to fully awakened awareness. They emphasize the urgency of starting meditation as soon as possible in this life as the progress made will be carried over into the next life. If meditation is postponed to the next life, the opportunity may not be there. The *10 Wheels Sutra* of Northern Buddhism states:

> There is greater merit in meditating for one day than in kalpas of copying, reading, listening to, explaining, or reciting the Dharma.

Organized Retreats

Some retreats are organized by the monastery over a weekend, a few days, a fortnight or longer. Generally people have to book to attend a particular retreat. Sometimes, if it is a popular teacher, the retreat may be fully booked a year ahead and there is often a waiting list. The number of people on the retreat depends on the accommodation available. The retreat is conducted under eight or Ten Precepts. The cooking is often done by volunteers who participate in the retreat in their free time.

This is a meditation retreat programme at a Buddhist monastery in the UK:

5.00 a.m. Wake-up bell. Hot drinks in the kitchen
5.30   Morning chanting and meditation
7.00   Breakfast in the kitchen
7.45   Working meditation

8.45   Morning meditation – sitting and walking
11.00   Food offering and meal
2.00 p.m.   Afternoon meditation – sitting and walking
5.30   Hot drinks in rhe kitchcn
7.30   Evening meditation, chanting and talk.

Many people are up by 4.30 a.m. to be ready for the early session. The evening programme ends at about 9.30 p.m. and lights are out at 10.00 p.m. In most meditation monasteries in Myanmar, Sri Lanka and Thailand the day begins at 3.00 a.m.

Individual Retreats

Some monasteries and retreat centres offer the possibility of personal retreats. The stay may be for a few days or a longer period of time (weeks or months), with the permission of the head monk or nun. The arrangements and programme may differ somewhat at the various monasteries. The retreat will be under the rules and customs that operate in the temple or monastery and will normally be under the Eight or Ten Precepts.

Below is a description of the author's experience of an individual retreat at a well-known meditation monastery in Sri Lanka.

Retreat in Sri Lanka

The monastery could accommodate about 70 meditators at a time – men and women living separately. In addition to the resident monks, there were visiting monks, nuns and lay people. On arrival, after registration, there was a brief and friendly interview with the head monk. He inquired about my acquaintance with Buddhist teaching and practice, including meditation, and welcomed me to the centre.

In the public area just inside the entrance to the centre there was a shrine room, a Bodhi tree and a *dagoba* (*stupa*). There was an administrative office, an alms food hall and a big building that housed the large pantry and kitchen, with a notice board outside indicating the number of persons for whom alms should be prepared the next day. There was also a large building that was the hall used for teaching.

The living area for meditators was separated from the public area by a fence of shrubs with a narrow entrance. The public were not expected to enter this area. The living accommodation for meditators was in long buildings arranged around a courtyard that

Meditators at the meditation monastery

had several stone benches. All around inside each building was a long corridor with a short connecting corridor in the middle. The corridors were used for walking meditation.

Each meditator was assigned a small *kuti* (room) of about seven by four feet. On one side was a bed made of concrete raised six inches above floor level, with a thin coir mattress and a mat. After sleeping five nights on this bed one felt the need for the attention of an orthopaedic surgeon. A small low-level table was the only other furniture. The light hanging from the ceiling had a 15 watt bulb because the meditators are not expected to do any reading. Hanging from a hook over the bed was the very necessary mosquito net, which could be unhooked and then hooked in the corridor just outside when communal meditation was done.

There were special paths outside the buildings for walking meditation. Down in the garden was a small glass-fronted room that housed a human skeleton. This was to be used as an object for meditation. There was a path leading away for a few yards, to be used for walking meditation, and at the end was a stone bench for meditators to sit upon and reflect on the reality of life.

The stay was according to strict Buddhist principles and practice. Lay people wore white with a white shawl draped over the left shoulder with the ends held by a safety pin under the right arm. This indicated that the person had undertaken the Ten Precepts. On arrival, after washing and changing into white clothes, the lay person attended at the small shrine room for a short devotion (*puja*) and one of the resident monks administered the Ten Precepts. It was rather like taking novice ordination for the duration of the stay, similar to the temporary ordination common in Myanmar and Thailand. Meditators quickly adjusted to living in this semi-monastic way and conforming to traditional norms. They came to appreciate the benefits of this environment for meditation. On leaving, the lay person undertook the Five Precepts, which then replaced the Ten Precepts.

The climate was hot and tropical, with daytime temperatures around 30°C and nights somewhat cooler. The many flowering plants, shrubs and trees gave the sense of living in a tropical forest. Numerous birds and squirrels had made their home in the trees and feasted off the berries and fruits. Monkeys of varying sizes swung overhead from branch to branch in the tall trees and chattered away to one another, quite oblivious of the height at which they lived.

The alms food was provided by lay supporters. Each day was booked by a different group, sometimes a family but more often several families or a whole village. The Buddhist community in Sri Lanka is so keen to give alms at this monastery that often after alms giving the same group booked the same day a year ahead. Generally, all of the days of the year ahead were booked at any given time. The people giving alms arrived about 4 p.m. the day before. They came from different parts of Sri Lanka, travelling in cars and coaches and bringing the necessary provisions with them. These lay supporters remained in the public area of the monastery. The resident monks conducted a *puja* (worship) at 6.00 p.m. and gave a *Dhamma* talk at

8 p.m. to the people who had arrived. These supporters then worked overnight preparing the alms food for the coming day. Having served the morning gruel, breakfast and lunch, they left at about 2.00 p.m., after having their own lunch. The group that had booked to give alms food the next day arrived later.

The waking up gong was at 3.30 a.m. and having washed and dressed, everyone continued with sitting and walking meditation. At 5.00 a.m. hot rice gruel cooked with vegetables was brought round and offered to the meditators. Meditation continued until 6.45 a.m. when breakfast was offered in the alms food hall. The meditators walked to the building in single file: the monks in order of seniority, then lay meditators in order of age, and took their place in the same order, sitting on benches at low tables. The alms food was offered and served by devotees, first to the monks and then to the lay meditators in strict order. Only after the senior monk began to eat did the others commence eating. The food was eaten in complete silence, this being a part of the meditation. There were rules regarding the eating of certain foods; for instance, a portion of the biscuits and sweets were broken off and that portion placed in the mouth rather than the whole being brought to the mouth and a portion been bitten off. Each person was provided with water for drinking and for washing his plate into the receptacle placed on the floor beside him. After everyone had finished eating, the senior monk led the way back into the meditation area, again in single file and in the same order.

There was formal communal meditation from 7.45 a.m. to 8.45 a.m. This was done individually. Each meditator placed a small mat and cushion outside his room in the corridor, hooked up the mosquito net and meditated seated inside the net. Some sat outside on the stone benches.

After this there was work to be done sweeping the room and corridor, collecting fallen leaves, sweeping the garden, cleaning the toilet block and so on. All this was done mindfully, as a continuation of meditation. At 10.00am, after the work was done, the meditators made their way to the well at the far end of the garden to bathe. The well was about eight foot by ten foot and about twelve feet deep. A kumbuk tree had been planted nearby so that its roots grew into the water to keep the water cool and crystal clear. Water was taken in small buckets and poured over oneself. Bathing in tropical sunshine with this cool water was so refreshing that it took much will power to end the bath. A good example of *Dukkha*.

At 11.15 a.m. the meditators proceeded in the same orderly manner to the alms food hall for the mid-day meal, the last meal of the day. Again alms food was offered and served by the devotees. The meals were substantial and vegetarian. From 12.30 p.m. to 1.30 p.m. was the second formal communal meditation of the day. During the afternoon the meditators met a senior monk on an individual basis for instruction, advice and guidance on progress made in meditation. The latter part of the afternoon was for further individual meditation.

At 6.00 p.m., while the resident monks arranged *puja* (devotions) for lay devotees who had arrived to prepare the *dana* for the next day, the lay meditators had devotions in the small shrine room in the residential block. After this there was the third hour of formal communal meditation from 6.15 p.m. to 7.15 p.m. By this time it was getting dark and a multitude of birds and bats made a terrific noise settling down in the trees for the night. This was also the time when the mosquitoes came out searching for victims. The meditators continued the sitting and walking meditation. Lights were out at 10.00 p.m. in the residential blocks, but the garden was lit by fluorescent lights throughout the night.

There were no regular courses or classes, so meditators were welcome to arrive on any day as arranged. The instruction and practice was ongoing and continued on an individual basis. An initial intensive training period of three weeks was recommended, but stays of shorter or longer periods could be arranged.

The training was in the Burmese tradition of *vipassana* or insight meditation. Most of the day was spent silently in individual meditation, alternating sitting and walking. All other activities, such as meals or personal needs, were also an important part of the practice as the cultivation of continuous mindfulness is very helpful for progress in meditation. Individual interviews were scheduled, usually on a daily basis, to enable meditators to report their meditation experiences and receive appropriate guidance from the teacher.

The centre literature explained that *vipassana* meditation is a process of investigation and observation through mindfulness (bare attention) that leads to a penetrating understanding of the true nature of reality. The ever-changing physical and mental phenomena arising in the meditators awareness are the objects of this investigation. The realization of their impermanence, *Dukkha* and selflessness gradually de-conditions the mind from unprofitable ways of thinking that can only lead to unhappiness. The total eradication of these unprofitable states of mind founded on attachment, ill will and ignorance is the ultimate goal of the practice; *Nibbana* the freedom from *Dukkha*, suffering, stress and imperfection. *Vipassana* or insight meditation is the central practice of Buddhism – a human being, alone, grappling with his mind to achieve a meaningful realization of reality.

Spending some days on such a retreat was strenuous, relaxing and profitable. Strenuous, because for those living a lay life it took a great deal of effort to follow the tight schedule of intensive training over successive days. Relaxing, because the day's programme was mapped out and one did not have to make decisions as to what to do throughout the day or have to deal with the ordinary matters of lay life. Profitable because by living, however briefly, a simple semi-monastic life with teachers on hand to give guidance, one began to understand the relevance and importance of mindfulness and meditation in understanding and accepting the ordinary daily lay life in the context of Buddhist teaching, in order to progress on the Buddhist path

Retreat in a Yangon Monastery

Sometimes the programme may be much more organized and rigorous, as is shown by this programme from a famous meditation monastery in Yangon, Myanmar. Here meditators train to a strenuous meditation programme, having two meals and about four hours of sleep a day.

3.00–4.00 a.m.	Waking up, washing and brushing
4.00–5.00 a.m.	Group sitting
5.00–6.00 a.m.	Walking meditation and breakfast
6.00–7.00 a.m.	Group sitting
7.00–8.00 a.m.	Walking meditation
8.00–9.00 a.m.	Group sitting
9.00–11.00 a.m.	Bath and lunch
11.00–12.00 noon	Walking meditation
12.00 noon–1.00 p.m.	Group sitting
1.00–2.00 p.m.	Walking meditation
2.00–3.00 p.m.	Group sitting
3.00–4.00 p.m.	Walking meditation
4.00–5.00 p.m.	Group sitting
5.00–6.00 p.m.	Bath and drink

6.00–7.00 p.m.	Group sitting
7.00–8.00 p.m.	Walking meditation
8.00–9.00 p.m.	Sitting meditation
9.00–10.00 p.m.	Walking meditation
10.00–11.00 p.m.	Sitting meditation
11.00–3.00 a.m.	Sleeping time.

Part IV

Community

Chapter 16

Ordained Sangha and Lay People

The Buddhist community is made up of ordained people, called the *Sangha* and lay persons or householders. Buddhists emphasize different inclinations in their practice: some scholarly, devotional, ascetic, contemplative and meditative. Each Buddhist is working towards the same goal, ending the Three Fires of attachment, ill will and ignorance, and transcending the cycle of life (*Samsara*) by attaining Enlightment and realizing *Nibbana*. The answer to the question 'who is a Buddhist?' is often given as 'a person who accepts the Triple Gem, the Buddha, the *Dhamma* and the *Sangha* as guides, has a present and continuing intention to live according to the *Dhamma* as a religion and makes an immediate and ongoing effort to do so'.

In Buddhist communities, the children of Buddhist parents are brought up as Buddhists and become members of the community. They do not make a concrete decision to become Buddhists: they cease to be Buddhists only if they take definite steps to embrace and follow another faith. People brought up in other faiths, or with no faith, may make a decision to follow Buddhist teachings and become members of the Buddhist community. There is no religious distinction between those who are born Buddhist and those who adopt the religion.

Generally there is no special ceremony to become a Buddhist. Often taking the Three Refuges and the Five Precepts is seen as an initiation, confirmation or reconfirmation of being a Buddhist. In some Japanese Buddhist traditions, however, there are simple ceremonies in which the person expresses the intention to live as a Buddhist. These ceremonies, varying with the tradition, are conducted by a Buddhist priest at a temple. For example, at Kikyoshiki the person takes the Three Refuges, and at Jukai the person takes the

Three Refuges and the Five Precepts. Within Tibetan Buddhism, a person may take the Three Refuges and thereby indicate his intention to live as a Buddhist. Later the person may take the bodhisattva vows indicating an intention to progress as a bodhisattva, and finally he may take the higher yoga tantric initiation by taking the tantric vows, leading towards the highest level of tantric Buddhist practice and achievement. The practice in some countries of taking novice ordination is understood to be a confirmation that the person is a Buddhist. It is technically not possible to be a Buddhist and follow another faith at the same time.

Ordained Sangha

Sangha means community. At first the Buddhist Sangha referred to the fourfold assembly of monks (bhikkhus), nuns (bhikkunis), laymen (upasakas) and laywomen (upasikas). Consequent to ordination rules, the ordained Sangha are considered to be directly descended in unbroken line from the Buddha. They are the living evidence of the teaching. Sometimes a distinction is drawn between the noble Sangha, who have achieved a stage of holiness, and worldlings, meaning monks and lay people who have not achieved that stage.

Current interpretation of Sangha varies according to tradition. Generally in South Asian countries, China and Korea, the Sangha, as the word is used now, consists of ordained monks and nuns. They live in temples and monasteries. In some Japanese traditions, in addition to monks and nuns, people can be ordained as priests or ministers; they marry and have families, live in temples and perform pastoral services for the supporters. In some Japanese traditions, such as the Tendai, the word Sangha has the wider original meaning of community of Buddhists and includes the ordained Sangha and lay members of the temple. In Tibet, in addition to the monks and nuns who live in monasteries and do not marry, there are monks who marry, have families and spend only a part of the year in the monastery. Also in Tibet, the community of bodhisattvas who have progressed a long way in their practice are considered to be part of the Sangha, as are lamas and gurus. These last three groups may or may not be ordained.

Tibet has the offices of the religious and political heads of the state vested in the office of His Holiness, the Dalai Lama. An incumbent Dalai Lama is considered to be a reincarnation of the previous holder of the office and also a reincarnation of Bodhisattva

Japanese Rinzai Zen monks processing out of Enkakuji temple in Kita-Kamakura to collect alms food.

Avalokatisvera. In Nepal there are scholar teacher priests in addition to monks and nuns. They follow professions outside the monastery, have families, live near the temple and perform pastoral duties for the supporters. The word *Sangha* is used in this chapter to mean the ordained *Sangha*.

Training

The rules of monastic discipline (*Vinaya*) govern the training, conduct and organization of the *Sangha*. These are strictly adhered to in Southern Buddhist countries but in some of the Eastern Buddhist traditions they are regarded not so much as definitive rules but as guidelines. They cover matters such as ordination, training, duties of teachers and novices, ways of dealing with differences of opinion and breach of the rules, lodgings, food, ceremonies and so on. They were formulated by the Buddha as the occasion arose and are a comprehensive guide to the life of the *Sangha*.

There are between 223 and 250 rules to be observed, depending on the tradition. Monks and nuns do not own anything apart from few personal possessions, such as robes and an alms bowl. They shave their heads or have very short hair and do not wear adornments such as ear rings, bangles or rings. They dress modestly in robes that are different colours depending on the style of Buddhism and country: orange in South Asian, grey in Korea, black in Japan and deep red in Tibet.

The Order

Entry into the order is by ordination: an elaborate religious and social ceremony. A person may take the Eight Precepts and live in the temple or monastery as a lay supporter (*anagarika*). Sometimes this is done to give the person an idea of ordained life.

In ordination proper, first there is the novice ordination when the person undertakes the Ten Precepts. If a child, the person must be over the age of seven and permission must have been given by the parents. After the age of twenty and a long period of study and training under a particular teacher, there is the higher ordination.. At least five senior members of the *Sangha* – monks for the ordination of a monk and nuns for the ordination of a nun – need to officiate at a ceremony giving full ordination. Where the lineage has broken in a country, the *Sangha* from another country have helped to restart the order. In the fifth century, nuns from Sri Lanka travelled to China to perform the full ordination ceremony for Chinese nuns and in the eighteenth century monks from Thailand travelled to Sri Lanka to perform the same reason.

Then the, now fully ordained, monk or nun has a further period of training with the teacher or another senior monk or nun lasting five years, before he can go out into the world independently as a member of the *Sangha*.

On ordination, in some traditions a person cuts off social and family ties, while in other traditions family relationships are maintained. Often the family continue to help the ordained member with robes, warm clothes, shoes, sandals, medicines, writing materials and the like, and perhaps these days with a laptop computer. The monk or nun is given a new Buddhist name and takes up residence in a temple or monastery.

Ordination is generally considered to be for life, but is voluntary and the person may leave the order and return to lay life at will. In some traditions ordination is considered a period of training but not necessarily for life. In South Asian countries such, as Myanmar and Thailand, men and women may take temporary ordination as novices under Eight or Ten Precepts intending to return to lay life afterwards. They live in the temple or monastery for a definite period of time of (days, weeks or months), sometimes for the three-month rainy season (*Vassa*) learning the *Dhamma* and tasting the life of the *Sangha*. Some take temporary ordination several times in a lifetime.

There is no central authority for the *Sangha*, however, in each country there are sub-orders, each headed by a senior member. In addition, each temple or monastery has a senior monk, abbot or nun. In Thailand the *Sangha* is organized as a national institution and the king appoints the head (*Sangha-raja*) of the *Sangha*. There is a special relationship between the *Sangha* and lay people. In South Asian traditions, affiliated temples and monasteries, the *Sangha* are not gainfully employed and lay people provide them with the necessities of life and meet the requirements of the temple. In return, the *Sangha* organize the religious life of the people, teach the *Dhamma* and perform pastoral duties. Many Buddhists consider it auspicious to receive blessings from the *Sangha* and the deities.

Nuns

The order of nuns dates from the time of the Buddha (see Chapter 2). In China, Japan and Korea, the ordination of nuns has continued unbroken and there are flourishing orders. In South Asian countries, full ordination has been broken due to technicalities in the ordination procedure: there were Eight or Ten Precept nuns living according to monastic rules. In about 1996, a full ordination ceremony was held in India. It was arranged by the Mahabodhi Society and officiated by Korean nuns. Several Sri Lanka nuns received full ordination. In 1998 a full ordination ceremony for monks and nuns from several Buddhist traditions was held at Buddha Gaya with nuns from the unbroken lineage of China officiating in the ceremony. Since then there have been other ordinations.

Outside Asia different ways of developing the ordination of nuns have evolved in various countries in including the UK and USA. In the Forest *Sangha* Tradition of Thailand in the UK, five nuns received the Eight Precept ordination in 1979. Then in 1983, with the permission of the Thai *Sangha*, they received the Ten Precept 'going forth' ordination, which formalizes the individual's determination to live the renunciate life. This tradition has developed a way of training, practice and ordination for women drawing on the rules of nuns and novices. The result is now known as the *Siladhara Vinaya* training and comprises some 120 rules and observances. In Los Angeles, California, 250 nuns and 50 monks were ordained at the

Hsie Lai Temple in 1998. An international congress on Buddhist women's role in the *Sangha* was held in Hamburg, Germany, initiated by His Highness the Dalai Lama to discuss ways to promote the ordination of nuns.

Westerners

Many Westerners over the years have gone to the East and been ordained as monks and nuns. Since the latter half of the twentieth century, full ordination has been conducted in the West. In addition, steps for partial ordination have been devised and some traditions have *Dharmacharies* (Buddhist teachers).

Lifestyle

The *Sangha* are divided broadly into those who live in temples in towns and villages among people and those who live secluded lives in monasteries or in the forest, away from people. All members of the *Sangha* lead strict lives of study, devotion, meditation and practice of the *Dhamma*. Generally they do not ask for anything directly from supporters but wait until it is given. Their day starts very early, generally before sunrise, with devotions and meditation.

Those who live in towns and villages, in addition to their personal practice, have a close relationship with lay people. They teach the *Dhamma*, arrange meditation classes, advise devotees on religious and other matters, organize Buddhist festivals and celebrations, participate in blessing ceremonies at birth, illness and death, visit people at home, in hospital and in prison on request, give talks in schools and colleges, receive visitors at the temple and participate in public, educational, religious and social conferences. In South Asian countries the temple in the town or village is often the focus of the religious, social and cultural life of devotees who live nearby. Further, most temples have a school for younger children where normal school subjects are taught until they are old enough to go to an established school. The temples have a library and a hall for meetings and gatherings. In the evening the *Sangha* in a temple come together for worship. This is done at a set time and lay people may also attend. It is sometimes possible for lay people to stay as guests in a temple or monastery, by arrangement, for some time. Some temples have a few lay people staying permanently to help with cooking, cleaning, gardening and other work in the temple.

In the Southern Buddhist tradition the *Sangha* have two meals a day: breakfast and the main meal, lunch, taken before mid-day. No solid food is taken after mid-day, only drinks such as tea or soup. In other traditions they may have an often uncooked evening medicinal meal. They depend on alms food provided by devotees and generally there is a roster of families providing alms food for the month. The practice is for the *Sangha* to go on an alms round to collect alms in the bowl. This is not begging but gives lay people an opportunity to show their support for the *Sangha* and gain merit. The practice of devotees bringing alms food to temples is growing. In Western countries often food has to be cooked in the temple, since devotees are not able to provide alms food on a regular basis. In Eastern countries too, temples have kitchens and cooking facilities that can be used when alms food is not provided on any day.

Meditation Orders

Some members of the *Sangha* lead ascetic lives away from people, in forests, small islands or secluded monasteries. The emphasis among them is mindfulness and meditation. Lay people may be able to stay as guests by arrangement in some monasteries. The lay people give them the necessary support, including the provision of alms food. Sometimes they are members of forest meditation orders. Meditation orders arrange meditation classes, workshops and retreats for lay people. Certain traditions, such as Zen, concentrate on meditation and ordinary daily tasks are carried out as meditations. In the Northern traditions, life in the temple includes chanting, worship and elaborate meditations and rituals.

Lay People, Laity and Householders

Lay people or householders form the vast majority, more than 95 per cent, of Buddhists. In Southern Buddhist communities there is a noticeable distinction between the lives of the laity and the *Sangha*. In other communities the distinction may be less marked. In all traditions the laity are considered important in that they give material support to the temples and monasteries and carry out daily work providing the economic foundation for the teaching and practice of Buddhism.

Birth, Naming and Growing up

It is common for the father and mother to visit the temple before a baby is born and arrange to receive blessings from the *Sangha* for the baby and themselves. Soon after birth, the baby may be taken to the temple again to receive blessings. There is generally no special initiation to be a Buddhist: if the parents are Buddhists, the baby is assumed to be a Buddhist and brought up accordingly. Many Buddhists choose names that begin with certain auspicious sounds for the children. Often a monk at the temple is consulted as to suitable names.

In some communities a cradle and clothes are prepared and the baby is then ceremonially placed in the cradle and gifts are placed around. Sometimes when the baby is about one month old, its head is shaved and sacred threads, which have been consecrated by a Buddhist ceremony, are tied around the wrists. At these ceremonies the *Sangha* arrange a short worship and are provided with alms food, after which they chant blessings.

Parents are keen that children should acquire a good Buddhist background. Generally there are no life transition ceremonies. In Japan the coming of age as an adult is sometimes celebrated with a special ceremony at the temple. In some traditions, for example in Myanmar and Thailand, teenage boys and girls take novice ordination and live for a short time in a temple, and this is seen as 'growing up'.

Marriage and Family life

Marriage is generally considered a secular matter. The social ceremonies celebrating marriage differ from one country to another. For instance, in Sri Lanka the bride and bridegroom dressed in good clothes stand on a dais, feed each other milk rice, exchange wedding rings and have the small fingers of their hands tied together with thread, to signify their union in marriage, while an older relative repeats certain ceremonial words. It is also customary to have young children chant blessings. Marriage is more a family affair that than one concerning the two people only. Often relatives and friends are invited to a wedding feast. The couple may visit the temple before or after the wedding to receive blessings from the *Sangha*. In Japan the couple may have a Shinto or Buddhist wedding. In the case of a Buddhist wedding ceremony at the temple, a priest officiates and the proceedings include paying homage to the Buddha, receiving holy water for dabbing on the hair, drinking holy wine, exchanging wedding rings and accepting a set of holy beads.

Today legal registration of marriage is the norm and Buddhists comply with the law of the land. Where a man and woman, even without registration of a marriage, live together with a long-term serious commitment to each other and their children, and according to Buddhist family values, they will be considered to be a family. By far the most common form of practice in Buddhist communities is a monogamous marriage. Buddhists and Buddhist families in the West try to lead good Buddhist lives.

In *RukkaDhamma Jataka* the Buddha explained the importance of family relationships and urged the laity to maintain family ties, together with the honour and dignity of the family as a social unit. He expressed the value of solidarity of the family, using the simile of trees in the forest that are able to withstand the force of a gale, while a single tree, however large, is unable to do so. The word 'family' will include two-parent and one-parent families, other relatives living in the household, people living alone and groups of people living in communities. Having an extended family is important among Asian Buddhists and the family is taken to be a supportive social foundation to an individual's life.

Specific Human Relationships

Sigala was the son of a Buddhist family residing in Rajagaha. His parents were devout followers of the Buddha but the son was indifferent to religion and only concerned with material prosperity. When the father was about to die he called his son and gave this advice 'practise dear son, after your morning bath worship the six quarters'. The father hoped that the Buddha would see his son and give him a suitable teaching.

Every morning young Sigala used to worship the six geographical directions – East, South, West, North, overhead and underfoot. One morning the Buddha saw him and asked him what he was doing. Sigala explained that his father had asked him to worship the six directions. 'Look here young man,' the Buddha said, 'Your father's advice is excellent, but the six directions he had in mind are parents, teachers, wife and children, friends, employees and religious persons. They are worthy of honour and respect and should therefore be worshipped by performing one's duties towards them.' Then, after giving him some general moral advice, the Buddha went on to explain these duties in a text called the *Sigalovada Sutta*. This advice teaches Buddhists the significance of learning to apply these values in a wise and compassionate way and helps them to establish a happy and harmonious Buddhist community.

Parents and Children

A child should support elderly parents, perform duties for them, maintain family traditions, be worthy of parents and perform the necessary funeral rites, including offering alms. A parent should guide children away from unskilful actions, encourage them to lead good lives, see to their education, advise them on marriage and hand over their inheritance to them.

Teachers and Pupils

A pupil should respect his teacher, attend on him, be eager to learn, do the work set by him and receive the teaching respectfully. A teacher should teach to the best of his ability, ensure that the pupils understand what is taught, instruct them in arts and sciences, introduce them to friends and associates, give good references and help them in later life.

Husband and Wife

A husband should honour and be courteous to his wife, love her, be faithful, delegate domestic matters to her and provide her with security and comfort. A wife should perform her duties well, be hospitable to relatives and friends, be faithful, manage the household and be skilled in her duties.

Friends, Relatives and Neighbours

A householder should be generous, courteous, helpful, impartial and sincere. In return they should protect him, protect his property, be a refuge from danger, not forsake him in times of difficulty and show consideration for his family.

Employer and Employees

An employer should assign work to employees according to their ability, pay adequate wages, care for them in sickness, share food and drink with them and grant adequate leave. Employees, in turn, should be loyal and industrious, only take their dues, perform their duties well and respect the employer.

Religious Persons

A householder should be respectful to them in deed, word and thought, hospitable and supply religious persons with the materials they need. Religious persons should restrain a lay person from unskilful actions, encourage him in good actions, show loving kindness to him, teach and clarify the teaching and point the way to *Nibbana*.

Death and Passing Away

Death or passing away has a special significance to Buddhists because of the idea of rebirth or rebecoming (see Chapter 8). The physical biological body comes to an end but the mental life energies leave the present body and, with some change, go on to the next life in another body. It is important that the person dies with a calm and peaceful mind, because that state of mind influences the next birth. So when a person is dying the *Sangha* or lay relatives recite or read suitable Buddhist texts to remind the person of the teaching. Often the text that is used is the *Satippattana Sutta*, the important text on meditation and mindfulness (see Appendix I).

The funeral service is not a sad or sombre affair. The atmosphere is one of love and warmth for the departed and a remembrance of the person's good qualities and actions. The *Sangha* conduct the service and chant selected texts dealing with the impermanence of life and other important aspects of the teaching. In Japan it is common to have a Buddhist funeral service. In the Pure Land tradition, the ceremony is considered to be an ordination ceremony to prepare the person to meet the Eternal Buddha. It is normal to cremate the body.

Family and friends arrange memorial services in the temple or at home shortly afterwards and often annually thereafter. The *Sangha* conduct the service either in the shrine room at the temple or at home, where a Buddha image and a small shrine brought by them from the temple will be placed on a table. First there is the offering of flowers, lights and incense and a plate of alms food as a token offering to the Buddha, with the recitation of appropriate words. Then there is a short talk about the deceased person. The alms food is next offered to the *Sangha*. A simple 'transference of merit' ceremony is then performed, with the pouring of water from a jug into a dish until it overflows. This is symbolic of the merit acquired by the ceremony being transferred to the departed one now living another life elsewhere. It is understood that the departed one benefits from this merit. The ceremony ends with the chanting, known as *pirith*, of Buddhist texts and tying of portions of the *pirith* thread on the wrists of the lay people as a blessing (see Chapter 12). The family and friends make gifts of money, books and other things required by the temple in memory of the departed one. Sometimes money is donated for the publication and distribution of books on the *Dhamma*. Some temples arrange a special day in the year when memorial services are held to remember the departed ones of many families.

In some Japanese traditions the family keep memorial tablets of wood, marble or china with the names of departed ones written on them at a small shrine at home. The Japanese festival of *Obon* is devoted to the remembrance of departed relatives.

Chapter 17

Arahats, Bodhisattas and Bodhisattvas

The ideal of the *Arahat* or 'worthy one' comes from the Vedas and is
known to Jainism as well as Buddhism. This is the aim in Southern
Buddhism for an ordinary lay Buddhist. The *Arahat* is one who has
realized *Nibbana* and attained Enlightment. He is comparable to the
Sravaka in Eastern Buddhism. In some countries, such as Myanmar,
certain *Arahats* are worshipped as a field of merit and source of
spiritual protective powers.

Bodhisatta (Pali) or Bodhisattva (Sanskrit) means someone
devoted to, or intent upon, full Enlightenment. The term is commonly
used in Southern Buddhism to refer only to someone seeking
supreme Enlightenment or *Samma-sambodhi*. Therefore Gotama
Buddha became a bodhisatta when he resolved, at the feet of
Buddha Dipankara, to work towards becoming a *Samma Sambuddha*. Three types of bodhisattas are known: the intellectual,
devotional and energetic. The spirit of service to others, compassion,
skill in means and loving-kindness are the predominant qualities of a
bodhisatta.

In Eastern Buddhism a bodhisattva, sometimes referred to in the
texts as a *mahasatta*, is one aspiring to become a fully Enlightened
Buddha. The reference, similarly, is to a *Samma Sambuddha* of
Southern Buddhism, however Eastern Buddhism has a broader
description of the bodhisattva as someone who has:

- taken the *Bodhisattva* vow, or
- developed *Bodhicitta* and is intent on Enlightenment in order to
  help others to progress towards Enlightened, or
- attained Enlightenment and is voluntarily reborn in the Sentient
  world in order to help others to progress towards Enlightenment
  and who has decided to postpone becoming a Buddha until all
  beings attain Enlightenment.

The vows taken by a bodhisattva are expressed a little differently in the different texts. Bodhisattva Samantabhadra, who personifies the transcendental practices and vows of the Buddhas, observed these ten vows set out in the *Avatamsaka Sutra* (Flower Garland Sutra) as follows:

- To worship the Buddhas
- To praise the *tathagatas*
- To make offerings to all the Buddhas
- To confess past sins
- To rejoice in the virtues and happiness of others
- To request Buddha to teach the law
- To request Buddha to live in the world
- To study Buddhism in order to teach it
- To benefit all beings
- To turn over the stock of merit to others.

Eastern Buddhism redefined and expanded the idea of the bodhisattva. It developed the idea of multiple, higher level, celestial bodhisattvas, far advanced on the path having achieved *Nirvana*, who are free from ordinary compulsive rebirth and can freely and voluntarily choose when and where they are to be reborn. They engage in rebirth only to save living beings. Southern Buddhism recognizes only one higher-level bodhisattva at any given time and he decides when and where to be reborn in the last human life in which *Nibbana* is realized.

Northern Buddhism refers to beings who achieve Enlightment, called *mahasiddhas* or *siddhas*. They embody the Northern Buddhism ideals of meditation, personal realization, the master-disciple relationship, the importance of the lay non-monastic life of the householder, and the concept of the wandering yogin. They are real persons of everyday life having transcendental and supernatural powers. They are like the bodhisattvas. They work for the benefit of Sentient beings and end as fully Enlightened beings. They are the main Northern Buddhist or tantric teachers and, on passing away, continue their lives in heavenly worlds. *Mahasiddhas* reappear in the human world from time to time and human beings worship them and may communicate with them.

Aims of Buddhist Practice

The general ultimate aim of Buddhist practice is Enlightment or

Nibbana. Often, Buddhists have a less ambitious intermediate aim, of birth in good circumstances.

In Southern Buddhism there are three types of Enlightment available, depending on a person's temperament, inclination and ability. They are:

- *Sravaka bodhi* or *Arahat bodhi.* The person seeks Enlightment under the guidance and with the help of a superior Enlightened teacher. The *Arahat* spends his life serving and teaching others. The main drawbacks of an *Arahat* are that he does not realize the supreme wisdom of a *Samma Sambuddha* and on passing away he is lost to the world and cannot teach any more. Eastern Buddhism explains that the individual has perceived the Four Noble Truths and realized *Nirvana.*
- *Pacceka bodhi, Pratyekka bodhi* or private *bodhi.* This is Enlightment by one's own efforts and without another teacher. Such a Buddha appears during a period when the teaching is not known to the world and does not go on to become a teacher of gods and humans. Eastern Buddhism says that this individual has seen the twelve links in the chain of causation.
- *Samma-sambodhi.* This is the Buddha who, by his own efforts and at a time when the *Dhamma* is not known, attains supreme Enlightment. The wisdom of a *Samma Sambuddha* is much greater than that of an *Arahat* or *pacceka* Buddha. He comprehends the *Dhamma* without any limitations and can teach it to heavenly beings and all other Sentient beings. A a *Samma Sambuddha* follows the bodhisatta path in all of the traditions (Eastern, Northern and Southern) and this path to help other beings to progress on the path of the Buddhas.

These are not three separate attainments but three stages in the same path. The Sanskrit writers referred to the three ways or *yanas* corresponding to the three *bodhis* as:

- *Sravaka yana*
- *Pratyeka Buddha yana*
- *Samma Sambuddha yana.*

In Eastern Buddhism the aim is to become a fully Enlightened Buddha, comparable in level to the *Samma Sambuddha* of Southern Buddhism. The path to this ideal is the bodhisattva path. Hence, the bodhisattva became the most important figure in Eastern Buddhism after a Buddha. The bodhisattva path came to be described with much elaboration and detail. That they wish to help others along the Buddhist path received much emphasis and became an important characteristic of the bodhisattva. Santideva says in the *Bodhicaryavatara*, about 725 (pp. 10.55):

> As long as space abides and as long as the world abides, so long may I abide, destroying the sufferings of the world.

This is an extension of the idea of compassion, common to all traditions.

Compared to the *Arahat*, who is represented as a saintly, austere and somewhat self-centred ascetic, the bodhisattva is represented as a friendly, warm and compassionate person whose main aim is to help people. This is, in fact, the same as the Southern Buddhist view of the bodhisatta: Gotama Buddha progressed through the bodhisatta path and became a Buddha for this same purpose of helping others. The characteristic of wanting to help others is common to bodhisattas both in Southern and Eastern Buddhism.

The Eastern Buddhism classification of the ideals is similar, but with the addition of a fourfold bodhisattva ideal:

- *Sravakas* or disciples
- *Pratyeka Buddhas*
- Bodhisattvas
- Buddhas *(Samma Sambuddhas)*.

These are again considered to be four attainments on the same path. The *Saddharma Pundarika* (Lotus) *Sutra* states:

> To those who sought to be Sravakas he taught response to the Law of the Four Noble Truths for escape from birth, old age, disease, and death leading finally to Nirvana; to those who sought to be Pratyeka Buddhas he taught response to the Law of the Twelve Causes; to Bodhisattvas he by means of the Perfect Enlightenment taught response to the Six Paramitas for perfecting Buddha wisdom.
>
> *Saddharma Pundarika Sutra*, pp. 42 and 290

The paths are referred to respectively as *Sravaka yana*, *Pratyeka Buddha yana*, and bodhisattva *yana*. Quite clearly the bodhisattva path became the most important, respected and sought-after path. It is this bodhisattva *yana* that later came to be called Eastern Buddhism.

Bodhisatta/Bodhisattva Virtues or Perfections

Southern Buddhism enumerates ten virtues (*Paramis*) that must be cultivated by a person to progress on the bodhisatta path. They are developed in the order in which they are enumerated and then practised all together, with practice becoming progressively deeper and more refined. The Buddhist scholar Venerable Narada Mahathera explains in his book *The Buddha and His Teaching*, 1964, that practice must be guided by reason, uninfluenced by selfish motives and cultivated with compassion towards all living beings. The *Jataka* stories (life stories of Gotama Buddha in the Pali Canon) describe how he, as a bodhisatta, developed and refined these perfections over many lifetimes (see Chapter 1)

The ten *Paramis* are as follows:

1. *Dana* (generosity). Working for the benefit of other beings, with no reward asked for or expected and without investigating whether they are worthy or not reduces selfishness, eliminates greed and increases loving-kindness towards others. The *Vyaghri Jataka* relates how the bodhisatta sacrificed his own life and gave up his body to provide food for a starving tigress. This *Parami* involves developing non-attachment to material or mental worldly things. The *Vessantara Jataka* relates how the bodhisatta, just one life away from the life when he would realize *Nibbana*, had developed the quality of non-attachment to such a high degree that, when tested by Sakra, the chief of the deities, he indicated a willingness to give away his children and wife, knowing through his developed mind that this would not in fact come about (see Chapter 1).

2. *Sila* (morality). This is living a virtuous and ethical life according to the Five Precepts and performance of duties towards others. The *Sigalovada Sutta* sets out the various duties and obligations relating to common social relationships. The importance of this *Parami* is indicated by the Bodhisatta's words, 'Apart from virtue wisdom has no worth', in the *Silavimamsa Jataka*.

3. *Nekhamma* (renunciation). This involves a renunciation of worldly pleasures (attachment to which is a hindrance to progress), leading the life of an ascetic and living in the present with few needs.

4. *Panna* (wisdom). The bodhisatta makes an effort to arrive at a

right understanding of the nature of life and the world in the light of impermanence, *Dukkha* and selflessness or *anatta*. Here wisdom means not only intellectual knowledge but also the higher wisdom that comes from mindfulness and meditation.

5. *Viriya* (energy). Mental strength and continuing persistent effort that develops strength of character and self-reliance.

6. *Khanti* (patience). Patient endurance of suffering, misfortune and unhappiness, forbearance for the wrongs of others and not being provoked to retaliation.

7. *Sacca* (truthfulness). To be trustworthy, sincere, honest, consistent and straightforward, and always truthful.

8. *Aditthana* (determination). Not to be put off by difficulties and misplaced criticism. The development of will power.

9. *Metta* (loving-kindness, benevolence, warmth). Respect, benevolence, goodwill and friendliness towards all Sentient beings. To identify oneself with all Sentient beings and not to discriminate between oneself and others (see Chapter 11).

10. *Upekkha* (equanimity, serenity). To view things justly and impartially without attachment or aversion. To develop an even temperament and perfect mental equilibrium and not react emotionally with love or anger at things, situations or persons, but without being cut off from them (see Chapter 15).

In addition to the above, the bodhisatta practises three modes of conduct, namely doing good with wisdom, working for the progress of family and relatives, and working similarly for all Sentient beings.

These *Paramis* are perfected over many lifetimes in which a bodhisatta is born as an animal, human being or deva (heavenly being). When the *Paramis* are perfected a bodhisatta seeks birth in the *Tusita* heaven until he decides that it is the correct time to be reborn in the human world for his last life, during which he will attain Buddhahood.

The *Prajna Paramita* (Perfection of Wisdom) *Sutra* and the *Saddharma Pundarika* (Lotus) *Sutra* set out six *Paramita*s in Eastern Buddhism. The later *Dasabhumika* (10-stage) *Sutra* adds another four, to give a total of ten *Paramitas*. These relate, in sequence, to the ten bodhisattva *bhumis*. The *Paramitas*, like the Southern Buddhism *Paramis*, are developed in the order of enumeration and practised all at once with increasing depth, concentration and refinement. They form a simple, accessible practice leading to stages of spiritual development unattainable in the world of ordinary human life. A systematic outline of bodhisattva practice is set out in Santideva's *Bodhicaryavatara*, about 725.

The ten *Paramitas* are:

1. *Dana* (generosity, liberality)
2. *Sila* (morality, discipline)
3. *Kshanti* (patience, patient endurance)
4. *Viriya* (energy)
5. *Dhyana* (contemplation, meditation, absorption)
6. *Prajna Paramita* (perfection of wisdom)
7. *Upaya* (skilful means)
8. *Pranidhana* (resolution)
9. *Bala* (power)
10. *Jnana* (knowledge).

Table of perfections

Southern Buddhism		Eastern and Northern Buddhism	
Order of perfections	Paramis	Order of perfections	Paramitas
1	*Dana* (generosity)	A	*Dana* (generosity) 1
2	*Sila* (morality)	B	*Sila* (morality) 2, 7
3	*Nekhamma* (renunciation) G	C	*Kshanti* (patience) 6
4	*Panna* (wisdom) J	D	*Viriya* (energy) 5
5	*Viriya* (energy) E, I	E	*Dhyana* (meditation) 5,9
6	*Khanti* (patience) F	F	*Prajna Paramita* (wisdom) 4
7	*Sacca* (truthfulness) B	G	*Upaya* (skilful means) 3,9,10
8	*Aditthana* (determination)	H	*Pranidhana* (resolution) 8
9	*Metta* (loving kindness) G, E	I	*Bala* (power) 5
10	*Upekkha* (equanimity) G	J	*Jnana* (knowledge) 4

Although there are slight differences in the wording, the *Paramis* in Southern Buddhism and *Paramitas* in Eastern Buddhism can be related to one another. The renunciation, loving-kindness and equanimity in Southern Buddhism can be related to the skilful means in Eastern Buddhism. The truthfulness in Southern Buddhism can be related to morality in Eastern Buddhism. Meditation in Eastern Buddhism can be related to energy and loving-kindness in Southern Buddhism; and the power and knowledge in Eastern Buddhism can be related to energy and wisdom respectively in Southern Buddhism.

Paths of the Arahat and Bodhisattva

Southern Buddhism gives details of the graded path of the *Arahat*, step by step, to *Nibbana*. It does not give a similar graded path of the bodhisatta, although it gives the ten virtues or *Paramis* that have to be practised by bodhisatta. Eastern Buddhism, because of the special place it gives to the bodhisattva, has developed a detailed step-by-step path of the bodhisattva through the bodhisattva *bhumis*.

The path of the *Arahat* is through the practice of the Noble Eightfold Path. This is divided into *sila* (morality), *samadhi* (mindfulness, awareness and meditation) and *panna* (wisdom). The pilgrim realizes that his existence is due to ignorance, craving, grasping, *kamma* (intentional actions) and physical food. He contemplates on *anicca* (impermanence), *Dukkha* (dissatisfaction or non-ease) and *anatta* (no self). He realizes that the stream of life is conditioned by internal and external causes and that mind and matter are in a state of constant change. When he realizes this he has a fleeting glimpse of *Nibbana*.

The Four Stages of Sotapanna, Sakadagami, Anagami and Arahat

Before entering the path, the person is referred to as a worldling. A pilgrim on the Path is referred to as an *ariya* or noble one. There are four stages in the path followed by an *ariya* on the way to realizing *Nibbana* and becoming an *Arahat* by eradicating the ten fetters or characteristics. The four stages are:

- The first is *sotapanna* (stream winner). The stream represents the Noble Eightfold Path and now the *ariya* is firmly established and has entered the stream leading to *Nibbana*. At this stage he overcomes three fetters, namely: a view of a permanent self; doubts about the Buddha, *Dhamma* and the *Sangha*; and adherence to rites and ceremonies. Now the individual will be reborn seven times at the most.

- The second stage is that of a *sakadagami* (once returner to the human world). The *ariya* now develops two characteristics: detachment from sense desires; and freedom from ill will. Should the *ariya* not attain arahatship in that birth itself, he will now be born only once more in the human world.
- The third stage is that of *anagami* (never returner). Now the *ariya* completely eradicates the first five fetters or characteristics and progresses to overcome the next five. These are: attachment to form realms; attachment to formless realms; pride; restlessness; and ignorance. It is understood that the *anagami* on passing away is reborn in the heavenly pure abodes (*suddhavasa*).
- At the fourth stage of *Arahat* all these fetters or characteristics are completely transcended and eliminated. In the first three stages, the *ariya* is referred to as a *Sekha* because he has to undergo more training. An *Arahat* is called an *asekha,* as he does not have to undergo any further training. The *Arahat* has now attained Enlightment and *Nibbana*. He is not wholly free from dissatisfaction or suffering because the *kammic* forces that produced his birth are not fully spent. He will not, however, accumulate any new *kamma* and will not be reborn. Until he passes away he lives in a peaceful and happy state, teaching others by example and *Dhamma* talks. The passing away of an *Arahat* at the end of his life is similar to the *Parinibbana* of a Buddha, in that it is the further *Nibbana* of one who has already attained *Nibbana*.

These four stages are explained similarly in Eastern Buddhism. The *Saddharma Pundiraka Sutra* (p. 270) refers to:

- *Srota-appana*, one who has entered the stream leading to *Nirvana*
- *Sakrdagamin*, one who returns or is reborn once more
- *Anagamin*, one who does not return
- *Arhat*, one who is free from all attachment and craving and, hence, from rebirth.

The paths of a *Pacceka Buddha* and *Samma Sambuddha* are the bodhisatta paths. In Southern Buddhist teaching it is not set out as a graded path. It consists of the development and refinement of virtues or *Paramis* given above and is demonstrated by the lives of Gotama Buddha.

The Ten Stages of the Bodhisattva Path

The aim in Eastern Buddhism is to become a fully Enlightened Buddha (*Samma Sambuddha*) and therefore the bodhisattva path has a special place. The *Avatamsaka, Bodhisattva Bhumi* and *Dasabhumika Sutras* set out the ten stages of the this parth, which are linked to the ten *Paramitas* and entered into after developing *Bodhicitta*. These are:

1. *Pramudita* (joyful). Rejoicing in bodhi and in the fact that he will help all beings the bodhisattva develops (*dana*, generosity).
2. *Vimala* (immaculate, pure). The bodhisattva develops *Sila* (morality) according to the Five Precepts.
3. *Prabhakari* (illuminating). The bodhisattva understands the reality of things and develops *kshanti* (patience).
4. *Arismati* (radiant). The bodhisattva overcomes ignorance and false ideas and develops *viriya* (energy).
5. *Sudurjaya* (difficult to conquer). The bodhisattva perfects his knowledge of the *Dharma* and develops dhyana (meditation).
6. *Abhimati* (face to face). Perfecting himself in *Prajna* (wisdom), the bodhisattva now understands the chain of causation, no-self and emptiness, and stands face-to-face with *Nirvana*. At this stage the Bodhisattva is equal in spiritual development to an *Arahat*. He can leave the round of rebirths and enter *Nirvana* at the end of his life. The ascetic Sumedha was at this stage when, at the feet of Buddha Dipankara, he renounced the aspiration to enter *Nirvana* and resolved, out of great compassion for beings, to become a Buddha like Buddha Dipankara and help other beings to progress on the Buddhist path. Likewise a bodhisattva, because of his great compassion for beings, decides to be reborn in order to help other beings. Once the bodhisattva has reached this stage there is no regression; the only way is forward.
7. *Durangama* (far going). At this stage the bodhisattva, now referred to as a *mahasattva*, goes beyond being reborn according to *karma*. The practical aspects of the bodhisattva's career are concluded. He is now able to assume different forms – animal, human, heavenly and so on – to assist others. He develops *upaya* (skilful means).
8. *Acala* (immovable). The bodhisattva enters Buddha land and is now certain of Buddhahood. He possesses supreme knowledge, masters the art of transfer of merit and is able to give spiritual

help to beings who pray to him. He can now appear in any form anywhere in the universe to teach beings. He develops *parinamana* (turning over merit).

9. *Sadhumati* (good mind, teacher of the *Dhamma*). The bodhisattva acquires the four *pratisamvidis* (elements of analytical knowledge) and gains insight into the character of beings. He teaches the *Dhamma*, is able to direct beings to Enlightment and develops *bala* (power).

10. *Dharmamega* (cloud of the Dharma) – The bodhisattva has now perfected the ten powers of a Buddha, becomes a *tathagata* and has all the characteristics, including *jnana* (knowledge) of a Buddha. He is enshrined in the *Dharma-kaya*, but is still a bodhisattva living in *Tusita* Heaven.

The last step is when the Bodhisattva attains Buddhahood, sometimes expressed as 'the *tathagatas* consecrate the bodhisattva to full Buddhahood'. According to Northern Buddhism teaching, the bodhisattva attains Buddhahood through tantric practice.

These ten stages or *bhumis* are common to most Eastern Buddhism traditions. Different traditions emphasize them differently and some traditions explain that Enlightment is a sudden radical development of the consciousness.

Southern Buddhism			Eastern and Northern Buddhism
Arahat Path	Paccekka Buddha Path	Bodhisatta path	Bodhisattva Path
1			1
			2
			3
2			4
			5
3			6
4			7
Arahat			8
	Pacceka Buddha		9
			10
		Samma Sambuddha	Samma Sambuddha

Named Buddhas, Bodhisattas and Bodhisattvas

Southern Buddhism accepts 28 named Buddhas, although there were many others before. The current teaching is that of Gotama Buddha, the twenty-eighth. The previous Buddha was Kassapa Buddha and the next Buddha will be Metteyya Buddha, who now lives as a bodhisatta in *Tusita* heaven. In Eastern and Northern Buddhism, Gotama Buddha is called Sakyamuni Buddha, and there are others such as Amitabha, Bhaisajya-guru and Vairochana, who are *dhyana* Buddhas, states of realization rather than persons. Northern Buddhism knows of numerous Buddhas, including Buddha Tara, a fully Enlightened female Buddha. These Buddhas continue to teach simultaneously in their own Buddha fields.

The Pali Canon refers to various *Arahats*, such as Theri Kisagotami and Venerable Rahula. The *Isigili Sutta* gives the names of several *paccekka* Buddhas in Southern Buddhism, for example Arittha, Yasassin, and Sudassana. The lives of Bodhisatta Gotama are given in the *Jataka* stories of the Pali Canon. According to Southern Buddhism, Bodhisatta Metteyya now lives in *Tusita* heaven and there are no other named current bodhisattas.

Eastern Buddhism acknowledges several bodhisattvas. Each has a special characteristic. For instance, Bodhisattvas Avalokatisvera (he who hearkens to the cries of the world) known for compassion (*karuna*), Manjushri for wisdom (*Prajna*) and Maitreya known for friendliness (*maitri*), who will become the next Buddha, and Tara, a female bodhisattva known for compassion. They are all tenth stage bodhisattvas or *mahasattvas*. Avalokatisvera manifests in Tibet as the male Chenrezi, in China in the female form of Kuan Yin and in Japan, again in the female form, of Kannon or Kanzeon. The male or female gender distinction is not relevant at this stage. Northern Buddhism refers to named *mahasiddhas*, for example, Ti-lo-pa (988–1069), Na-ro-pa (1016–1100) and Vajrabodhi (about the eighth century).

Chapter 18

The Buddha

The current Buddha *Sasana* (dispensation) was firmly established in the lifetime of Gotama Buddha. During Emperor Asoka's reign in India, third century BCE, there began some discussion and speculation about the personality of the Buddha. The concept of the Buddha became one of the most important and intellectually exciting topics of discussion in the history of Buddhist thought. From its original meaning of teacher or *Arahat*, the concept went through several stages of development, refinement and extension. In the present day its meanings include 'absolute reality' and the 'Buddha nature' in each living being (see summary at the end of this chapter).

The word 'Buddha' has been used in different religious traditions in India to describe those who have had a transforming and liberating insight into the nature of reality. For instance, the Jain religion applies it to *Mahavira*. It is not a proper name but a generic name that places a person within a class and essentially indicates a move to the highest level of consciousness.

The Pali word '*Budh*' means to wake up, understand or perceive. So a Buddha is one who has awakened, eliminated greed, hatred and ignorance and realized the truth or absolute reality. We say that the person has realized *Nibbana* (*Nirvana*) or Enlightenment or release from *Dukkha*, meaning suffering, dissatisfaction, imperfection and mental non-ease. *Nibbana* does not mean the cessation of life (see Chapter 5). It means the acquisition of that wisdom in which one is free from *Dukkha* in the midst of the *Dukkha* of birth, life, illness, ageing and passing away, and the peace of mind resulting from the acquisition of this wisdom. It is a state of consciousness.

In understanding a Buddha to be one who has attained *Nibbana*, in other words a living being whose consciousness has realized absolute reality, Southern Buddhism recognizes three types of Buddhas, namely:

- *Arahat* (*savaka*, listener, disciple) Buddhas who attain *Arahat bodhi*
- *Pacceka* Buddhas who attain *Pacceka bodhi*
- *Samma Sambuddhas* (universal, fully, perfectly Enlightened Buddhas) who attain *Samma Sambodhi*.

The *Arahat* attains *Nibbana* at a time when Buddha teaching prevails in the world and with the guidance and help of the teaching of a *Samma Sambuddha*. The *Pacceka* Buddha attains *Nibbana* solely by his own efforts at a time when the teaching is not known in the world. Neither the *Arahat* nor the *Pacceka* Buddha goes on to establish a Buddha *Sasana*. The *Samma Sambuddha*, the highest level of Buddhahood, attains *Nibbana* by his own efforts at a time when the teaching is not known in the world. He has the greatest powers and goes on to teach and establish a Buddha *Sasana* that carries on in the world for several thousand years after him.

Saddharma Pundarika Sutra (pp. 42 and 290) explains that Eastern and Northern Buddhism, likewise, recognize *Sravaka* Buddhas (*Arahats*), *Pratyeka* Buddhas (*Pacceka* Buddhas), and perfectly Enlightened *Samma Sambuddhas*, and describes them in similar terms (see Chapter 17). Eastern Buddhism developed the idea of innumerable Buddhas and teaches of celestial Buddhas, cosmic Buddhas, *Dhyani* Buddhas (transcendental Buddhas) and an *adi* Buddha (primary Buddha or Buddha principle). Eastern Buddhism also developed the idea of the Eternal Buddha – the earthly form being a temporary manifestation of this Eternal Buddha – and explains the Buddha under the three aspects of the *Trikaya*.

In all the traditions, by custom the use of the word Buddha by itself, refers to a perfectly Enlightened *Samma Sambuddha* or Universal Buddha (this practice is followed in this chapter). The *Arahats* (*Sravakas*), *Pacceka* (*Prateyka*) Buddhas, Bodhisattvas and *Samma Sambuddhas* are considered attainments on the same path. On being questioned by a Brahmin called Dona, Gotama Buddha said: 'I am not a deity ... nor a heavenly musician... nor a demon... nor a human being... but a Buddha.'[1]

Therefore we understand that a *Samma Sambuddha* is a very special category of living being. Some Eastern Buddhism traditions consider the Buddha to be an active, living, dynamic spiritual force who could ease the path of a Buddhist pilgrim towards Buddhahood.

Lobsang Phuntok Lhalunga explains the view in Northern Buddhism:

> When a Tibetan takes refuge in the Buddha he is vowing to attempt to reach Buddhahood, to follow the career of a Bodhisattva. There have been in the past, are now in the present, and will be in the future, many Buddhas. When a human being has attained the highest development possible of the love, wisdom, intuition, resolution, spiritual power, and other qualities of a Buddha such a human being can only be compared to other Buddhas [...]. Tibetans believe that the Lord Buddha is still spiritually active and that he continues to guide, inspire, and protect the spiritual life...' (Lhalungpa, 1956)[2]

Nowhere in any of the schools or traditions is the Buddha equated to a God or Creator of the world or a saviour of human beings or one who can either punish or forgive sins or transgressions.

Other respectful terms are used to refer to the Buddha. For instance:

- *Baghavat* – awakened one
- *Tathagata* – one who has attained the truth
- *Arahat* – one worthy of offerings
- *Sugata* – well gone
- *Lokavidu* – knower of worlds
- *Awakened one* – awakened from the sleep of ignorance.

Multiple Buddhas

Southern Buddhism teaches that a bodhisatta becomes Enlightened as a Buddha and establishes a Buddha *Sasana* community that carries on for a time and then comes to an end. No Buddha appears until the *Sasana* of the previous Buddha has ended. There is a cycle – a series of Buddhas one after another. Twenty-eight Buddhas over different cosmic periods are named by Southern Buddhism. In the present cosmic period there are three before Gotama Buddha, including Buddha Kassapa who immediately preceded him, and the fifth Metteyya (Maitreya) who is yet to come. Gotama Buddha referred to the Teaching as 'the way trodden by the ancient Buddhas,' and said that there had been many Buddhas before and there were many to come.

Southern Buddhism points to a unity among Buddhas. The word 'Buddha' is taken to refer to all Enlightened ones: 'There is no distinction in form, morality, concentration, wisdom, freedom [...] among all the Buddhas, because all the Buddhas are the same in respect of their nature' (Horner, 1964).[3] Their common identity is expressed in two ways namely:

- The special characteristics associated with the Buddha
- Buddhahood expressed through the language of the Buddha bodies, e.g. a body 'born of *Dharma'*.

The teaching of the different Buddhas is the same – all Buddhas teach the same eternal truths. This teaching is a part of nature and is the absolute reality so far as Buddhism is concerned. This idea that the teaching remains the same although there are many different Buddhas was developed by Eastern Buddhism into the *Trikaya* doctrine.

Although there can be only one *Samma Sambuddha* in a Buddha *Sasana* and no *Paceka* Buddhas can arise in that period, there may be *Arahats*. An *Arahat* is technically a Buddha and an *Arahat* Buddha may exist during the life of a *Samma Sambuddha*. Therefore according to Southern Buddhism it is also possible to have more than one Buddha at a given time.

Eastern Buddhism developed the idea of multiple Buddhas living and teaching simultaneously in different worlds: human and heavenly. It also developed the idea of a Universal or Eternal Buddha. All Buddhas were reduced to a unity, each associated with the same teaching or *Dharmakaya*. All of these Buddhas, past, present and future living in different worlds realize and teach the same *Dharma*.

The original Buddhist community consisted of monks, nuns, laymen and laywomen. Southern Buddhism texts reflect the social order in India at the time of Gotama Buddha and do not specifically refer to women attaining Buddhahood. However, considering the doctrine of rebirth – where a being of one gender can be born in the next life in the other gender, and that in certain higher worlds gender difference is irrelevant – Southern Buddhism does not exclude the possibility of women aspiring to Buddhahood. Eastern Buddhism teaches that women can attain Buddhahood, the Buddha nature being common to all living beings. It points out that because of the universal concept of *sunyata* (emptiness), gender difference is also made empty and irrelevant. In the *Saddharma Pundarika Sutra* (p. 216), the Buddha addresses Bhikshunis Mahaprajapati and Yasodhara and predicts that both of them will in time become Buddhas (see Chapter 2). Further, it should to be kept in mind that at the final stage, Enlightment is simply a change in consciousness.

Historical Buddha

The current teaching is that of Gotama Buddha or Sakyamuni Buddha, the historical Buddha common to all schools and traditions. He lived about the sixth century BCE. (see Chapter 2). The main features of the lives of other Buddhas are similar to the life of Gotama Buddha. The Enlightment he achieved was the same as that of other Buddhas past and future and his teaching is the same.

Even after Enlightment he was subject to the *Dukkha* of hunger, thirst, illness and old age. Although dying will be *Dukkha* in the case of an ordinary being, it will not be so in the case of a Buddha attaining *Parinibbana* because it is not followed by rebirth or anything else.

Southern Buddhism emphasizes the human nature of Gotama Buddha even after Enlightment and refers to him as an extraordinary human being. Over the many lives previous to his last birth as a bodhisatta in the human world, he had developed and perfected the qualities, *Paramis*, which marked his progress to becoming a Buddha (see Chapter 1). Finally he came to live in the *Tusita* heaven, from where the bodhisatta was able to observe the human world. This was a time when the Buddha *Sasana* of the previous Buddha Kassapa had come to an end and the teaching was not known in the world. The bodhisatta, at the invitation of the deities, understanding the need of human beings for the *Dhamma*, decided to come down to the human world in order to attain Enlightenment and teach the *Dhamma*. At the time of his birth in the human world as a prince, his mind would have been highly developed and refined as a bodhisatta, but needed a little more refinement to attain Enlightenment as a *Samma Sambuddha*.

Even among human beings we notice wide differences of intellect, mental refinement and spirituality. Therefore, although Southern Buddhism refers to him as a human being, there must have been a substantial difference between his consciousness and that of an ordinary human being even at the time of his birth. The next Buddha, Buddha Metteyya (Maitriya), recognized as such by all traditions, now lives in the *Tusita* heaven until it is time to be born in the human world to become Enlightened as a Buddha.

Eastern Buddhism likewise teaches that Sakyamuni Buddha had, over many previous lives as a bodhisattva, perfected the qualities, *Paramitas* (same as the Southern Buddhism *Paramis*, see Chapter 17) that prepared him for Buddhahood and progressed through the ten stages of the bodhisattva path. As a tenth-stage bodhisattva he was living in the Buddha world (heavenly world) until the time was ripe for him to appear in the human world as a human being. When he did appear in the human world it was as a *Nirmanakaya*, a manifestation of the *Dharmakaya*, or Eternal Buddha, and the only purpose was to teach the *Dharma* to living beings and lead them on the path to Buddhahood.

Qualities of the Buddha

These are recollected as a part of Buddhist worship (see Chapter 12). The Pali Canon sets out further qualities of the Buddha gained by the practice of *Sila* (morality), *samadhi* (contemplation, mindfulness and meditation) and *panna* (wisdom). These are:

1. *Tivijja*. The threefold knowledge:
   - Memory of one's former births
   - Knowledge of the appearance, disappearance and re-appearance of beings
   - Knowledge to achieve the total eradication of passions.
2. *Chalabinna*. The sixfold higher knowledge. The above three, plus:
   - Psychic power
   - Divine ear
   - Ability to see into the minds of others.
3. *Dasabala*. Ten intellectual powers that consist of knowing:
   - What is a causal situation
   - Actions and their results (*kamma*)
   - Course that leads to *Nibbana*
   - World of various and diverse elements
   - Various characters of beings
   - Varied spiritual nature of beings
   - Defilements and purification from them by meditation and mindfulness
   - The threefold knowledge above.
4. *Catu-vesarajja*. The fourfold self-confidence regarding:
   - Perfection of his Enlightenment
   - Total eradication of passions by self-effort

- The hindrances on the path
- Nature, quality and effectiveness of the middle path he taught.
5. Further attributes of the Buddha, namely:
  - Five eyes of knowledge and wisdom
  - Omniscience not obstructed by anyone or anything
  - Fourteen areas of special knowledge.

Development of the Buddha Concept

Gotama Buddha's followers considered him an incomparable teacher. Superhuman intellectual, moral, and physical qualities were attributed to him even while alive and many followers thought of him as a *deva* or deity. A monk, Venerable Vakkali used to come and gaze at Gotama Buddha. When questioned why he did this he replied that it was because Gotama Buddha looked so attractive. The Buddha responded: 'What does it mean to you ... this body of mine which you see before your eyes. Whoever sees the Dhamma sees me, and whoever sees me sees the Dhamma.[4]

No Buddha passes away until the *Sasana* is firmly established. The *Dhamma* continues after the passing away of a Buddha. In time the knowledge and practice gradually diminishes and is finally lost to humans. There is a time when it is not known to the world until another bodhisatta achieves Enlightment as a *Samma Sambuddha* and begins to teach. During the period of time when teaching is unknown, the laws of the teaching still operate in the universe.

From early times Southern Buddhism distinguished between the two bodies of the Buddha:

- The *Rupakaya*, the physical body
- The *Dhammakaya*, body of truth.

Venerable Nagasena says, '... it is possible to point to the Lord (Gotama Buddha) by means of the body of Dhamma, for the Dhamma (Dhammakayena)... was taught by the Lord.' (Horner, 1964).[5]

Spiritualization seems to be indicated in the Pali Canon and has been developed in Pali commentaries. If the historical Buddha Gotama was born in the world through his own wish and decision and because of his compassion for all beings in order to teach them the path to *Nibbana*, was there not a fundamental Buddha as the foundation of the historical Buddha?

According to the law of *anatta*, Gotama Buddha who appeared in this world was a grouping of the five aggregates or energies, namely: body, feelings, perceptions, volitions and consciousness. The *Dhamma* or teaching must have been an element of those feelings, perceptions, volitions and consciousness.

The Pali commentaries argue that since the historical Buddhas realize *Nibbana* or attain Enlightment by realizing the *Dhamma*, the *Dhamma* or teaching is permanent and continuing, and is revealed through the personal form of a historical Buddha. Consequently the *Dhamma* is the fundamental Buddha and the Buddha is the *Dhamma* personified.

Sanskrit writers expanded on the special qualities of the Buddha, fundamentally similar,but more elaborate and detailed than in the Pali Canon. Eastern Buddhism developed the idea that Buddhahood should be the aim of every person. It explained the bodhisattva path, the gradual development of the individual in ten stages, *dasa bhumi*, ending in Buddhahood. They noted the Buddha's special powers that enabled him to appear among different kinds of beings in different forms. Among humans he appeared as a human being and among deities as a deity (see Chapter 17).

About the year 200, pious followers began to consider him as being above normal human standards. A teacher possessed of numerous qualities not even possessed by *Arahats*, they argued, he must be far above the status of even an extraordinary human being. Texts like the *Mahavastu* and *Lalitavistara* indicate that the Buddha is above the laws and conditions of normal human existence. He appeared as a human being by his own powers and acted as human being in order to conform to the customs of the world but was really above all human needs and weaknesses. His appearance and behaviour as a human being was an illusion.

Eastern Buddhism developed the ideas of immortality, multiplicity/infinity of Buddhas, simultaneous existence of numerous Buddhas, spiritualization of Buddhas and cosmic body.

Immortality

According to the Pali tradition the Buddha after *Parinibbana* was not known to humans and deities. The Sanskrit texts lengthened the life span of the Buddha until the Buddha was credited with immortality. They argued that a being with the qualities of the Buddha must be divine and continue to exist, being eternal. Buddha explains that he became Enlightened countless eons ago. Over the ages since then he had already appeared on Earth in the form of past Buddhas, such as Dipankara, and taught according to peoples' spiritual capacities. Buddhas pass into *Nirvana*, beyond contact with human beings in order to ensure that people do not become overly dependent on Buddhas, but use the teaching instead. *Saddharma Pundarika Sutra*, states:

> Since I attained Buddhahood,
> The kalpas through which I have passed
> Are infinite thousands of myriads . . .
> Yet truly I am not [yet] extinct
> But forever here preaching the Law
> I forever remain in this [world] . . .
> *Saddharma Pundarika Sutra*, Ch. XVl, p. 254

In *The World of Tibetan Buddhism*, 1995 (p. 100), Tenzin Gyatso the XVl Dalai Lama states that:

> In order to actualize the omniscient mind of the buddhahood, it is necessary to realize the nature of the mind. This mind, whose nature we realize in order to actualize omniscience, must be a very special type of mind, which, in terms of its continuity, is eternal.

Multiplicity

The number of Buddhas was multiplied and finally it was stated that the Buddhas were infinite in number, 'Countless like the sands on the Banks of the Ganges.' (*Lalitavistara*, p. 273).

Simultaneous Existence

Eastern Buddhism developed the idea of the simultaneous existence of numerous Buddhas.

Spiritualization

If the Buddha is immortal his physical body does not represent his true body, it was said, and therefore he must be a divine and spiritual being who assumes a physical form in order to teach living beings. This corresponds with the Southern Buddhist view that the physical body, *Rupakaya*, does not represent his true body. Sanskrit writers distinguished between the heavenly Buddha Sakyamuni, an eternal being, and earthly Buddha Sakyamuni, a manifestation projected into earthly life by the transcendent heavenly Buddha.

Cosmic Body

Eastern Buddhist writers said that Buddha represents the *Dharma*, which is his real body; and that his real body is a cosmic body also. They named the Buddha's spiritual and cosmic body *Dharmakaya*. This idea was seen in Southern Buddhism, for instance, when Gotama Buddha advised Venerable Vakkali to look at the *Dhamma*, and in the *Mahaparinibbana Sutra*: '... Ananda, for what I have taught and explained to you as Dhamma and discipline will, at my passing, be your teacher.' (Walshe, 1995, p. 270).[6]

Sanskrit writers developed these ideas further. The *Dharmakaya* was linked with the constituents of the universe and the *Dharma* teaching as a part of nature and the universe. The next step was to say that all living beings live within, and have their being in, the *Dharmakaya*. Finally they said that the *Dharmakaya* was the same as absolute reality. In the Pali Canon the Buddha is identified with the *Dhamma* and also with absolute reality. The three factors Buddha, *Dhamma* and *Pratityasamutpada* were mutually identified, 'Whoever sees the Pratityasamutpada sees the Dharma, whoever sees the Dharma sees the Buddha.'

Northern Buddhists said that the Buddha was capable of forming a mind-made body that enabled him to visit the heavens and could form exact replicas of his physical form. Southern Buddhism also speaks of the Buddha visiting *Tavatimsa* heaven, where his mother was living, in order to teach the deities, including her, the *Dhamma* and *Abhidhamma*. Buddhists understand that Gotama Buddha visited several places in South Asia, including Kelaniya and Nagadipa in Sri Lanka.

Eastern Buddhist Teaching

Eastern Buddhism now had to reconcile five ideas:

- Oneness and plurality of the Buddha
- Buddha being a permanent spiritual cosmic principle and the appearance of earthly Buddhas
- Presence of innumerable Buddhas in different worlds

- Appearance of the Buddha in different forms
- Connection between the Buddha and living beings.

This was done by formulating the *Trikaya* doctrine. The triple nature of the *tathagata* is that it is at one with the absolute, one actively pursuing the welfare of bodhisattvas and one actively pursuing the welfare of human beings. This is the philosophical basis for the *Trikaya* doctrine, which explains that the Buddha has three kinds of bodies:

- *Dharmakaya* – one immortal *Dharma* body
- *Sambhogakaya* – many non-immortal bliss bodies
- *Nirmanakaya* – many non-immortal transformation bodies.

The many Buddhas in the form of *Sambhogakaya* and *Nirmanakaya* are spiritually united in the *Dharmakaya* or absolute reality. Buddhahood unites all Buddhas in one wisdom and one aim. The Buddha is not different from other beings. The essence of the Buddha is in each being and every being has the capacity to attain Buddhahood (meaning Enlightenment). At this point we find that Buddhahood, Enlightenment and *Nirvana* mean the same thing.

The *Dharmakaya* was too abstract a concept to become an object of religious consciousness. Hence it was personified and materialized in the *Sambhogakaya* and *Nirmanakaya*. It was said that all religious or spiritual teachers of whatever religion were expressions of the *Dharmakaya*.

Dharmakaya (Prajna Dharmakaya, Unmanifested Body)

In the *Mahaparinibbana Sutta*, Gotama Buddha said, '... Ananda, for what I have taught and explained to you as Dhamma and discipline will, at my passing, be your teacher'. The teaching that takes the place of the teacher is designated the *Dharmakaya*. '... it is possible to point to the Lord (Gotama Buddha) by means of the body of the Dhamma (Dhammakayena), for the Dhamma [...] was taught by the Lord.'[7]

Dharmakaya is the body of teaching on a metaphysical level, the truth of the teaching and essence of Buddhahood. It includes the other two bodies of the Buddha. It is the permanent, undifferentiated, comprehending truth. The true body of the Buddha is his spiritual body, free of mental defilements, the *Dharmakaya*. This is the real nature of every Buddha and every being. It has to be realized by spiritual practice and experience by every being for oneself. As a rule only a bodhisattva can hope to realize it fully. According to the *Saddharma Pundarika Sutra* it is the true meaning of Buddhahood . It is identical with the essential nature of all beings. Further, the *Dharmakaya* is the essence of existence, absolute wisdom, essence of the universe and absolute reality.

Sambhogakaya

This is a manifestation of the Buddha or *Dharmakaya* for the benefit of all bodhisattvas. It is an expression of the *Dharmakaya*, personifies wisdom, is a symbol of transcendental perfection, and is visible to the bodhisattvas although beyond the reach of human perception. Only those who have knowledge of the *Dharma* have followed and practised the *Dharma* and have progressed somewhat on the path can understand the teaching of a *Sambhogakaya*, who leads them along the path of the Buddha to ultimate Enlightment.

Nirmanakaya

These are earthly Buddhas, such as Gotama Buddha. The Universal Buddha or *Dharmakaya* manifested in the world of Sentient beings as Buddhas, bodhisattvas, deities and ordinary beings, often in humble circumstances, and sometimes in concrete form, for example paintings or images. They are representatives of the absolute reality but now appearing in the sense world, adapting to earthly conditions and possessing earthly bodies. The earthly bodies are in reality transcendental and are not subject to the operation of laws like *kamma*. The *Nirmanakaya* is mind-made and can multiply and transfer from place to place at will. It is understood that Gotama Buddha visited several South Asian countries and the capacity of the *Nirmanakaya* explains how such travel took place.

The appearance of a Buddha on Earth is not an accident. It is a deliberate descent of the *Dharmakaya* as a human being. His form is an illusion and his life and acts from birth to passing away are a make-believe act designed to create a sense of kinship with human beings.

Buddha Nature

This is the potential ability in all beings to achieve Enlightment. It has a special emphasis in Eastern and Northern Buddhism, where it is called *Bodhicitta*.

In Southern Buddhism, Buddha Nature is specifically associated with bodhisattas. Since anyone can aspire to become a bodhisatta, all human beings must possess this quality. Further, because of the doctrine of rebirth stating that animals can be reborn as humans, they too must possess this quality. In other words, all living beings have the quality of Buddha Nature. Ascetic Sumedha resolved before Buddha Dipankara to become a *Samma Sambuddha*. The resolution gave focus to his aspiration, but the latent ability to become a *Samma Sambuddha* must have been already within his consciousness.

Eastern and Northern Buddhism teach that Buddha Nature is in operation all the time, *Mahaparinirvana Sutra* states that:

> Buddha Nature in all beings dwells and unalterable, throughout all transmigrations, ever ready to develop itself no sooner the opportunity presents itself.
>
> *Mahaparinirvana Sutra*

Buddha Nature is present in every form of consciousness. It comes to fruition through practice of the teaching. It is not a mechanical process but a living force in the consciousness of a living being. It is developed in different individuals to different degrees. In some Eastern and Northern Buddhist traditions, Buddha Nature is taken to be the *Dharmakaya* covered with defilements. Enlightenment, and therefore Buddhahood, is the recovery of this pure, original state of being that is identical with ultimate reality itself. The *Dhamma* a Buddha teaches is the expression of Buddha Nature in its total and pure form.

Summary

In the history of the current Buddhist teaching, the concept of the Buddha has gone through a process of development, refinement and then extension of the original meaning. New meanings have been added to former meanings. This may be summarized as:

- A development from teacher/*Arahat* to an extraordinary human being;
- Then to a superhuman transcendental being;
- a permanent living being;

- Then as the embodied *Dharma*/teaching, the ultimate or absolute reality;
- Finally not as something external to be achieved but the potential ability within each living being to achieve Enlightment.

Part V

Buddhism

Chapter 19

Past, Present and Future

Buddhism can be seen as the golden thread that adorns the fabric of the civilizations of Asia. There is no country in Asia that has not been significantly influenced for the better, at one time or another, by Buddhism. Bhutan, Cambodia, Japan, Korea, Laos, Myanmar, Mongolia, Nepal, Sri Lanka, Taiwan, Thailand and Vietnam remain strongly Buddhist countries. China was once mainly a Buddhist country. It has been on the decline there, but now the number of Buddhists and Buddhist temples is increasing. In India also the number of Buddhists is on the increase.

Buddhism has been the primary inspiration behind many successful civilizations, the foundation of great cultural achievements, the source of much peace of mind and tranquillity, the basis of extensive devotion and worship, and a profound guide to the very purpose of life and meaning of death for millions of people. Buddhist teaching, practice and customs have played an important part not only in the private lives of the people, but also in State matters. The *Sangha* has had an important and respected position in the State and the Buddhist temples and monasteries often received State support. Even in the early stages the famous Buddhist universities of Taxila and Nalanda and medical centres for both human beings and animals were established.

The spread of Buddhism has always been peaceful, more a case of the teaching being available to those who came to it than an active propagation. Buddhists can be proud that no war has been waged, no human rights breached, no living beings harmed and no environment desecrated in the name of Buddhism. It has developed and existed harmoniously and without conflict with other religions, whether they were the original religions in the country or new religions that arrived later. A well-travelled religion, it has shown that it can take root in any soil, provided its spirit rather than its form was transplanted, and its subsequent growth has always enriched the native culture.

The period from the sixteenth century to the mid-nineteenth century saw a decline in the influence of Buddhism in Asian countries for various reasons, mainly political. The Buddhist communities had to withstand the spread, often backed by force and political might, of other religions.

Since the mid-nineteenth century there has been a resurgence of Buddhism in Asia. Many Buddhist schools, universities and organizations have been established and this has been a catalyst for an increase in the teaching, study and practice of Buddhism at all levels. There has been an increase in the number of publications on Buddhism in local and foreign languages. There has been greater communication between Buddhists in different Asian countries at both individual and organization level. Several international organizations, such as the World Fellowship of Buddhists founded in 1950, have been created to facilitate the liaison between different communities of Buddhists by arranging conferences and sponsoring co-operative activities. Other organizations have also been active in promoting such ventures. An International Buddhist University has been established in Bangkok. An increasing number of people have come to Buddhist Asia from other parts of the world to study Buddhism at universities and temples, to learn and participate in meditation, and some to become ordained as monks and nuns. Some of them have made significant contributions to the development of Buddhism through their teaching and publications, both in Asia and other parts of the world.

Adverse conditions have not prevented some of them from carrying on their chosen task. For instance, Venerable Nyanatiloka was a German national ordained as a Buddhist monk and living in Sri Lanka. His now famous *Buddhist Dictionary* was written during the 1939–1945 war in the Central Internment Camp in Dehra-Dun, India where, being an alien enemy he was interned for the duration of the war, as a guest of the government of the time.

In recent times many Buddhists in the Asian countries have become very concerned by the aggressive incursions of proselytizing sections of other religions aimed mainly at poorer Buddhists using unethical methods and being generously funded by foreign organizations. There has been much discussion about this. One of the problems in curbing such practices is the difficulty of framing legislation that will stop them but still leave people free and independent to decide for themselves which religion to follow. There is no doubt, however, that the Buddhist communities in these countries have the strength and vitality to maintain their position in the face of such incursions.

Buddhism has spread from the Asian countries in which the current teaching was born, grew and flowered to other countries across the world. Today, large numbers of men and women from diverse backgrounds in different countries throughout the world follow the teachings of Gotama (Sakyamuni) Buddha. They are attracted to Buddhism because of the excellence of its teaching, the gentleness of its outlook, the incisiveness of its practice and the sophisticated and civilized way of life it promotes. In the West it was scholars, especially in France, Germany, the UK and US, who took the initial interest in Buddhism from the early nineteenth century. Gradually, the translation of texts, communication with Asian Buddhists, discussions at the Parliament of World Religions in Chicago in 1893, followed by the centennial conference in 1993 (again in Chicago) and the establishing of Buddhist temples and monasteries have created an interest in Buddhism as a personal religion. In the twentieth century the many Asian Buddhists who went to live in the Americas, Australasia, Europe and the UK took Buddhism with them. Many Buddhist temples, monasteries and organizations have been established in these regions. Buddhist festivals are celebrated and Buddhism is practised as a living religion by the newcomers and a growing number of the indigenous people. Buddhism was brought to Sri Lanka by Venerable Mahinda (see Chapter 3). After some years the king asked him whether Buddhism had become established in Sri Lanka. Venerable Mahinda replied that Buddhism becomes established in a country when the people of that country learn the *Dhamma* in their own language and a *Sangha* is established. This has happened in regions outside Asia, so that Buddhism is now a worldwide religion.

The main teaching of Buddhism is at temples and monasteries. It is now a subject of study and research in many universities across the world. In some countries Buddhism is taught in schools as an academic subject, for instance in the UK there are official published syllabi for the study and examination of Buddhism in national school examinations. Growing numbers of people are interested in Buddhist meditation and attend meditation classes, meetings and retreats. Sometimes joint meditation sessions are arranged between ordained Buddhists and Christians. Today Buddhist meditation has been taken up in medicine, psychology and the care services in, for example, Australia, the UK and the US as part of mainstream treatment for stress-related and psychiatric illnesses and for general well being.

In Asian countries Buddhism in any one country is generally confined to one school or tradition. An interesting feature in the countries outside Asia is that generally the different schools and traditions are represented. There are temples, monasteries, monks and nuns, library materials, teaching, supporters and celebration of the festivals of the different traditions. In addition there are new movements that may develop into new traditions in time. In its 2007 edition, the *Buddhist Directory* published by The Buddhist Society in London lists 649 Buddhist centres, groups and organizations of various traditions in the UK and Republic of Ireland.

From earliest times Buddhists have been happy to engage in discussion and dialogue with those of other religions. This continues in the present day, often in an organized manner among both ordained and lay persons. In the UK Buddhists are represented at national level on the Religious Education Council of England and Wales and at a local level on the Standing Advisory Councils on Religious Education. In the UK and US the armed forces have appointed Buddhist chaplains. In the UK there is a Buddhist chaplaincy service operating in prisons and hospitals. Buddhist monks and nuns visit hospitals and hospices to give religious comfort to patients.

Buddhism has been and continues to be a multi-ethnic and multi-cultural religion. As Buddhism looks to the future, Buddhists will have to consider issues relating to animal rights, conservation, corporate liability, economic matters, environment, global warming, equal opportunities, human rights, imbalance of wealth in the world and peace movements. Buddhists are confident that the framework of the teaching is sufficiently wide and comprehensive to meet these and any other challenges.

Notes

Introduction

1 In this context the term 'world' implies *Dukkha*.

Chapter 2

1 Different dates, months and years are given by different traditions and by different scholars for the birth. Buddhists of different traditions celebrate the main events of his life on different days. There is no known evidence of written records at this time. These differences are due to inaccuracies in dating, cultural differences and imprecision resulting from conversion of the lunar calendar and time keeping used during the Buddha's time to the calendars used today in different Buddhist communities. These differences are mainly of academic interest to Buddhists. The traditional Southern Buddhist (*Theravadin*) chronology is used in this book for simplicity.

2 Many Buddhists in the South Asian countries believe that Princess Yasodhara who became the wife of the bodhisatta, Kaludayi his boyhood friend, Channa his friend and charioteer and Kanthaka his horse were born on the same day. They also believe that the pipal tree, later known as the Bodhi tree, began to grow from seed on that day.

3 In his first teaching Gotama Buddha referred to birth, ageing, illness and death as being the causes of imperfection and *Dukkha*. This is called the cycle of life or *Samsara*.

4 It is interesting to note the non-human element appearing in various places in the story of the life of the Buddha.

5 A few years later the Buddha recited the Dhamma while the king passed away.

6 In this context, the term 'world' implies *Dukkha*. See also the explanations of the five aggregates in Chapter 6, the Three Signs of Being and the four subjects of mindfulness in the *Satipattana Sutta* in Chapter 15.

Chapter 6

1 *Dukkha* has a range of meanings, as explained in Chapter 5. In the Four Noble Truths and later in this chapter it is convenient to use the word *Dukkha* where possible rather than another word.

2 This text should be compared to the text of the *Prajna Paramita Sutra* set out below.

3 *Dukkha* is explained in detail in Chapter 5.

4 This text should be compared to the text of the *Anattalakkhana Sutta* set out above.

Chapter 7

1 Translated by Narada Thera, Taiwan, The Corporate Body of the Buddha Educational Foundation, 1993.

2 *The Path of Purification*, Ch. XIX, para. 20.

3 Translated by John Blofeld and published by The Buddhist Society, London, 1978.

4 Vol. iii. 2.10, p. 228 of *Buddhism in Translations,* translated by Henry Clarke Warren.

Chapter 8

1 See Appendix II for an interesting case of rebirth.

Chapter 9

1 This section must be read together with the section on Different Planes of Existence in Chapter 8.

2 The section on Planes of Existence in Chapter 8 gives the detailed advantages of being born as a human being.

3 The section on Planes of Existence in Chapter 8 gives details of life in this plane.

4 For further details, see the explanation of Dependent Origination in Chapter 6.

Chapter 10

1 This verse refers to the ethical state of an *Arahat*.

2 Here *brahmana* means one who has won Enlightment

Chapter 11

1 Vol. 1, p. 190, Sri Lanka, BPS, 1973.

Chapter 12

1 *Maha Parinibbana Sutta*, Sacred Books of the Buddhists, vol. III, p. 150.

2 See Chapter 11 on the lay person's morality for detailed explanations.

3 Note Gotama Buddha's last words above.

4 Master Daito being the founder of one of the great training monasteries in Kyoto-Daitoku-ji.

5 *Prayer and Worship, The Wheel*, vol. vii, No. 139, p. 19.

6 *Zen Traces*, vol. 25.2, p. 224.

Chapter 15

1 Summarized in Chapter 11 in the section on general moral values.

2 pp. 7.8.50.

Chapter 18

1 *Gradual Sayings*, PTS, Pt. ii, pp. 44–45 and *Anguttara Nikaya*, PTS, Pt. ii, p. 37.

2 Chapter on Buddhism in Tibet, by Lobsang Phuntsok Lhalungpa, in *The Path of The Buddha*, Ed. Kenneth W Morgan, New York, Ronald Press Co, 1956, p. 276.

3 *Milinda's Questions,* translated by I. B. Horner, London, Luzac & Co Ltd, 1964, vol. 11, p. 110.

4 *Kindred Sayings*, PTS, 1954, vol. 111, p. 103.

5 *Milinda's Questions*, vol.1, p. 100.

6 *The Long Discourses of the Buddha,* translated by Maurice Walshe , Boston, MA, Wisdom, 1995, p. 270.

7 *Milinda's Questions*, p. 100.

Glossary

The classical languages of Buddhism, in which the teachings were first expressed, were Pali and Sanskrit. As Buddhism spread throughout the East, the teachings came to be expressed in many different languages, which today includes the indigenous languages of Asia, such as Chinese, Burmese, Japanese, Korean, Sinhalese, Thai and Tibetan. Much of the material has been translated into English and some of it into European languages, such as French and German. More details on this topic are given in Chapter 4. The glossary is arranged to give the corresponding Pali and Sanskrit words and the explanation. Some English words in common use among Buddhists are given in the column of Pali words. This glossary is based on the one published in 1994 by the School Curriculum and Assessment Authority, London, together with other materials on different religions. It was written by the Buddhist Working Group, of which the author was the chairperson.

Pali	Sanskrit	Explanation
Abhidhamma	*Abhidharma*	Further of higher teaching of the philosophy and psychology of Buddhism in abstract, systematic form
Abhidhamma Pitaka	*Abhidharma Pitaka*	This is the third of the three principal sections of the Pali Canon. It is a systematic, philosophical and psychological treatment of the teachings given in the *Sutta Pitaka*
	Amitabha, amitayus	Also *amida* (Japanese). Buddhas having unlimited light and life respectively
Anapanasati	*Anapanasmrti*	Mindfulness of the breath. The practice most usually associated with the development of concentration and calm (*samatha* meditation), but also used in the training of *vipassana* (insight) meditation

Anatta	*Anatman*	Selflessness, no self, no soul. Insubstantiality. Denial of a real or permanent self
Anicca	*Anitya*	Impermanence. Instability of all things, including living beings
Arahat, Arahant	*Arhat*	Enlightened disciple. The fourth and highest stage of realization recognized by the Southern Buddhist tradition. One whose mind is free from all attachment, ill will and ignorance
Ariya		A noble one
Asoka	Ashoka	Emperor of India in the third century. A great supporter of Buddhism
Atta	*Atman*	Self, soul
Bhikkhu	*Bhikshu*	Fully ordained Buddhist monk
Bhikkhuni	*Bhikshuni*	Fully ordained Buddhist nun
Blessing		Good fortune. Wishes for good fortune
Bodhi tree		The tree *(Ficus religiosa)* under which the Buddha realized Enlightment. It is known as the tree of wisdom
Bodhisatta		A Wisdom Being. One intent on becoming, or destined to become, a *Samma Sambuddha*. Gotama Buddha in his lives before his Enlightenment as the historical Buddha (Southern Buddhism)
	Bodhisattva	A being destined for Enlightenment. Also one who has attained Enlightenment but post-pones final attainment of Buddhahood in order to help living beings (Eastern and Northern Buddhism)
Brahma Viharas		The four divine worlds, sublime states: loving-kindness, compassion, sympathetic joy and equanimity (evenness of mind)
Buddha	Buddha	Awakened or Enlightened one
Buddha *Sasana*		Buddha's dispensation. Buddhist teaching, practice and community. Buddhism
Buddhayana		Buddha path/career. A combination of the teachings of all the Buddhist schools and traditions
Canon		A collection of sacred books
Citta		Mind and heart
Conditioned		Made up of other things
Consecrated		Dedicated in a religious way

Dalai Lama (Tibetan)		Spiritual and temporal leader of the Tibetan people
Dana	Dana	Generosity, giving, gift. Specially the offering of the morning and mid-day meal to the *Sangha*
Deities		Devas, people born on a higher plane
Devotee		Person following a religious way of life
Devotional		In the nature of worship
Dhamma	*Dharma*	Universal law. Ultimate or absolute truth. The teachings of the Buddha. A key Buddhist term
Dhammapada	*Dharmapada*	Famous scripture of 423 verses
Dukkha	*Duhkha*	Imperfection, unsatisfactoriness, suffering, ill will. The nature of existence according to the First Noble Truth
Enlightenment		See *Nibbana*
Four Noble Truths		Fundamental Buddhist teaching
Gompa (Tibetan)		Monastery; place of meditation
Gotama	Gautama	Family name of the Buddha
Jataka		Birth story. Accounts of the previous lives of the Buddha. Illustrating Buddhist ethical ideas
Jhana	*Dhyana*	Also Ch'an (Chinese) and Zen (Japanese). Advanced stages of meditation
Kamma	*Karma*	Action. Volitions. Intentional actions that affect one's circumstances in this and future lives
Karuna	*Karuna*	Compassion
Kesa (Japanese)		The robe of a Buddhist monk, nun, or priest
Khandha	*Skandha*	Heap. Aggregate. The five *khandhas* together make up the 'living being' (form, feeling, perception, volitions and consciousness). Includes thoughts and emotions
Khanti	*Kshanti*	Patience, forbearance
Kilesa	*Klesa*	Mental defilement or fire, such as attachment, ill will and ignorance
Koan (Japanese)		A technical term used in Zen Buddhism referring to enigmatic or paradoxical questions used to develop intuition. Also refers to religious problems encountered in daily life
Kwan-yin (Chinese)		Also, Kannon (Japanese). Bodhisattva of Compassion, depicted in female form.

		Identified with Chenrezi (Tibet) and Bodhisattva Avalokitesvara
Lama (Tibetan)		Teacher or one who is revered
Lay person		A person who is not ordained
Loving-kindness		Affectionate consideration for others. *Metta*
	Lotus Sutra (*Saddharma Pundarika Sutra*)	A scripture of major importance to Eastern and Northern Schools. It describes the virtues of the Bodhisattva and emphasizes that all Sentient beings possess Buddha-Nature and can attain Enlightenment (*Nirvana*)
Magga	Marga	Path leading to cessation of *Dukkha*. The Fourth Noble Truth. Noble Eightfold Path
	Mahayana, Eastern Buddhism	Great Way or Vehicle. Teachings that spread from India into Tibet, parts of Asia and the Far East, characterized by the bodhisattva ideal and the prominence given to the development of both compassion and wisdom
Mala		Also, *juzu* (Japanese). String of 108 beads used in Buddhist meditation practice (like a rosary)
Mandala		Pictorial diagram of the teaching
Mantra		A set of words having a religious meaning
Mara		Evil. Temptation. A malevolent deity
Meditation		Mental control and development leading to concentration, calmness and wisdom
Mindfulness		Mental concentration and awareness
Metta	Maitri	Loving-kindness. A pure love that is neither grasping nor possessive
Metta Sutta		Buddhist scripture that describes the nature of loving-kindness
Metteya	Maitreya	One who has the nature of loving-kindness. Name of the next Buddha
	Mudra	Ritual gesture, as illustrated by the hands of Buddha images
Mudita	Mudita	Sympathetic joy. Welcoming the good fortune of others
Nibbana	Nirvana	Blowing out of the fires of attachment, ill will and ignorance, and the state of secure perfect peace that follows. Awareness of absolute reality. The Third Noble Truth. A key Buddhist term

Nirodha	*Nirodha*	Cessation (of *Dukkha*, suffering). The Third Noble Truth
Noble Eightfold Path		The path to be followed by a Buddhist, the Middle Way, the Fourth Noble Truth
Non-attachment		Not being attached to persons and things
Ordination		Ceremony on becoming a member of the *Sangha*
Panna	*Prajna*	*Wisdom*. Understanding the true nature of things
Parami	*Paramita*	A perfection or virtue. One of the six or ten perfections necessary for the attainment of Buddhahood
Parinibbana	*Parinirvana*	Final and complete Nirvana reached at the passing away of a Buddha or *Arahat*
Patimokkha	*Pratimoksha*	The training rules of a monk or nun – 227 in the case of a Southern Buddhist monk
Pirith (*Pirit*)		Selected scriptures. Chanting the scriptures
Prajna		Wisdom in relation to the Buddhist teaching
Pitaka		Basket. Collection of scriptures (see *Tipitaka*)
Precepts		Rules of conduct, guidelines
Rebirth, Rebecoming		Continuity of life after death
Rupa	*Rupa*	Form. Used for an image of the Buddha. Also, the first of the five *khandhas*
Sakyamuni	Shakyamuni	Sage of the Shakyas (the family community of the Buddha). Title of the historical Buddha
Samadhi	*Samadhi*	Meditative absorption. A state of deep meditation
Samatha	Samatha	A meditative state of concentrated calmness. Style of meditation (see *vipassana*)
Samsara	*Samsara*	Everyday life. The continual round of birth, sickness, old age and death that can be transcended by following the Eightfold Path and Buddhist teaching
Samudaya	*Samudaya*	Arising, origin (of *Dukkha*, suffering). The Second Noble Truth
Sangha	Sangha	Community; assembly. Often used for the Order of bhikkhus and bhikkunis in Southern Buddhist countries. In the Eastern Buddhist countries, the Sangha includes lay devotees and priests, eg in Japan.

Sankhara	*Samskara*	Mental/*karmic* formation. The fourth of the five *khandhas*
Sanna	*Samjna*	Perception. Third of the five *khandhas*
Savaka	*Sravaka*	Disciple, listener, hearer
Satori (Japanese)		Awakening. A term used in Zen Buddhism
Siddattha	Siddhartha	Wish-fulfilled. The personal name of the historical Buddha
Sila	*Sila*	Morality, Virtue, moral Precepts
Stupa		Dagoba. A circular structure containing Buddhist relics
Sukha		Happiness, pleasure, ease
Sunyata		Emptiness, selflessness, insubstantiality
Sutta	*Sutra*	A *Dhamma* text. The word of the Buddha
Sutta Pitaka	*Sutra Pitaka*	The second of the three collections – principally of teachings – that comprise the Pali Canon of Southern Buddhism. The wisdom and practice teachings
Tanha	*Trishna*	Attachment, thirst, craving. Attachment (rooted in ignorance) is the cause of *Dukkha*. The Second Noble Truth
Tathagata	*Tathagata*	Another epithet for the Buddha
Theravada (Southern school)	*Sthaviravada*	Teaching of the elders. A principal school of Buddhism, established in Sri Lanka and South East Asia. Southern Buddhism. Now also found in the West
Thupa/ cetiya	*Stupa*	Reliquary (including pagodas), *dagoba*
Tipitaka	*Tripitaka*	Three baskets. A threefold collection of texts – *Vinaya*, *Sutta* and *Abhidamma* – in Southern Buddhism
Tiratana	*Triratna*	The Triple Gem, Three Refuges. The Buddha, the *Dharma* and the *Sangha*. Another way of referring to the three jewels
Tulku (Tibetan)		Reincarnated lama
Upaya		Any skilful means, e.g. meditation on loving kindness, to overcome anger
Upekkha	*Upeksa*	Equanimity. Evenness of mind
	Vajrayana	Thunderbolt, diamond way. Teachings promulgated later, mainly in India and Tibet. Another term for esoteric Buddhism
Vassa		Seclusion during the rainy season

Vedana		Feeling. The second of the five *khandhas*
Vesak or *Wesak*	*Wesak*	Buddha Day. Name of a festival and a month. In Southern Buddhist countries the birth, Enlightment and passing away of the Gotama Buddha is celebrated on the day of the full moon in May. Some traditions celebrate these events on other days
Vihara		Dwelling place of the *Sangha*. Monastery, temple
Vinaya		The rules of discipline of monastic life
Vinaya Pitaka		The first of the three collections of the Pali Canon of Southern Buddhism, containing mostly the discipline for monks and nuns, with many stories and some teachings
Vinnana	*Vijnana*	Consciousness. The fifth of the five *khandhas*
Vipassana	*Vipashyana*	Insight into the true nature of things. A particular form of meditation. Insight medi tation (see *samatha*)
Viriya	*Virya*	Energy, exertion
Zen (Japanese)		Meditation. Derived from the Sanskrit 'dhyana'. A tradition of Eastern Buddhism that developed in China (called Ch'an) and Japan

Bibliography

Anandamaitreya, Ven. B. (1997) *Buddhism, Lectures and Essays*. Taiwan: The Corporate Body of the Buddha Educational Foundation.

Anandamaitreya, Ven. B. (1995) *Nine Special Qualities of the Buddha and Other Essays*. London: World Buddhist Foundation.

Bechert, H. and Gombrich, R. (1991) *The World of Buddhism*. London: Thames and Hudson. (A scholarly book for the library.)

Buddhaghosa, (1979) *The Path of Purification (Visuddhimagga)*. Translated by Nanamoli Bhikkhu, Kandy: Buddhist Publication Society.

Chan, K. S. (2006) *Buddhism Course*. Kuala Lumpur, Malaysia: Majujaya Indha Sdn. Bhd.

Croucher, P. (1989) *Buddhism in Australia*. Kensington, NSW Australia: NSW University Press.

Gampopa (1998) *The Jewel Ornament of Liberation, The Wish-fulfilling Gem of the Noble Teachings*, translated by Khenpo Konchog Gyaltsen Rinpoche, New York: Snow Lion Publications.

Gombrich, R. F. (1988) *Theravada Buddhism*. London: Routledge & Kegan Paul Ltd.

Goonewardene, A. D. (1996) 'Buddhism' in Cole W. O. (ed) *Six World Faiths*. London: Continuum, p. 104.

Gunasekara, O. (1979), 'The Spread of Buddhism Throughout the Ages' in *The Ven. Narada Mahathera Felicitation Volume*. Sri Lanka: Buddhist Publication Society.

Guruge, A. W. P. (1984) *Buddhism – the Religion and its Culture*. Sri Lanka: The World Fellowship of Buddhists.

Gyatso, T. HH The XIV Dalai Lama (1975) *The Buddhism of Tibet*. Jeffery Hopkins J (transl), New York: Snow Lion Publications.

Gyatso, T., HH The XIV Dalai Lama (1995) *The World of Tibetan Buddhism*. Boston, MA: Wisdom Publications.

Harvey, P. (1990) *An Introduction to Buddhism*. Cambridge: Cambridge University Press.

Higgins, M. M. (1984) *Jatakamala*. Colombo, Sri Lanka: Lake House Bookshop.

Horner, I. B. (transl) (1964) *Milinda's Questions*. London: Luzac & Co Ltd.

Humphries, C. (1990) *Buddhism*. London: Penguin Books.

Kato, B., Tamura, Y. and Miyasaka, K. (transl) (1975) 'Saddharma Pundarika (Lotus) Sutra', in *The Threefold Lotus Sutra*. New York/Tokyo: Weatherhill/Kosei.

Korean Buddhist Chogye Order (1988) *Korean Buddhism*. Seoul, Korea.

Kuruppu, R. (2000) *Facing Death with a Smile*, Sri Lanka: Tharanjee Prints.

Kuruppu, R. (2003) *Buddhism: Its Essence & Some Relevant Approaches*. Sri Lanka: Public Trustee Department.

Kuruppu, R. (2005) *The Essence of Dhamma*. Sri Lanka: Tharanjee Prints.

Mahasi Sayadaw, Venerable, Agga Mahapandita U Sobhana (1978) *Practical Vipassana Meditational Exercises*. Rangoon (Yangon): Buddhasasananuggaha Association. (A talk to disciples).

Malalasekera G. P. et al. (eds) (1961–2008) *Encyclopaedia of Buddhism*. Colombo: The Government of Sri Lanka, Colombo (vol.1, 1961 to vol.8, 2008).

Mendis, N. K. G. (ed) (1993) *The Questions of King Milinda*. Kandy: Buddhist Publication Society.

Mircea Eliade, M. et al. (eds) (1987) *The Encyclopedia of Religion*. New York: Macmillan. (Vol. 2, the section under Buddhism gives a detailed scholarly account.)

Morgan, K. W. (ed) (1956) *The Path of the Buddha*. New York: The Ronald Press Company. (Chapters on different traditions by authors from the tradition.)

Muthukumarana, N. et al. (2004) *Guide to the study of Theravada Buddhism, Book 1*. Sri Lanka, Colombo Y M B A.

Muthukumarana, N. et al. (2005) *Guide to the Study of Theravada Buddhism, Book 2*. Sri Lanka, Colombo: Y M B A.

Narada, Thera (transl) (1972) *The Dhammapada*. London: John Murray.

Narada, Thera (transl) (1993) *The Dhammapada*. Taiwan: The Corporate Body of the Buddha Educational Foundation.

Narada, Thera (1949) *A Manual of Buddhism*. Colombo, Sri Lanka: Associated Newspapers of Ceylon Ltd.

Narada, Thera (1980) *The Buddha and His Teachings*. Kandy, Sri Lanka: Buddhist Publication Society.

Narada, Thera (ed and transl) (1979) *A Manual of Abhidhamma*. Kuala Lumpur, Malaysia: Buddhist Missionary Society.

Nyanaponika, Thera (1960) *Devotion in Buddhism*. Kandy, Sri Lanka: Buddhist Publication Society, The Wheel Publications, vol. 1, no. 18.

Nyanaponika, Thera (1962) *The Heart of Buddhist Meditation*. London: Rider & Company. (Contains the text of the *Satipatthana Sutta*.)

Nyanatiloka Venerable (1972) *Buddhist Dictionary*. Colombo, Ceylon (Sri Lanka): Frewin & Co Ltd.

Oliver, I. P. (1979) *Buddhism in Britain*. London: Rider & Company.

Piyadassi, Nayaka, Thera (1994) *The Buddhist Doctrine of Life After Death*. Taiwan: The Corporate Body of the Buddha Educational Foundation.

Powell, A. (1989) *Living Buddhism*. New York: Harmony Books. (A book for the library – well written, with beautiful photographs.)

Rahula, W. (1959) *What the Buddha Taught*. London: Gordon Fraser.

Rhys Davids, Caroline A. F. (1989) *The Stories of the Buddha*. New York: Dover Publications, Inc.

Saddhatissa, H. (1971) *The Buddha's Way*. London: George Allen & Unwin Ltd.

Saddhatissa, H. (1976) *The Life of the Buddha*. London: Unwin Paperbacks.

Santideva (725) *The Bodhicaryavatara*. Crosby, K and Skilton A. (transl. 1995), Oxford: Oxford University Press.

Shinnyo – En (2005) *Morning & Evening Chanting*, Tokyo.

Snelling, J. (1987) *The Buddhist Handbook*. London: Rider.

Stevenson, I. and Maitreya, B. A. (1974) *Twenty Cases Suggestive of Reincarnation*. Virginia: University Press of Virginia.

Sugatananda, Anagarika (Story, F.) (1964) *The Case for Rebirth*. Sri Lanka: Buddhist Publication Society, The Wheel Publications, vol.1, nos. 12/13.

Sugatananda, A. (Story, F.) (1973) *The Buddhist Outlook*. Vol. 1. Sri Lanka: Buddhist Publication Society.

Sujatha, U. (1988) *Jataka Stories*. Colombo, Sri Lanka: Evangel Press Ltd.

Sujato, Bhikkhu (2005) *A History of Mindfulness*. Taipei, Taiwan: The Corporate Body of the Buddha Educational Foundation.

Suzuki, B. L. (1981) *Mahayana Buddhism*. London: George Allen & Unwin.

Suzuki, D.T. (transl) (1981) 'Prajna Paramita Sutra (The Heart Sutra)', in B.L. Suzuki, *Mahayana Buddhism*. London: George Allen & Unwin.

Takakusu, J. (1947) *The Essentials of Buddhist Philosophy*. Honolulu: University of Hawaii.

The World Fellowship of Buddhists (1994) *Unity of Diversities. Nine Lectures on Buddhism*. Bangkok: The World Fellowship of Buddhists. (Has chapters on the different traditions.)

Tsering, Geshe Tashi (2005) *The Four Noble Truths*. Boston: Wisdom Publications.

Tushita Med. Ctr. (1985) *International Buddhist Directory*. London: Wisdom Publications.

Upali, M. (1991) *Methods and Benefits of Meditation*. Sweden: Casimir and Eva Amon. (Sometime principal teacher at the Meditation Centre, Kanduboda, Sri Lanka. This was a talk given to the University of Colombo under-graduates.)

Warren, H. C. (1922) *Buddhism in Translations*. Vol. 3. Harvard Oriental Series, Cambridge, Mass: Harvard University Press.

Williams, P. (1989) *Mahayana Buddhism*. London: Routledge.

Note: Some of these books have been reprinted and republished several times and in different countries. There may be earlier or later editions of these books.

There is a wealth of material on Buddhism on the internet. The author has looked at the following websites and can recommend them as giving authentic and accurate information about Buddhist life, including talks (printed and spoken), meditation classes, chanting, celebrations, photographs, connections to other websites and so on. These websites are being continually updated.

1. www.dhammatalks.org.uk
2. www.forestsangha.org
3. www.londonbuddhistvihara.org
4. www.thebuddhistsociety.org
5. www.worldbuddhistfoundation
6. www.srisaddhatissainternationalbuddhist.centre

Appendix I

Facing Death with a Smile

Rajah Kuruppu, Vice President, Colombo Young Men's
Buddhist Association, Editor of 'The Buddhist'
Sometime President, Servants of the Buddha, Sri Lanka.

In this presentation, by smile, we mean a gentle smile similar to the smile of the Buddha, a smile of understanding and wisdom. It is a gentle smile that indicates an awareness of life in its true nature as *anicca*, *Dukkha* and *anatta* – impermanence, unsatisfactoriness and the absence of a lasting and unchanging self.

Death is one factor that is common to all living beings. Just as a bullet once fired from a gun has to find its destination, a living being once born has to proceed to its logical conclusion, which is death. Among the many uncertainties of life the only certainty is death. Death is also a great equalizer, since all living beings have to face it without exception and discrimination.

We face two kinds of death in life. One is the death of those whom we love, the near and the dear, and the other is our own death.

Loved ones

From the Buddhist standpoint, we have to accept the death of loved ones philosophically as a part of nature. Wailing and weeping or even being deeply depressed will do no good. The acceptance of such loss with the outstanding Buddhist quality of equanimity – *upekkha* – will enable one to bear the loss with less suffering and understanding.

In the event of an untimely death, a remark often heard is that while death is inevitable to all, what is unacceptable is that the loved one should die at so young an age. It is important to remember, however, that at the time of birth no guarantee was given that one would live up to a ripe old age. So a wise person should be acutely aware of this fact of life before such tragedies occur.

The Buddha in previous lives as a boddhisatta, one aspiring to be a Buddha, displayed no grief at the death of dear ones. In one previous life as a farmer he did not grieve over the death of his only son. Instead he contemplated, 'What is subject to dissolution is dissolved and what is subject to death is dead. All life is transitory and subject to death.'

A Brahmin, who attended the funeral, inquired why he did not grieve – was he hard-hearted with no feelings for his only son? The Bodhisatta replied that his son was dear to him but grieving would not bring him back to life. 'No lamenting can touch the ashes of the dead. Why should I grieve?'

In another life, the Bodhisatta did not cry over the death of his brother and was accused of being hard hearted. He replied that they did not understand the eight vicissitudes of life, *atta loka Dhamma*, namely: gain and loss, repute and ill-repute, praise and blame, success and failure. These vicissitudes, pleasant and unpleasant, are common to all. All existent things are transient and must eventually pass away. So he explained that on account of their ignorance they cry and lament but why should he, who understands, also join them and weep?

In still another life the Bodhisatta lost his young and pretty wife but did not shed a tear on that account. Instead he reflected as follows. 'That which has the nature of dissolution has dissolved. All existences are impermanent', and went about his normal day-to-day tasks with equanimity but very mindfully from moment to moment. Some said that they hardly knew the deceased but the sight of a beautiful woman dead at so young an age moved them to tears. They were amazed that he was able to remain so calm in such a situation. The Bodhisatta explained that although his wife was very dear to him, she was destined to live with him for a limited period and not for all time. So when the time for parting comes one should face it with understanding and a sense of balance.

These incredible stories of the previous lives of the Buddha should inspire us to contemplate well and deeply on the teachings of the Buddha, understand the truth of impermanence and accept philosophically the fact of death. Actually, when we face the loss of loved ones, we too should reflect, as the Bodhisatta did, and maintain our composure.

The Buddha, when about to pass away, advised Venerable

Ananda, who had not attained the Buddhist goal of *Nibbana*, not to grieve and said that one should accept the fact that death and separation from all that we love is inevitable. The last words of the Buddha are most significant, '*VayaDhamma sanakara. Appamadena Sampadetha*'. (All conditioned things are subject to dissolution. Strive on with diligence. *Dhiga Nikaya, Mahaparinibbana Sutta*)

It is good for Buddhists and even others to ask themselves the question for whom we actually feel sorry with the passing away of a loved one. In all probability we feel sorry for ourselves for having lost a good and helpful friend. As far as the dead one is concerned we cannot be certain whether the death was for his good or otherwise. Under the natural law of *kamma*, the law of cause and effect, one could be born after death in a more pleasant and congenial place. Thus, we actually mourn our own loss rather than the loss of the friend.

To those whose company we value, it is advisable to indicate to them that we appreciate their company before they die. Otherwise, we could have a guilt complex if they die suddenly without forewarning.

The Buddha explained how a wise man should accept the death of a close associate as follows. 'Seeing the nature of the world the wise do not grieve. Weeping and wailing will lead to only more suffering and pain. It cannot bring back the dead. The mourner becomes pale and thin. He is doing violence to himself and his mourning is pointless.'

If there is wisdom and understanding, the death of a loved one will not assail us. Not that we are heartless and without feelings but that the right understanding of the nature of existence and death would enable us to accept the loss with a sense of equanimity as an integral part of life.

If we reflect deeply we realize that our grief on the death of a loved one is largely due to our attachment. The development of a sense of detachment and the acceptance of the inevitability of death would enable us to bear these with equanimity.

We could also respond to these deaths positively and resolve to live a noble and exemplary life in honour of the departed one. When the Buddha was about to pass away, it is said that heavenly flowers and sandal wood powder fell from the sky in his honour However, the Buddha indicated that he did not wish for that kind of honour. 'It is not thus that the *thathagatha* is honoured in the highest degree. But, Ananda, whosoever abides by the *Dhamma*, lives upright in the

Dhamma, walks in the *Dhamma*, it is by such a one that the *thathagatha* is honoured in the highest degree.'

Moreover, our departed loved ones would not wish that we lose our self-control and be deeply depressed by their death but would prefer that we accept their demise gracefully. Having taken a new life in the long sojourn through *Samsara* they would not wish us to continue mourning and weeping, which will be of no benefit to them. Instead of grieving we could respond to the death of a loved one positively, as stated earlier, by resolving to lead an exemplary and noble life to honour the memory of the loved one. The wholesome *kamma* generated by such action we could share with the departed loved one and that sincere wish may be helpful to the dead in certain circumstances.

Those of us who are mature in years have considerable experience of the loss of loved ones, but despite this experience we are deeply moved by the subsequent deaths of close associates, especially if they occur without warning. Thus to abide by the *Dhamma* we should make a firm resolve to face the death of loved ones with equanimity and wisdom and evaluate our reactions to such deaths in the future.

In death the loved one, who may have given sincere and valuable advice on many occasions in the past, conveys a final invaluable piece of advice apparent to the wise. 'Just as much as I have died, you will also die, sooner or later.' We are living on borrowed time and should therefore act with a sense of urgency to lead a noble life in accordance with the *Dhamma*, which itself will be helpful at the time of our departure from this world.

Preparing Loved Ones for Death

In the preparing a terminally sick loved one for death, we should establish a serene atmosphere taking into consideration his preferences. If he likes flowers, then there should be flowers by his bedside. If he prefers to pass away in his own room at home rather than in a hospital, accommodate these wishes if it is feasible to do so. Otherwise, make his surroundings in hospital as serene and peaceful as possible, to approximate the home atmosphere.

On the other hand, if a loved one who is terminally sick reveals signs of anxiety and worry, an effort should be made to eliminate or mitigate such anxieties. Often there is concern for the welfare of family and close dependents who may suffer when the loved one is no more.

During the time of the Buddha there was Nakulapita and his wife,

Nakulamata, both very devoted to each other in the material and spiritual fields. When Nakulapita was seriously ill and close to death, Nakulamata observing his anxieties advised her husband not to die with any regret or attachment to anything. She added that the Buddha has said that it is unwise to die in such a manner. Noticing the concern of Nakulapita for the family, she reassured him stating that he may think that when he is gone she will not be able to support the children and keep the family fires burning, however, she declared that she is capable of spinning cotton and carding wool and could stand on her own feet and consequently requested him to be at peace. She further assured him that she would always remain virtuous and practise the *Dhamma* until attaining Enlightenment. Comforted by these assurances, Nakulapita recovered from his illness. Later the Buddha, when the couple met him, told Nakulapita that he was very fortunate to have a wife like Nakulamata, who had so much love and compassion for him and also had the capacity to suitably counsel him at a time of crisis.

If the loved one indicates a fear of death, those close to him should provide the confidence to face death. One could gently remind the dying that all those not facing imminent death at present will also have to experience it in the years to come, sooner or later. Moreover, all the great people of the world, including the Buddha himself, have had to face death. One could also remind the dying of their good deeds of the past and encourage them to do good now by cultivating noble thoughts of wishing for the happiness and welfare of all living beings. This would be facilitated by persuading them to make up with enemies, if they have any, so that it would be possible to depart from this world with goodwill to all and malice to none. Some enemies of the past may be dead and one may not have access to some of the others. In that event one should make the effort to eliminate from the mind any feelings of bitterness or hatred towards them.

In preparing terminally sick and aged people for death, their children and those dear and close to them should ensure that they are well cared for with warmth, kindness and consideration. The physical faculties of the aged and terminally ill may fast deteriorate, such as sight, hearing and memory. Those caring for them should have great patience to deal with these adverse factors without permitting aversion and resentment to surface. Children could recall with gratitude the love and care bestowed on them by their parents when they were growing up and could not fend for themselves. Now the roles are reversed, the parents becoming the dependents because of their physical and mental deterioration and the children becoming responsible for looking after them. This is an opportunity to repay their debt to the parents for all they had done for them.

While those who are near and dear should extend all support to the dying, they should not reveal their own anxieties to the patient or cry in his presence as that would adversely affect the dying person. If they find it difficult to control themselves, they should reflect on the *Dhamma* and consider that death is inseparable from life. Where there is life there is death and this fact should be accepted gracefully. They could also think that when a loved one is terminally sick, in pain and beyond redemption it is better for the loved one to be freed of this life. This kind of selfless reflection, thinking not of one's own personal loss but the welfare of the loved one would enable them to regain their composure and help the dying person to make a dignified and serene departure.

Our Own Death

With regard to our own death, many are reluctant to think or talk of it, considering it an unpleasant subject. Our greatest possession is our own life and contemplation of the end of that life is not a pleasant experience. By such an attitude of mind one cannot wish away death, however. If death is unpleasant, the only way to overcome it is to prevent birth, by realizing the Buddhist goal of the deathless state of *Nibbana* by following the Noble Eightfold Path enunciated by the Buddha.

The Buddha, on the contrary, advocated frequent contemplation of death because of its many benefits. If one is irritated or frustrated, then contemplate that life is short and soon we will all be dead. So why argue, quarrel and loose one's sense of balance over comparatively trivial and mundane matters? Actually, in these circumstances, it would be far better to maintain peace with oneself and others. If agitated and worried about something, one could consider that life takes its natural course and death awaits everyone and therefore it is better to live a life in accordance with the *Dhamma*. Again, one could reflect that with or without worries we grow old and die. It is better to grow old without worries and indeed worries may even shorten one's life. Thinking of death will also encourage the development of the noble qualities of tolerance and patience, both with oneself and others. Moreover, with death in the forefront of one's thoughts there will be less attachment to material things, less wish to acquire such things and less envy of others' fortune. There would also be the tendency towards greater generosity and sharing and caring to bring happiness to others.

Moreover, the correct contemplation of death would give rise to *sanvega*, a sense of urgency to prepare for death. The Buddha once posed a question to King Pasenadi of Kosala: 'What would you do, O king, if you are told that four huge mountains, one each from the north, south, east and west, are heading in the direction of your kingdom, crushing every living thing in sight, and there is no escape?' The King replied: 'Lord, in such a mighty disaster, what else can I do but lead a righteous life and do good deeds.' The Buddha then drove home the point 'O king, old age and death are rolling in upon you. What are you going to do?' The King replied that in such circumstances it was all the more urgent for him to lead a righteous life and do good deeds. The King thus acknowledged that all the power, prestige, wealth and sensual pleasures that he enjoyed as king would be useless in the face of death.

This is wise attention – *yoniso manasikara* – to the subject of death is emphasized in Buddhism. On the other hand, unwise attention – *ayoniso manasikara* – would make one morose, frightened and depressed when thinking of death. Wise reflection leads to a sense of solidarity with all other living beings as they all have to face death. The reflection of death as advocated in Buddhism would enable one to live more wisely and compassionately.

If one is fearful of death, the advice of the Buddha is to perform wholesome deeds. In this connection, the words of the Buddha as recorded in *The Dhammapada* and given below are significant:

The doer of good rejoices in this world;
He rejoices in the next world;
He rejoices in both worlds.

Reflection on the doctrine of rebirth that all living beings are caught in a cycle of births and deaths, called *Samsara*, whose beginning is inconceivable, is also helpful when facing death. By such reflection one would realize that death is no stranger to us and that death in this life is not our first experience of death. We have experienced death on numerous occasions in our long journey through *Samsara*. This also provides a motivation to proceed along the Noble Eightfold Path to the deathless state of *Nibbana*.

In order to face death with equanimity it would also be helpful, as stated earlier, to contemplate the fact that all living beings are subject to death: the wealthy, the prestigious, the powerful and even the saintly, including the Buddha himself.

With and Without Notice

One could face one's own death in two ways, namely, with or without notice. When one faces death with notice, one becomes aware of its imminence on account of being afflicted with a serious terminal ailment. Doctors and nurses, who are close to such people just prior to their deaths, report that usually the old and terminally ill patients tend to be selfish. They think and talk only of their own problems. Even from a health angle, it is endorsed by medical opinion that it is better not to think too much of one's own sickness or old age but to concentrate on other matters, such as the welfare of others and society.

There are some terminally ill patients, however, who are more concerned with the welfare of others than with their own problems. They are able to accept death with greater equanimity and philosophical acceptance. Towards the turn of the century, King Hussain of Jordan, a few months prior to his death, announced to his people over the electronic media that he had only a short time to live on account of cancer but declared that he would continue to serve his people as long as he was able to do so. For the sake of those suffering from the state of war in the Middle East, he undertook a long journey to Washington in the US, at great personal discomfort, to add his weight to the peace negotiations initiated by the US President between the Prime Minister of Israel and the Palestinian Leader.

Several years ago a senior and eminent lawyer told his junior at a morning consultation that he had had an unusual but exhilarating experience the previous day when he went to visit a friend who was terminally ill at the Maharagama Cancer Hospital in Sri Lanka. He was surprised that his friend was not to be seen on his usual bed or any other bed in the ward at visiting time and made inquiries. He was told that his friend was on a mat in the corridor of the ward. Considerably angered by this kind of treatment to an incurable patient, he approached his friend who greeted him with a smile and said that he had voluntarily surrendered his bed to a new patient since the latter had some hope of recovery while he had none.

The late Prime Minister, S. W. R. D. Bandaranaike, of Sri Lanka, when he was shot several times on that fateful day in September 1959 issued a public statement appealing to his family and the people at large to extend compassion and not harm the assailant. This is the practice of Buddhism at its sublime best. Even faced with death there is consideration for those who had seriously harmed one.

One could also look at death as a phenomenon one experiences from moment to moment, for in reality we are dying every moment and being reborn the next. Thoughts and consciousness are arising and ceasing all the time – on the dissolution of one thought another immediately arises and this process is ceaseless. Thus, one experiences death all the while, the arising and ceasing of mental and physical phenomena. In Pali, the language of Theravada (Southern) Buddhism, it is called *khanika maranam* (momentary death). According to Buddhist philosophy, at death the last thought of this life is followed immediately by the first thought in the new life when the first mental stirrings occur.

When facing death with notice, as a terminally sick patient or in old age with sharply deteriorating faculties, one should be mindful of the good work of those who are looking after you, be they relatives, friends or hired personnel. They are often performing a very difficult and unpleasant job that should not be made more difficult by unreasonable demands. The kindness and patience of those who nurse should be gratefully acknowledged. Thoughts of appreciation and goodwill should be directed towards them that would be of benefit to oneself and those nursing one.

Guilt Complex

A terminally sick person, apart from the physical pain of the disease, could also suffer from a guilt complex for serious unwholesome actions of the past. From a Buddhist standpoint, one should not regret the past over which there is no control whatsoever. What should be done by a Buddhist is to note the misdeeds of the past and ensure with firm determination that such actions do not happen in the present or future, over which one has considerable control. The wise recollection of the past unwholesome actions could be an incentive and a spring board to engage in wholesome actions from now onwards.

Some may question what good action could a person condemned to death by an incurable ailment and confined to bed perform? In

Buddhism, *kamma* or intentional activities include not only physical and verbal actions but also thoughts. So whatever physical and bodily constraints of the terminally ill, if they are mentally in a reasonable state, they could accumulate wholesome *kamma* by wholesome thoughts. Perhaps such patients are in a better position to perform good mental actions than others who have full physical and mental control but are running hither and thither with no time for relaxation, contemplation and reflection. In fact, it is said in Buddhism that *bhavana* or mental culture and development is the highest form of meritorious action. As a meritorious action, *bhavana* surpasses *dana* and *Sila,* generosity and virtue.

Let not the Mind be Sick

When one is dying and there is no hope of recovery one could console oneself with the words of the Buddha that the 'body may be sick but let not the mind be sick'. One may not be able to do much for the body but can do much for the mind when mental faculties have not seriously deteriorated. Even when seriously ill, one could keep one's mind steady: be mindful and, if one has pain, observe the rise and fall of pain and observe how it comes and goes in waves. One can understand the nature of suffering and learn that there is no permanent self but a constant change of arising and passing away, similar to the ceaseless flow of water in a river. One can understand that it is our ignorance, craving, attachment, anger, fear and similar such emotions that are the cause of one's suffering. This understanding could be helpful in take pain in one's stride and remaining calm and tranquil without depression. At the highest levels, one could respond to pain as the Buddha taught – without anger and aversion – and rise above it with mindfulness and peace of mind. The Buddha says that life is unsatisfactory, but one could rise above it and by so doing could smile at imminent death.

When a person is dying or close to death, he could radiate thoughts of *metta,* loving kindness or the sincere wish for the happiness and welfare of all living beings. 'May all living beings be well and happy. May they be healthy and free from disease. May they be free from mental and physical suffering. May they lead a life in accordance with the *Dhamma*.' Having such noble thoughts of *metta* to all living beings reigning supreme in his mind would be a noble way to die. It is said in Buddhist literature that a person who radiates *metta* on a regular basis will, among many other benefits, die very peacefully like falling into a pleasant sleep. If such a person does not realize *Nibbana* in this life itself, and consequently is born again, he will be born in a heavenly abode.

Meditation (*Bhavana*)

As stated earlier, meditation is very helpful to a person facing death with notice. *Bhavana* is mental development or culture, purifying the mind, eradicating all its defiling thoughts and visualizing reality in its true perspective as *anicca*, *Dukkha* and *anatta* – impermanence, unsatisfactoriness and the absence of an everlasting and unchanging self.

There are two forms of meditation. One is *samatha* meditation, or calming and tranquillizing the mind by its concentration on one wholesome subject to the total exclusion of other thoughts. The other is *vipassana*, or insight meditation to proceed beyond ordinary vision and mere appearances, to see the three characteristics of *annica*, *Dukkha* and *anatta* in all phenomena.

The art of meditation should be cultivated early in life. One can then make the best use of the knowledge and experience of meditation to engage in it when one is facing death with notice. In the case of *anapanasati* meditation, one would have already identified the point of sensation of in and out breathing at or around the tip of the nose. When one is physically weak and mentally depressed it would be difficult, but not impossible, to engage in meditation for the first time.

Right Attention

In the case of the death of loved ones, as stated earlier, it is possible to evaluate one's progress in facing such deaths. However, regarding one's own death, with or without notice, one cannot do so since it only happens once. Still, with the right contemplation of death and a large fund of wholesome actions (thoughts, words and deeds) as well as purification and development of the mind, the chances are that one would be able to face death with dignity and composure.

Taking all these factors into consideration one can extend right attention – *yoniso manasikara* – to the subject of death so that one will be able to face death of our loved ones and our own death with wisdom and understanding.

Appendix II

An Interesting Case of Rebirth

This is an extract from a small book *The Buddhist Doctrine of Life after Death* (1981, The Corporate Body of the Buddha Educational Foundation, Taiwan) by the late Nayaka Thera Piyadassi of Vajirarama temple, Bambalapitiya, in Sri Lanka.

This is the story of a mother and son, and it was related to Venerable Piyadassi by the mother in her flat not far from Hyde Park Corner in London. The story began when she showed him a photograph of a grave in Kuala Lumpur, Malaysia. It was the grave of her five-year-old son and the headstone bore an inscription that is unique. Beneath the life-size effigy of a bonny child these words were carved:

> To the glory of God
> and to the sweet memory
> of our dear son
> Philip Pryce Smith
> Born October 22nd, 1920
> Died November 22nd, 1925
> Reborn February 23rd, 1927.
> God moves in a mysterious way
> His wonders to perform.

Here is the story that Mrs Smith describes as the 'the greatest experience of my life'.

I went out to Malaysia as the bride of an engineer and Philip was our first baby. He was a handsome, happy child and of course was the world to me. Then, in the steaming rain of a November monsoon, he fell suddenly ill. He had been stricken with dysentery and after an illness of only eight days he died; a month to the day after his fifth birthday.

I was crazed with grief. I had, I hope, always been a devout God-fearing woman, but I could not understand why a loving God should take my only child from me.

After the funeral my husband sent me on a cruise to Myanmar but I remained inconsolable. I spent most of the time in the ship on my knees in my cabin in worship or weeping uncontrollably on my bunk. One day, early in December, as the ship was moving towards the Burmese port of Moulmein, when I was torn by anguish from the lack of sleep, I knelt on the floor of the cabin once more.

I poured out my heart to God and when I arose I felt in the grip of a strange impulse. I felt it was imperative for me to talk to a certain Burmese person whom I had seen on board. I did not know him and had never spoken to him. It was an impulse that had to be obeyed. I did not even wait to dress. I just threw a kimono around me and dashed out of my cabin and made my way on deck.

There was the Burmese standing beside the rail gazing out across the water to Moulmein. I looked too. I saw a pagoda gleaming in the sun. It was difficult to open a conversation. I felt tongue-tied. But finally my eyes sought the pagoda. I gestured towards it and asked him its name. When he had told me I boldly asked, 'In your religion what do you believe happens to a child after it dies?' His reply was simple 'We believe', he said, 'the child dies and then is born again'. Quite suddenly I seemed to understand everything. I felt I had been purposely directed to this man and that he had been led to give me the message for which I had sought and prayed. Suddenly I knew that all was going to be well, that my lost boy would be returned to me.

Back again in Malaysia I told my friends of my experience and of the firm belief that had come to me. They were, quite naturally, sceptical. They thought my sorrow had gone to my head. I, too, began to wonder whether I had merely clutched at this belief because I was grief-stricken and needed comfort.

As these doubts began to arise I almost began to despair again. Then further signs were given to me. I dreamt of my boy. He spoke to me, with his arms around my neck, 'I am coming back to you mummy', he said. I found something that seemed to me, and still seems to me, a further sign: a picture book that had belonged to him. He was too young to write words, but he could print letters. Running through this book one day I found he had printed with a pencil the word 'PAGODA'. I was astonished. I could not understand how he had ever come across this word. I could only take it as a further sign of the strange things that were happening.

Then in a dream sometime in March 1926, some 14 weeks after Philip's death, he told me again that he was coming back. I saw him in a dream and he said, 'I will be back with you two months after Christmas Mummy'. It was nearly 12 months later, in February 1927, that that happened. Philip was born to me again. If I ceased to believe that my Philip was the Philip who died reborn, I could not believe in God.

This is Mrs Smith's astonishing story. She and Venerable Piyadassi understood that sceptics would not accept the reality of this story; however, her firm belief was that her child was born twice to her. Philip was educated in England and worked as an engineer in Australia.

Index